Indefinite Objects

Linguistic Inquiry Monographs

Samuel Jay Keyser, general editor

A complete list of books published in the Linguistic Inquiry Monographs series appears at the back of this book.

Indefinite Objects

Scrambling, Choice Functions, and Differential Marking

Luis López

A Bradford Book
The MIT Press
Cambridge, Massachusetts
London, England

© 2012 Massachusetts Institute of Technology

All rights reserved. No part of this book may be reproduced in any form by any electronic or mechanical means (including photocopying, recording, or information storage and retrieval) without permission in writing from the publisher.

This book was set in Syntax and Times New Roman on InDesign by Asco Typesetters, Hong Kong.

Library of Congress Cataloging-in-Publication Data

López, Luis, 1965–
Indefinite objects : scrambling, choice functions, and differential marking / Luis López.
   p. cm.—(Linguistic inquiry monographs)
Includes bibliographical references and index.
ISBN 978-0-262-01803-6 (alk. paper)—ISBN 978-0-262-51785-0 (pbk. : alk. paper)
1. Grammar, Comparative and general—Topic and comment. 2. Grammar, Comparative and general—Syntax. 3. Semantics. 4. Discourse markers. 5. Typology (Linguistics) I. Title.
P298.L67   2012
415—dc23   2012007129

Contents

Series Foreword   vii
Preface   ix
Acknowledgments   xiii

1 **Introduction: Remarks on the Grammar of Indefinite Objects**   1
   1.1 Indefinites: Their Readings, Scopes, and Peculiar Morphologies   3
   1.2 Spanish Marked Objects   12
   1.3 Conclusions   29

2 **Scrambling and Differential Object Marking**   31
   2.1 Theoretical Assumptions   31
   2.2 Short Scrambling and A-Dependencies   39
   2.3 The [Context] of Accusative A   59
   2.4 Conclusions   64
   Appendix: On Incorporation of Indefinite Objects   65

3 **Scrambling and Semantic Composition**   69
   3.1 Introduction   69
   3.2 Restriction, Saturation, and the Structure of Transitive Predicates   72
   3.3 Empirical Consequences   84
   3.4 Conclusions   97

4 **Crosslinguistic Predictions**   101
   4.1 Introduction   101
   4.2 Dependent-Marked DOM: Persian   106
   4.3 Dependent-Marked DOM: Hindi-Urdu   118
   4.4 Head-Marked DOM: Kiswahili   133
   4.5 Dependent- and Head-Marked DOM: Romanian   138
   4.6 No (Apparent) Marking: German   144
   4.7 Conclusions   149
   Appendix: Inuit   151

Notes   155
References   163
Index   171

Series Foreword

We are pleased to present the sixty-third in the series *Linguistic Inquiry Monographs*. These monographs present new and original research beyond the scope of the article. We hope they will benefit our field by bringing to it perspectives that will stimulate further research and insight.

Originally published in limited edition, the *Linguistic Inquiry Monographs* are now more widely available. This change is due to the great interest engendered by the series and by the needs of a growing readership. The editors thank the readers for their support and welcome suggestions about future directions for the series.

Samuel Jay Keyser
for the Editorial Board

Preface

I always wanted to be somebody.
Now I see that I should have been more specific.
—Lily Tomlin

The polyvalent behavior of indefinites has always been a matter of curiosity among linguists. For instance, in (1), the indefinite object *a philosopher* may take scope outside the conditional, with the meaning that there is a certain philosopher such that if Bert invites him, Lud will be upset. Since conditional clauses are strong islands for extraction, the wide scope reading suggests that the scope of indefinites depends on a semantic operation rather than on Quantifier Raising. In (2), we do not know whether Mary is looking for just any individual who has the properties of being a manager and speaking German or whether she is looking for a specific individual—known to herself or to the speaker—whom we happen to identify by using these properties.

(1) If Bert invites a philosopher, Lud will be angry.

(2) Mary is looking for a manager that speaks German.

In this monograph I discuss three approaches to accounting for the grammar of indefinites. Linguists working in the tradition of differential object marking (DOM) (see Bossong 1985; Aissen 2003) have connected a piece of morphology with a specific interpretation. For instance, in the Spanish sentence (3), the presence of *a* before the indefinite object makes a specific reading possible; without *a*, the specific reading is impossible.

(3) María está buscando (a) un gestor.
    María is seeking   a manager
    'María is looking for a manager.'

Other linguists—in particular, Diesing (1992)—have linked specificity with scrambling. The subject's position to the right of the adjunct particles in the

German example (4a) facilitates a nonspecific reading of *zwei Cellisten* 'two cellists', whereas its position to the left in (4b) forces a specific reading.

(4) a. ... weil   ja doch zwei Cellisten in diesem Hotel abgestiegen sind.
               because indeed two cellists   in this   hotel have.taken.rooms
     b. ... weil zwei Cellisten ja doch in diesem Hotel abgestiegen sind.
        (Diesing 1992, 78)

Finally, Reinhart (1997) and many others have argued that indefinite DPs obtain wide scope by means of choice functions—consequently making the scope of indefinite nominal phrases independent of their structural position.

Of particular interest for our purposes are Chung and Ladusaw's (2004) proposals, according to which indefinite nominal phrases have two modes of semantic composition available to them: Restrict and Satisfy. Restrict combines the indefinite nominal phrase as a restrictive modifier without saturation of the predicate argument structure and leads to narrow scope. Satisfy involves a choice function and Function Application, giving rise to a variety of scopes.

In this monograph, I synthesize the three traditions. The gist of my proposal is shown schematically in (5) (where $EA = external\ argument$, $DO = direct\ object$).

(5) [$_{vP}$ EA v [$_{\alpha P}$ DO.DOM α [$_{VP}$ V DO]]]
                   ↑   ↑
               Satisfy   Restrict

That is, DOM and wide scope of indefinites entail scrambling. I substantiate this claim using data from Spanish, Persian, Hindi-Urdu, Kiswahili, Romanian, and German.

The main theoretical contribution of this research project is that it allows us to develop a more nuanced view of the syntax-semantics interface. Diesing and many others have argued that syntactic positions are linked to semantic interpretations. A rigid mapping is the only option within a theory of syntax-semantics mapping in which Function Application is the only operation that can build a semantic structure out of a syntactic structure. However, recent years have seen the development of other operations of semantic composition such as Kratzer's (1996) Event Identification and Chung and Ladusaw's (2004) Restrict, as well as other innovations in semantic theory relevant to the present project such as Van Geenhoven's (1998) Semantic Incorporation. These developments in semantic theory call for a renewal of our theory of the syntax-semantics interface. Thus, I argue that there is no rigid "syntactic position–semantic interpretation" mapping; instead, the effect of the syntactic configuration is to limit the range of possible modes of semantic composition, a restriction that in turn limits the range of possible semantic representations.

In this book, I also uncover and provide analyses for some DOM data that have not been discussed in the literature so far, and I develop analyses for well-known data that have lacked a satisfactory account.

Acknowledgments

I would like to thank Karlos Arregi, Angel Gallego, Remus Gergel, Kay González-Vilbazo, Manuel Leonetti, Silvina Montrul, and the members of the Temple of DOM reading group for numerous comments on a previous draft of this monograph and valuable advice thereafter. The comments and suggestions of three referees for MIT Press were likewise illuminating and provided crucial help in turning my submitted manuscript into a publishable monograph. I would also like to thank the audiences at the Workshop on Differential Object Marking at the University of Zurich (October 2008), the Patterns and Algorithms talk series at Freie Universität Berlin (June 2009), the UICTiL (February 2010), and the University of Iowa (March 2010) for their questions and comments.

I am grateful to the Alexander von Humboldt Foundation for financial support while this book was being written. I would also like to thank everyone at the Institute of Romance Philology at the Freie Universität Berlin, in particular my host Guido Mensching, for their hospitality during the summer of 2009 and fruitful discussions on everything linguistic.

I would like to express my deepest gratitude to the language consultants without whose generous help this project would never have come to fruition: Muhammad Belverdi, Rajesh Bhatt, Vicki Carstens, Ioana Chitoran, Jonathan Choti, Veneeta Dayal, Haig Der-Houssikian, Remus Gergel, Jila Ghomeshi, Edward Göbbel, Kay González-Vilbazo, Zeyana Hamid, Jutta Hartmann, Gholamhossein Karimi-Doostan, Inga Kohl, Manuel Leonetti, Guido Mensching, Dennis Ott, Elisabeth Stark, Susanne Winkler, and Anja Weinberger. Any misunderstandings of the data, and any shortcomings in the book, are solely my responsibility.

Finally, I would like to thank Yasmin Mehta for her help in preparing the final manuscript as well as, last but not least, Anne Mark for impressive copyediting work.

1 Introduction: Remarks on the Grammar of Indefinite Objects

Consider the examples (1), (2), and (3).

(1) John ate an apple.

(2) Mary is looking for a manager that speaks German.

(3) If Lud invites a philosopher, Bert will be offended.

In (1), we do not know whether *an apple* refers to an individual apple or to apples in general (the second reading becomes more prominent with additional context, as in *John ate an apple whenever he saw one*). In (2), we do not know whether Mary is looking for just any individual who has the properties of being a manager and speaking German or whether she is looking for a specific individual—known to herself or to the speaker—whom we happen to identify by using these properties. In (3), the indefinite *a philosopher* may take scope outside the conditional, resulting in the meaning that there is a certain philosopher whom Lud would do better not to invite. A conditional is a strong island and therefore a quantifier cannot escape it by Quantifier Raising (QR). In fact, strong quantifiers are not able to widen their scope with the freedom that weak quantifiers have (see, e.g., Reinhart 1997).

When we add languages with *differential object marking* (DOM) to the discussion, the data at first appear more complex. On deeper examination, however, it turns out that DOM can make things clearer. I introduce here some data to arouse the reader's curiosity. Spanish indefinite objects may be introduced by a particle that I refer to as *accusative A*. Adding or subtracting accusative A to an indefinite object has interpretive consequences.

(4) María buscó **a/Ø** una gestora que hablara alemán.
María sought a manager that spoke.SUBJ German
'María was looking for a manager that spoke.SUBJ German.'

(5) María buscó **a**/*Ø una gestora que hablaba alemán.
María sought a manager that spoke.IND German
'María was looking for a manager that spoke.IND German.'

(6) a. Si Lud invita **a** un filósofo, Bert se ofenderá.
'If Lud invites a philosopher, Bert will be offended.'
∃ > →
→ > ∃
b. Si Lud invita Ø un filósofo, Bert se ofenderá.
'If Lud invites a philosopher, Bert will be offended.'
*∃ > →
→ > ∃

(7) Un hombre ama **a**/*Ø toda mujer.
'A man loves every woman.'
∃ > ∀
*∀ > ∃

Let us start with (4). The direct object (DO) in (4) includes a relative clause with a verb in the subjunctive mood. It is a well-known property of Spanish grammar that the presence of the subjunctive mood in a relative clause ensures that the noun modified by the relative clause can only be interpreted as nonspecific (Rivero 1979). Thus, *gestora* 'manager' can only be nonspecific. In this context, the DP *gestora* may either be introduced by accusative A, or not (I indicate absence of accusative A with Ø). In (5), the verb in the relative clause is indicative and the DP can only be interpreted as specific. In this context, accusative A is obligatory. Taken together, (4) and (5) indicate that unmarked objects cannot be specific while marked objects can be (but do not have to be). In (6), the indefinite can take wide scope *only* if it is introduced by accusative A. Thus, (6) suggests that accusative A has the property of widening scope. (7) shows that a strong quantifier in object position cannot take scope over the subject. Even though the object is introduced by accusative A, the strong quantifier cannot take wide scope. Thus, accusative A allows wide scope only if it prefixes an indefinite DP.

This chapter is composed of two sections. In section 1.1, I present three traditions in the study of indefinites that I build upon or contest in later chapters; one goal of this monograph is to synthesize some of the findings from all three traditions.[1] In this section, I also initially present the hypothesis that I argue for throughout. In section 1.2, I present the Spanish data that will be the focus of chapters 2 and 3.

1.1 Indefinites: Their Readings, Scopes, and Peculiar Morphologies

1.1.1 Indefinites and Tree Splitting

In an influential monograph, and in subsequent work, Diesing (1992, 1996; Diesing and Jelinek 1995) proposes to approach the study of specificity by linking the specific interpretation to a certain position or positions in the syntactic tree.

Diesing takes indefinites to be lexically ambiguous between strong and weak (for the strong/weak distinction, see Milsark 1974). Weak indefinites are not quantifiers proper; they are variables that need to be bound by some quantifier (Lewis 1975; Heim 1982). In (8a), the indefinite is bound by an existential quantifier; in (8b), it is bound by a universal quantifier; and in (8c), it is bound by a generic quantifier.

(8) a. Mary saw a cat.
   $\exists x \; cat(x) \land$ Mary saw x
   b. Every cat that likes a kitten licks it.
   $= \forall x,y \; [cat(x) \land kitten(y) \land likes(x,y)] \rightarrow licks \; (x,y)$
   c. Girls like a cat.
   $GEN_x \; [x \; a \; cat]$ girls like x

Diesing further argues that weak indefinites must find themselves in situ—within the VP—at LF. In that position, they are bound by an existential quantifier. Consider example (9). If the determiner *some* is pronounced without stress, this sentence has the meaning expressed in (9b). This meaning is mapped from the syntactic structure in (9a). Since English subjects are forced by the Extended Projection Principle (EPP) to raise to the specifier of T (Spec,T) by S-Structure, the mapping from S-Structure to LF must involve lowering. In some languages, weak quantifier subjects do show up superficially in a predicate-internal position, making Diesing's view more plausible (see the discussion of Dutch in Diesing 1992, 80–85).

(9) Some men arrived. (*some* pronounced without stress)
   a. [$_{TP}$ t(some men) T [$_{VP}$ some men arrived]]
   b. $\exists x \; man(x) \land arrived(x)$

If the determiner bears stress, it is strong. Strong indefinites are quantifiers. As such, they scramble or undergo QR out of VP and into TP. Strong quantifiers create Heimian tripartite structures (Heim 1982) composed of the quantifier itself, a restrictor, and a nuclear scope. The restrictor is "presuppositional," which in the case of indefinites means that it is interpreted as specific or generic. Thus, (10) could be paraphrased as 'Some of the men arrived'. *Some men* is in Spec,T at LF, and the resulting semantics is as shown in (10b).

(10) Some men arrived. (*some* pronounced with stress)
    a. [$_{TP}$ some men T [$_{VP}$ t(some men) arrived]]
    b. some x [x a man]   x arrived
              ↑   ↑
        Restrictor Nuclear scope

Indeed, on the basis of the empirical evidence provided (mostly) by German object scrambling and Dutch subjects, Diesing proposes a direct, rigid mapping from syntactic form to semantic interpretation, which she formulates as the Mapping Hypothesis.

(11) *Mapping Hypothesis*
    a. Material from VP is mapped into the nuclear scope.
    b. Material from IP is mapped into a restrictive clause.
       (Diesing 1992, 10)

Diesing's syntactic evidence for object scrambling is based on adverb position. Certain types of adverbs are generally assumed to demarcate the upper limit of VP; consequently, objects that appear to the left of these adverbs must have left the VP. It is precisely these objects, according to Diesing, that have strong readings. The objects in situ have weak readings (with a caveat that I introduce shortly).

(12) a. ... DO [$_{VP}$ Adv [$_{V'}$ V]]
       ↑
      Scrambled → in restrictor → specific, generic, etc.
    b. ... [$_{VP}$ Adv [$_{V'}$ DO V]]
                 ↑
      In situ → in nuclear scope → nonspecific

This approach to the study of indefinites has been very popular and different versions have been proposed, based on a variety of languages (see Mahajan 1989, 1990, 1992; Bhatt and Anagnostopoulou 1996; de Hoop 1996; Ramchand 1997). In (13a), I summarize the common denominator of these approaches (except de Hoop's, as her approach varies somewhat from the schematic picture I paint here). In (13a–e), the two positions indicated in the tree as bearing a value for the feature [specific] are intended to represent two alternative positions for an argument. (13a) is the configuration that Diesing

Introduction

predicts and argues for. (13b–d) are configurations that are ruled out by the Mapping Hypothesis.

(13) a.

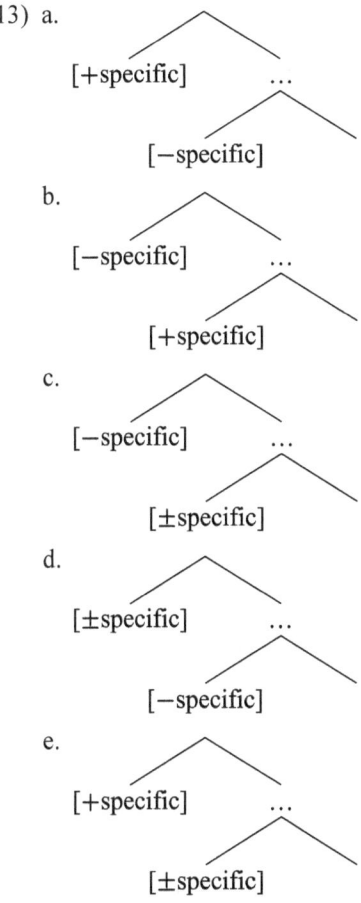

As far as I know, (13b) and (13c) are undocumented. Since intensive research has been carried out in this area for at least twenty years, I think it is safe to assume that if these syntax-semantics configurations existed, they would have been found.

Configuration (13d) does exist. In this monograph, I discuss an example extensively: Spanish objects. In Spanish, objects that stay in situ cannot be specific. Objects that undergo scrambling, even if it is short, can be specific; but they do not have to be. How could this be accounted for within the Mapping Hypothesis? As mentioned, Diesing (1992) considers the possibility of "LF lowering" for English subjects. We could apply "LF lowering" to (13d) and simply claim that nonspecific indefinite objects can raise overtly and lower covertly. It is fair to say that this is a technical solution that does not get to the heart of the problem. Moreover, as I will show, "LF lowering" would make the wrong empirical prediction because it is possible to show that scrambled nonspecific objects remain in a relatively high position at LF.

Thus, it is tempting to take (13d) as a counterexample to the "specific is higher" approach and adopt the position that there really is no connection between syntax and specificity. But the fact that (13a) is found in many languages and (13b) and (13c) are unattested should give us pause. Thus, I take (13d) to show that the direct Mapping Hypothesis cannot be true as stated but that there is a correlation between the syntactic position of the indefinite and the possibility of specific readings. I distance myself from Diesing's approach by acknowledging that the mapping between configuration and semantic interpretation is not direct; rather, it is mediated by the types of operations that can be applied to build the compositional meaning of a verb and its complement. Understanding the syntax-semantics interface in this manner turns out to yield a wide range of empirical consequences.

Regarding (13e), Diesing (1992) admits that there are object indefinites in German that do not appear to scramble yet have a specific reading. De Hoop (1996) uses these data to mount a critique of Diesing's approach. But more recently, Frey (2001) provides a fine-grained analysis of the positions of indefinites in German, using a wider variety of adverbs than Diesing or de Hoop. Frey shows that strong objects indeed scramble in German, even though this scrambling might be very short. I discuss Frey's findings, and my own take on them, in chapter 4.

Next, let us look at the modes of semantic composition that may affect indefinites.

1.1.2 Indefinites, Choice Functions, and Restrict

A central concern regarding indefinites is their ability to take scope over islands, as exemplified in (14). In (14a), it is possible to interpret *a philosopher* as referring to one particular philosopher such that if Lud invites him, Bert will be offended. In order to obtain this reading, the indefinite *a philosopher* must take scope outside the conditional phrase, which is a strong island for movement. In (14b), the indefinite *a friend of mine* can have the widest scope (there is a friend of mine such that every woman is convinced . . .), or the sentence can have an intermediate reading in which the existential quantifier takes scope within the universal quantifier but still outside the conditional (for ample discussion of—and controversy about—intermediate readings, see, e.g., Abusch 1994; Kratzer 1998; Reinhart 1997). The intermediate reading is the one I choose to represent.

(14) a. If Lud invites a philosopher, Bert will be offended.
∃x [Lud invites philosopher(x) → Bert will be offended]
'There exists a philosopher x such that if Lud invites x, Bert will be offended.'
b. Every woman is convinced that if John invites a friend of his to the party, it will be a disaster.
∀x∃y [woman(x) ∧ friend (John,y) → convinced (x, [invite (John,y,party) → disaster (party)])]
'For every woman x there exists a friend of John's y such that if John invites y to the party, x is convinced it will be a disaster.'

This sort of example has been taken to provide evidence that QR should not be part of the theory of grammar. Reinhart (1997) instead proposes to maintain QR, at least for strong quantifiers, which do not have this scopal freedom. But for weak quantifiers, she does agree that a purely semantic mechanism is called for in order to handle examples like (14a,b). This semantic mechanism is the *choice function*.

Take indefinite nominal phrases to be properties of type ⟨e,t⟩ (McNally 1997 et seq.). A choice function variable lifts an indefinite from type ⟨e,t⟩ to type ⟨e⟩, which can then be composed by regular Function Application. In Reinhart's view, the choice function variable is bound by an existential quantifier. This existential quantifier can be merged at different points in the tree structure, giving rise to different scopes for the indefinite DP. For instance, the wide scope for indefinites contained in a conditional clause is represented as follows:

(15) a. If Lud invites a philosopher, Bert will be offended.
∃**f** [CH(**f**) ∧ [Lud invites **f**(philosopher) → Bert will be offended]]
'There exists a (choice function that picks out a) philosopher such that if Lud invites the philosopher picked out by the choice function, Bert will be offended.'
b. Every woman is convinced that if John invites a friend of his to the party, it will be a disaster.
∀x∃**f** CH(**f**) [woman(x) → convinced (x, [invite(John,**f**(friend-of-mine),party) → disaster(party)])]
'For every woman x there exists a (choice function that picks out a) friend of John's such that if John invites the friend picked out by the choice function to the party, x is convinced it will be a disaster.'

Choice functions have engendered intensive debate (e.g., Kratzer 1998; Matthewson 1999; Chierchia 2001; Winter 2007). In particular, Kratzer (1998) and others have argued that intermediate readings are pragmatically triggered and that the semantic representation should not have an existential quantifier closing the choice function variable. I do not have anything to contribute to this debate. I adopt Reinhart's approach for perspicuity, but my results do not depend on it.

A related concern involves the fact that certain types of indefinites obligatorily take the narrowest possible scope. Van Geenhoven (1998), for instance, studies three such nominal phrase types: incorporated nouns in Kalaallisut/West Greenlandic, split topics in German, and bare plural objects in English. Chung and Ladusaw (2004) add to this list indefinite nominals in Maori bearing the determiner *he* (as opposed to indefinite nominals headed by *tētahi*, which allow for wide or narrow scope readings and are interpreted by means of choice functions). Consideration of these data has led these authors to argue for novel views of semantic composition. The Montagovian tradition only allowed for one mode of composing arguments with a predicate, Function Application, which has the form $\lambda x[P(x)](a) \rightarrow P(a)$. Van Geenhoven argues that a weak indefinite can combine with a predicate by Function Application only if the verb is type-shifted so it can combine with properties, while Chung and Ladusaw argue for a new mode of semantic composition called *Restrict*. Restrict combines the indefinite object with its selecting predicate by means of conjunction, with the result that the predicate is not saturated. The outcome of Restrict is then closed by existential closure. An indefinite nominal interpreted by this mechanism is necessarily interpreted with narrow scope.

(16) (Mary has) seen a man.
 $\lambda e \lambda x.\ [seen(e)(x)]\ (man)$
 Restrict $\quad \lambda e \lambda x.\ [seen(e)(x)] \wedge man(x)$
 ∃-closure $\quad \lambda e\ \exists x\ [seen(e)(x) \wedge man(x)]$

I adopt as my theory of semantics roughly that of Chung and Ladusaw (2004, 2006), without trying to argue either in favor of it or against its competitors. Readers who are convinced that Chung and Ladusaw's approach to indefinites is promising, as I am, can read this monograph as a theory of how a syntactic structure is mapped onto the type of semantics that these authors propose. Otherwise, readers are free to take what I say about semantics as an *exemplum*, since many of the proposals offered in these pages can be easily translated into other semantic frameworks. I would like to emphasize that I will not attempt to contribute to the semantic debates concerning specificity, choice functions, or the modes of semantic composition. These debates now involve a complex database, and there are enough developed alternatives that even a critical summary would involve a full monograph.

Instead, my goal here is to show that these new semantic possibilities open the door to new ways of regarding the syntax-semantics interface, beyond the traditional direct mapping between a syntactic position and a semantic interpretation. In particular, I propose to pair syntactic positions with modes of semantic composition. This way of looking at the interface yields empirical dividends and, I believe, helps us understand some of the problems that concern semanticists and syntacticians alike.

To connect the ideas from the previous section and this one: According to Diesing and other linguists, the semantic interpretation of an indefinite depends on its syntactic position. However, the semanticists who discuss the wide scope of indefinites seem to leave their syntax aside. In Chung and Ladusaw's (2004, 2006) approach, an indefinite can be interpreted by means of a choice function or Restrict regardless of its position in the syntactic tree. In Van Geenhoven's (1998) approach, type-shifting of the verb resolves any mismatches and there is no need for a syntactic operation like scrambling. Finally, in Reinhart's (1997) analyses, application of choice functions is not restricted by syntax in any way. How can we reconcile the findings of syntax with these semantic proposals?

In this monograph, I argue that syntax is crucial: I show evidence that indefinite objects that stay in situ can only be composed by Restrict, while indefinite objects that scramble can only be interpreted by choice functions. Moreover, the sort of scrambling that I discuss cannot be confused with QR. The QR approach to scope assumes that the scope of an operator equals its c-command domain (May 1985). However, the scrambling movement that I discuss here can be very short, moving the object to a position where it does not c-command the external argument (EA) or any scope-taking operators in the clause. However, the scrambled indefinite DO is able to take scope over anything in the clause and even outside the clause, thus revealing the intervention of a choice function.[2]

Before closing, I should remark that the existence in the grammar of $\langle e,t \rangle$ and type-shifted $\langle e \rangle$ indefinites does not preclude the possibility of quantificational indefinites. These would be indefinites that would undergo QR and take scope over other sentential operators but not outside an island. Although I have very little to say about strong indefinites in this monograph, they will reappear briefly in my discussion of Romanian in chapter 4.

1.1.3 Differential Object Marking

It has been observed that the grammars of many languages include a piece of morphology, attached to a DO or to the lexical verb, that plays a role in the interpretation of the DO. Following the seminal work of Bossong (1985), it has become customary to refer to this phenomenon as *differential object marking* (DOM). DOM is often related to specificity: in many languages, indefinite objects with such a marker are (or can be) specific, while unmarked objects are not. Spanish is one such language.

(17) María busca **a/Ø** un traductor de alemán.
 María seeks a translator of German
 'María is looking for a German translator.'

The object in this sentence can be prefixed by accusative A. With accusative A, it can have a specific reading. Without accusative A, it can only be nonspecific.

The mainstream analyses of DOM, revitalized by Aissen (2003), have two properties in common: (i) they make a direct connection between a piece of morphology and an interpretation; and (ii) the distribution of DOM can be accounted for by means of scales, such as the definiteness scale in (18).

(18) *Definiteness scale*
 Personal pronoun > Proper name > Definite NP > Indefinite specific NP > Nonspecific NP

As for (i), the specific interpretation is only optional in some languages, like Spanish. Since a DO prefixed by *a* in Spanish is not necessarily specific, one could wonder whether this relationship between morphology and semantics is really so direct.

Concerning (ii), I will argue that the analyses of DOM in terms of scales are missing crucial ingredients for understanding the phenomenon. Consider small clause complements. In all the languages that I have looked at, the argument of a small clause complement is obligatorily marked.

(19) Considero **a/*Ø** un estudiante inteligente.
 consider.1SG a student intelligent
 'I consider a student intelligent.'

This is not the only type of argument that bears obligatory DOM: the same holds for affectees in clause union (CU) and objects that control PRO. Since none of these constructions involves obligatory specificity, it is clear that something is going on beyond the definiteness scale. I will argue, in fact, that conditions for DOM are created in syntax by means of scrambling. The actual phonological realization of marked morphology depends on environmental conditions surrounding the object, hence giving the appearance of scales.

Preempting likely criticism, I should clarify that the purpose of this monograph is not to provide a comprehensive description of the contexts in which

DOM may appear universally or in any given language. Rather, it is to contribute to our understanding of the morphology-syntax-semantics interface, using indefinite objects and the DOM phenomenon as a database that allows falsifiable predictions to be formulated.

1.1.4 Is It Possible to Unify?

To summarize: The possibility of strong readings—in particular, specific readings—has been treated in the Diesing tradition from a syntactic point of view: a certain syntactic configuration maps into a certain semantic configuration. In the DOM tradition, a connection has been made between a piece of morphology and an interpretation. Both traditions see the connection between syntax and semantics or between morphology and semantics as direct. Reinhart and other linguists have focused on the wide scope readings of indefinites and have supplied a purely semantic operation, the choice function, to account for them. The question is whether it is possible to present an analysis of the grammatical properties of indefinites that synthesizes the findings of all three traditions.

Generative grammar drafts a path for this synthesis:

- A particular functional category/feature (FC/F) may be included in the structure of a nominal phrase.
- FC/F triggers a syntactic operation that yields a new configuration.
- Type-shifting of the nominal phrase takes place within the frame of the new syntactic configuration.
- FC/F may take phonetic shape in a postsyntactic morphology module if it appears in a certain context (animate noun, telic predicate, object-affecting verb, etc.). A nominal phrase with a spelled-out FC/F is a marked object.

The main goal of this monograph is to connect these three strands of research on the morphology, syntax, and semantics of indefinites. First, I argue that there is a connection between morphology and syntax: marked objects undergo short scrambling out of VP to a vP-internal position (they may scramble further, but I am interested only in showing that a minimal scrambling is associated with DOM). Second, I maintain Diesing's insight that there is a connection between configuration and interpretation; but unlike Diesing, I argue that this connection is indirect. The syntactic position of an indefinite object affects the mode of semantic composition, which in turn may affect the final interpretation of the sentence. I will argue that only DOs that stay in situ are interpreted by means of Restrict, while scrambled indefinite objects are interpreted by means of choice functions (CH).

(20) [vP EA v [αP DO α [VP V DO]]]
           ↑   ↑
          CH   Restrict

Third, I will argue that the connection between syntactic position and mode of semantic interpretation can be derived from the nature of the system.

1.2 Spanish Marked Objects

In this section, I discuss the contexts in which marked objects may appear, must appear, or cannot appear in Spanish. It is often asserted that accusative A can only be associated with animate nouns. This is true for most cases, but there are some systematic exceptions (see García 2007 and López 2011 for analyses of accusative A with inanimates in Spanish, as well as section 2.3). In the examples that I use in this monograph, the objects are always animate in order to control for this factor. Whenever I say, "Accusative A is obligatory/optional/prohibited in this example," it should be understood that I am abstracting away from animacy, as well as other factors such as telicity and perfectivity. For an overview of factors involved in accusative A, see Torrego 1999. The claims made here have been tested with Peninsular Spanish speakers.[3]

1.2.1 Obligatory Contexts: Strong Quantifiers, Definite DPs, Proper Names, and Pronouns

Accusative A is obligatory with strong quantifiers, definite (referential) DPs, proper names, and pronouns (see, e.g., Pensado 1995; Torrego 1999). This is shown in the following examples:

(21) *Strong quantifiers*
   a. Juan vio **a**/*Ø todas las chicas.
      'Juan saw all the girls.'
   b. Juan vio **a**/*Ø la mayoría de las chicas.
      'Juan saw most of the girls.'

(22) *Definite (referential) DPs*[4]
   a. Juan vio **a**/*Ø la chica.
      'Juan saw the girl.'
   b. Juan vio **a**/*Ø su hija.
      'Juan saw his daughter.'

(23) *Proper names*
   María visitó **a**/*Ø Pedro.
   'María visited Pedro.'

(24) *Pronouns*
 María me vio **a/*Ø** mí.
 María CL.1SG saw me
 'María saw me.'

1.2.2 Indefinite Objects and Scope

Accusative A is optional with indefinite nominal phrases, including all of the weak quantifiers. The presence of accusative A leads, unsurprisingly, to changes in interpretation. To begin with, marked objects can have wide scope over other quantifiers and sentence operators, while unmarked objects cannot. Marked indefinite objects can have wide scope with respect to conditionals, quantifiers, or negation.[5]

(25) a. Todo hombre amó **a** una mujer.
 every man loved a woman
 = For every man, there was a woman that he loved.
 = There was a woman that every man loved.
 $\exists > \forall$
 $\forall > \exists$
 b. La mayoría de los hombres amó **a** una mujer.
 the most of the men loved a woman
 'Most men loved a woman.'
 $\exists >$ Most
 Most $> \exists$
 c. Juan no amó **a** una mujer.
 Juan NEG loved a woman
 $\neq$ Juan did not love any woman.
 = There was a woman Juan did not love.
 $\exists > \neg$
 $*\neg > \exists$
 d. Juan no amó **a** ninguna mujer.
 Juan NEG loved no woman
 'Juan loved no woman.'
 $*\exists > \neg$
 $\neg > \exists$
 e. Si Lud invita **a** un filósofo, Bert se ofenderá.
 if Lud invites a philosopher Bert SE offend.FUT
 = If Lud invites a philosopher, Bert will be offended (Bert wants to be the only philosopher at the party).

= There is a philosopher such that if Lud invites him, Bert will be offended.
∃ > →
→ > ∃

f. Todo el   mundo está convencido de que si invito   a un amigo
   all   the world is   convinced of that if invite.1SG a friend
   mío a la fiesta, será   un desastre.
   mine to the party be.FUT a disaster
   'Everybody is convinced that if I invite a friend of mine to the party, it will be a disaster.'
   ∀ > → > ∃
   ∀ > ∃ > →
   ∃ > ∀ > →

Examples (25a) and (25b) show that accusative A can have broad or narrow scope with respect to a subject quantifier. (25c) shows that accusative A must have wide scope with respect to negation if the indefinite is the regular indefinite *una* 'a$_{[fem]}$'. However, accusative A is perfectly compatible with narrow scope: all we have to do is replace *una* with *ninguna*, a negative concord item, as shown in (25d).[6] (25e) shows that accusative A can take scope over a conditional. (25f) shows that this scope over the conditional does not need to be the widest possible. A reading in which every person is paired with a friend of mine is also possible.

In the following examples, the object is unmarked. In no case is wide scope possible.

(26) a. Todo hombre amó   una mujer.
      every man   loved a woman
      = For every man, there was a woman that he loved.
      ≠ There was a woman that every man loved.
      *∃ > ∀
      ∀ > ∃

   b. La mayoría de los hombres amó   una mujer.
      the most   of the men   loved a   woman
      'Most men loved a woman.'
      *∃ > Most
      Most > ∃

   c. Juan no   amó   una mujer.
      Juan NEG loved a   woman
      = Juan did not love any woman.

≠ There was a woman Juan did not love.
*∃ > ¬
¬ > ∃

d. Juan no amó ninguna mujer.
Juan NEG loved no woman
'Juan loved no woman.'
*∃ > ¬
¬ > ∃

e. Si Lud invita un filósofo, Bert se ofenderá.
if Lud invites a philosopher Bert SE offend.FUT
= If Lud invites a philosopher, Bert will be offended (Bert wants to be the only philosopher at the party).
≠ There is a philosopher such that if Lud invites him, Bert will be offended.
*∃ > →
→ > ∃

f. Todo el mundo está convencido de que si invito un amigo mío
all the world is convinced of that if invite.1SG a friend mine
a la fiesta, sera un desastre.
to the party be.FUT a disaster
'Everybody is convinced that if I invite a friend of mine to the party, it will be a disaster.'
∀ > → > ∃
*∀ > ∃ > →
*∃ > ∀ > →

The wide range of possible scopes for marked indefinite objects in Spanish contrasts with the scope rigidity of strong quantifiers. In Spanish, strong quantifiers in object position cannot take scope over weak quantifiers in subject position. This is the case even though strong quantifiers in object position must be marked with accusative A. In (27) and (28), the subject is in postverbal position and still the universal quantifier cannot take scope over it (i.e., the sentences have no reading in which female prisoners are paired with different men).

(27) Ayer visitó un hombre **a** toda mujer prisionera.
yesterday visited a man every female prisoner
'Yesterday a man visited every female prisoner.'
∃ > ∀
*∀ > ∃

(28) Ayer   visitó un hombre **a** la mayoría de las mujeres prisioneras.
    yesterday visited a man   the most of the female   prisoners
    'Yesterday a man visited most of the female prisoners.'
    ∃ > Most
    *Most > ∃

Strong quantifiers cannot take scope over negation, either.

(29) No visité   **a** todo hombre.
    NEG visited.1SG every man
    'I didn't visit every man.'
    ¬ > ∀
    *∀ > ¬

Moreover, a strong quantifier in object position cannot bind a variable contained within the subject.

(30) Ayer   visitó su*ᵢ hijo **a** todaᵢ mujer prisionera.
    yesterday visited her son   every female prisoner
    'Yesterday her son visited every female prisoner.'

(31) Ayer   visitó su*ᵢ hijo **a** la mayoríaᵢ de las mujeres prisioneras.
    yesterday visited her son   the most of the female   prisoners
    'Yesterday her son visited most of the female prisoners.'

The possibility of wide scope readings for Spanish weak quantifiers in object position, in contrast with the scope rigidity of strong quantifiers in the same position, strongly suggests that choice functions are available in the grammar of this language. This conclusion is reinforced by the lack of sensitivity to islands that indefinite wide scope exhibits. Since only *marked* objects take wide scopes, we are led to the conclusion that there must be some connection between choice functions and DOM.

1.2.3 Indefinite Objects and Specificity

A marked object can be specific; an unmarked object cannot be. Thus, in (32a) *a una gestora* can be read as specific or nonspecific, while in (32b) *una gestora* can only be read as nonspecific.

(32) a. María busca **a** una gestora.
        María seeks   a   manager
        'María is looking for a manager.'
    b. María busca una gestora.

There are several approaches to the notion of specificity in the theoretical literature, and even a concise summary here couldn't possibly do justice to all of them (for that purpose, see von Heusinger 2011). Moreover, as far as I can tell, there is no one set of properties that are agreed by all researchers to constitute specificity. Thus, I adopt an approach that I hope the reader will find reasonable: I take two popular concepts of specificity as canonical, *epistemic specificity* and *partitive specificity*, and then show that marked objects in Spanish qualify as potentially specific according to either definition. Unmarked objects, on the other hand, are shown to be unambiguously nonspecific. Thus, the purpose of this section is (i) to highlight the difference between marked and unmarked objects with regard to this aspect of the interpretation of indefinites and (ii) to develop tests that allow us to tease them apart.

Let me start with *epistemic specificity* (following Farkas's (1994) and von Heusinger's (2002) terminology). It involves the state of knowledge of the speaker or the referent of the subject. The following example shows the contrast:

(33) a. Ayer   vi   a/Ø un estudiante en la   biblioteca.
       yesterday saw.1SG   a   student   in the library
       'Yesterday I saw a student in the library.'
   b. Ayer   vi   a/*Ø un hijo mío en la   biblioteca.
       yesterday saw.1SG   a   son mine in the library
       'Yesterday I saw a son of mine in the library.'

In (33a), the presence of accusative A is optional, since the student we are talking about could be known to the speaker or not. In (33b), accusative A is obligatory because 'a son of mine' is (most likely) known to the speaker.

The modifier *certain*, as in *a certain man*, highlights epistemic specificity by forcing the referent of the DP to be salient in the speaker's mind (Hintikka 1986). The Spanish equivalent of *certain* is *ciert-*. In (34), inserting *ciert-* within the DP forces accusative A.

(34) Juan buscó a/*Ø un cierto futbolista.
     Juan sought   a   certain soccer.player
     'Juan looked for a certain soccer player.'

The nominal modifier *cualquiera* has the opposite effect: it forces a nonspecific reading. I gloss *cualquiera* as 'no matter who'.[7]

(35) Juan buscó a/Ø un futbolista   cualquiera.
     Juan sought   a   soccer.player no.matter.who
     'Juan looked for a soccer player, no matter who.'

Thus, with *ciert-* and *cualquiera* we have two tests for specificity in Spanish.

Enç (1991) develops a theory of specificity based on *partitivity*. Her leading idea is that determiners may select implicit or explicit partitive complements, which are anaphoric with respect to a discourse antecedent. In (36), the partitive object also requires accusative A.

(36) [Context: Some gentlemen came into the room.]
    a. Me   presentaron   **a** uno de ellos.
        1SG.DAT introduced.3PL   one of them
        'I was introduced to one of them.'
    b. *Me   presentaron   uno de ellos.
        1SG.DAT introduced.3PL one of them

The partitive construction does not entail discourse connectedness. It can be used to classify the DP into a (possibly stereotypical) class. If that is the case, accusative A is not obligatory.

(37) No sé   si te   acuerdas.   Ahí vimos   **a/Ø** uno de esos
     NEG know.1SG if 2SG.DAT remember.2SG there saw.1PL   one of those
     tipos que andan   siempre . . .
     guys that walk.3PL always
     'I don't know if you'll remember. In that place we saw one of those guys who are always . . .'

Thus, accusative A is obligatory with partitives only in cases of real discourse connectedness.

We have seen that *ciert-* and *cualquiera* force a specific or nonspecific reading on the nominal phrase that includes them. In other words, they can be used as tests of specificity. Another test involves mood, as mentioned in the introduction to this chapter. If a nominal phrase includes a relative clause, the mood of the relative clause depends on specificity (Rivero 1979). If the mood is subjunctive, the nominal phrase is nonspecific. If the mood is indicative, the nominal phrase is specific. Accusative A is compatible with both indicative and subjunctive, while unmarked objects are compatible only with subjunctive.

(38) a. María buscó **a** una gestora que habla/hable alemán.
        'María looked for a manager that speaks.IND/SUBJ German.'
    b. María buscó una gestora que *habla/hable alemán.

The subjunctive test can be combined with the lexical items *ciert-* and *cualquiera*, with the expected results. *Ciert-* requires indicative mood and accusative A.

(39) María buscó **a/*Ø** una cierta gestora que habla/*hable alemán.
    'María looked for a certain manager that speaks.IND/SUBJ German.'

Cualquier- requires subjunctive mood and can be a constituent of marked or unmarked objects.

(40) María buscó **a/Ø** una gestora cualquiera que *habla/hable alemán.
    'María looked for a manager (no matter who) that speaks.IND/SUBJ German.'

A marked object can introduce a new discourse referent and be used as antecedent for a discourse anaphor. This is not surprising if marked objects are not obligatorily specific. In this respect, marked and unmarked objects behave alike.

(41) a. Vi   un niño$_i$ cruzando la calle.
        saw.1SG a boy   crossing the street
        pro$_i$ no parecía tener   ningún miedo.
            NEG seemed have.INF no   fear
        'I saw a boy crossing the street. He did not seem to be afraid at all.'
    b. Vi **a** un niño$_i$ cruzando la calle. *pro$_i$* no parecía tener ningún miedo.

The final question I would like to address in this section is the connection between specificity and wide scope. The two notions are often casually equated. However, some linguists (see in particular Hintikka 1986; Farkas 1994, 1997; von Heusinger 2002) have made a point of differentiating specificity from wide scope. Their evidence comes from examples in which it is possible for an indefinite to be specific and to take narrow scope with respect to another quantifier. Consider (42a): the modifier *certain* forces the object to be specific. At the same time, it is possible for it to have a narrow scope reading. In (42b), the negative polarity item is necessarily within the scope of negation, but it is also specific according to any definition. In (42c), the Spanish *n*-word *ninguno* must also be within the scope of negation even though it is specific, as confirmed by the obligatory indicative mood in the relative clause.

(42) a. According to Freud, every man unconsciously wants to marry a certain woman—his mother.
        Possible reading: $\forall > \exists$, [+specific]
        (Hintikka 1986, 332)
    b. I didn't buy any of these books.

c. Yo no   compré ninguno de los libros que le   gustan/*gusten a
   I   NEG bought any   of the books that CL.3SG please.IND/SUBJ DAT
   Juan.
   Juan
   'I did not buy any of the books that Juan likes.IND/SUBJ.'

Although I have not seen it discussed anywhere, the opposite sort of case is also found: a wide scope indefinite that is nonetheless nonspecific. Consider the following example:

(43) Sherlock concluded that every man loved a woman.
     Possible reading: ∃ > ∀, [−specific]

Sherlock has gathered evidence at the crime scene—recent opera tickets, wilted roses, a perfumed handkerchief—that leads him to conclude that all the men in the story are in love with the same woman—although the speaker or even Sherlock himself has no idea who this woman is.

Thus, specificity and wide scope are conceptually and empirically distinguishable. However, there is a connection: unmarked objects in Spanish cannot be specific or take wide scope; marked objects can be specific and take wide scope. This issue is taken up in chapter 3.

1.2.4 Prohibited Contexts: *Haber*, *Tener*, and Bare Plurals

A marked object is ungrammatical as the complement of *haber* 'have' (existential) and *tener* 'have' (possessor or relator).[8]

(44) En el patio hay   *a/Ø un niño.
     in the yard HABER   a   boy
     'There is a boy in the yard.'

(45) María tiene *a/Ø tres hijos.
     'María has three children.'

Marked objects cannot be bare plurals.[9]

(46) Yo contrato *a/Ø traductores.
     'I hire translators.'

The data surrounding *tener* are extremely intricate. *Tener* can mean something close to 'hold' or 'get', in which case a marked object is possible. The VP headed by *tener* can include a secondary predicate, in which case a marked object is again possible.

(47) ¡Ya   tengo   **a/Ø** uno!
    already have.1SG   one
    'I got one!'

(48) María tiene **a/Ø** un hijo en el ejército.
    'María has a son in the army.'

Bleam (2005) has aptly teased apart the two types of *tener* into an individual-level version, exemplified in (45), and a stage-level version, exemplified in (47) and (48).

The existential verb datum has occasionally been used as evidence that marked objects are specific. Indeed, existential and possessor predicates have been shown to exhibit definiteness (or specificity) effects in many languages, including Spanish. Likewise, bare plurals can only be interpreted as nonspecific (and nongeneric) indefinites in Spanish. However, the conclusion that the ungrammaticality of the examples with accusative A follows from a specificity requirement is incorrect. As we have seen, marked objects are compatible with nonspecific readings. Therefore, as far as I know, the contrasts in (44)–(48) remain unaccounted for.

1.2.5 Spanish and Maori Indefinite Nominals

As described by Chung and Ladusaw (2004), there are two types of indefinite determiners in Maori, *he* and *tētahi*. The properties of *he* parallel very precisely those of Spanish unmarked objects, while the properties of *tētahi* parallel those of marked objects. Like the Spanish unmarked object, *he* can only take narrow scope with respect to other operators and is compatible with the existential predicate. *Tētahi* can take either narrow or wide scope and is incompatible with the existential predicate. (Chung and Ladusaw do not discuss specificity.) Both *he* and *tētahi* can introduce new discourse referents and become antecedents for discourse anaphora. Here are some of the examples that Chung and Ladusaw provide:

(49) Tērā   [he tangata], ko   Rua-rangi te ingoa, ko   Tawhaitū te
    over.there a person   IDENT Rua-rangi the name IDENT Tawhaitu the
    ingoa o tana hoa.
    name of his friend
    'Once there was a man called Rua-rangi. Tawhaitu was the name of his wife.'
    (Chung and Ladusaw 2004, 32)

(50) Na terā   [tētehi wahine puhi], ko   Pare te ingoa, he tino
     now over.there a   woman virgin IDENT Pare the name a very
     rangatira taua   wahine.
     chiefly the.aforementioned woman
     'Now, once there was a woman, called Pare, who was a virgin. This
     woman was of high birth.'
     (Orbell 1992, cited in Chung and Ladusaw 2004, 32)

Chung and Ladusaw (2004, 34–41) argue that both determiners in Maori can take narrow scope with respect to conditionals, universal quantifiers, and negation, but only *tētahi* can take wide scope. This is shown in the following examples with negation. In (51) and (52), the most natural reading is for the determiner to take narrow scope. As for (53), Chung and Ladusaw argue that the context makes clear that *tētahi* takes wide scope.

(51) Kaore a   au e pīrangi kia kite he tangata.
     T.not PERS I T want   T   see a person
     'I don't want to see anyone.'
     (Chung and Ladusaw 2004, 36)

(52) Kaore anō te nuinga o ngā   tamariki nei kia kite i tētahi tereina.
     T.not yet the majority of the.PL children this T see DO a   train
     'Most of the children hadn't seen a train before.'
     (Chung and Ladusaw 2004, 37)

(53) Kaore ia i kite i   tētahi hō e takoto ana i roto   i ngā   karaehe.
     T.not he T see DO a hoe T lie   at inside at the.PL grass
     'There was a hoe he didn't see lying in the grass.'
     (Chung and Ladusaw 2004, 41)

Interestingly, *he* is compatible with existential sentences while *tētahi* is not, making the parallel with the Spanish phenomena almost perfect.[10]

(54) Kit e ai   he toxi.
     if exist an axe
     'If there should be an axe.'
     (Chung and Ladusaw 2004, 43)

Chung and Ladusaw use the Maori data to argue that some indefinites can be composed by means of Restrict, while others are composed using the choice function mechanisms sketched above. In particular, *he* indefinites are composed by Restrict, which accounts for their narrow scope properties, while *tētahi* indefinites are composed by means of choice functions. The parallelism

Introduction 23

with the Spanish objects invites a parallel analysis, which I undertake in chapters 2 and 3.

One final property of Maori indefinite nominal phrases that I would like to mention is this: although internal arguments can be headed by *he* or *tētahi*, external arguments can only be headed by *tētahi* (Chung and Ladusaw 2004, 56).

(55) I   whiu tētahi/*he wahine i   tāna mōkai ki   te moana.
     PAST throw a   woman DO her pet   into the ocean
     'A woman threw her youngest child into the ocean.'

This requires an account—and, as far as I can tell, nothing in Chung and Ladusaw's (2004) system provides one. It will turn out that the account requires taking syntax into consideration (see section 2.3.5).

1.2.6 Obligatory Contexts: Small Clauses, Clause Union, and Object Control

As far as I know, the literature on Spanish DOM has not discussed the interaction of this phenomenon with small clauses, clause union, and object control. Nonetheless, the judgments are clear. The nominal phrase in the small clause must be introduced by accusative A.

(56) El profesor   consideró   **a/*Ø** un estudiante inteligente.
     the professor considered   a student   intelligent
     'The professor considered a student intelligent.'

Bare plurals are not possible as small clause arguments (for the equivalent Italian phenomenon, see Belletti 1988; de Hoop 1996, 89).

(57) *El profesor   consideró   **a/Ø** estudiantes inteligentes.
      the professor considered   students   intelligent
      'The professor considered students intelligent.'

Notice that the data in (56) and (57) are consistent. If small clause arguments require accusative A and bare plurals reject accusative A, it follows directly that bare plurals cannot be found as small clause arguments. (Instead, (57) becomes fully grammatical with a plural indefinite determiner and accusative A.)

Likewise, accusative affected arguments (the *affectee*) in clause union also need accusative A and reject bare plurals. I start with the *causee* of a causative construction. The causee of an intransitive predicate is accusative. This accusative is obligatorily introduced by accusative A and cannot be a bare plural.

(58) a. María hizo llegar tarde **a/*Ø** un niño.
         María made arrive late   a boy
         'María made a boy be late.'
     b. *María hizo llegar tarde **a/Ø** niños.
         María made arrive late   boys
         'María made boys be late.'

(59) a. María hizo trabajar los domingos **a/*Ø** un empleado.
         María made work   the Sundays   an employee
         'María made an employee work on Sundays.'
     b. *María hizo trabajar los domingos **a/Ø** empleados.
         María made work   the Sundays   employees
         'María made employees work on Sundays.'

In (60), the complement of the causative predicate is a transitive predicate. The causee of the transitive predicate is also prefixed by *a*, but in this case it is the dative case marker.[11] The internal argument is not required to be introduced by accusative A. For perspicuity, the causee in (60) is plural, in agreement with a dative plural clitic.

(60) María les   hizo visitar **a/Ø** un enfermo **a/*Ø** unas empleadas.
     María CL.PL.DAT made visit   a   sick   DAT   some employees
     'María made some employees visit a sick person.'

The same holds for the affectee of a permissive construction.

(61) María dejó llegar tarde **a/*Ø** un niño.
     María let arrive late   a boy
     'María allowed a boy to be late.'

(62) María dejó trabajar los domingos **a/*Ø** un empleado.
     María let work   the Sundays   an employee
     'María allowed an employee to work on Sundays.'

(63) María dejó a   una empleada visitar **a/Ø** un enfermo.
     María let DAT an employee visit   a sick
     'María allowed an employee to visit a sick person.'

Again, the same facts hold of perception verbs.

(64) María vio caer **a/*Ø** un niño.
     María saw fall   a boy
     'María saw a boy fall.'

(65) María vio trabajar **a/*Ø** un niño.
    María saw work   a boy
    'María saw a boy work.'

(66) María vio a una empleada visitar **a/Ø** un enfermo.
    María saw DAT an employee visit   a sick
    'María saw an employee visit a sick person.'

Finally, the object of an object control predicate also needs to be introduced by accusative A.

(67) Juan forzó **a/*Ø** un niño a hacer los deberes.
    Juan forced   a boy to do.INF the homework
    'Juan forced a boy to do his homework.'

The obligatoriness of accusative A in any of these contexts does not follow from any specificity requirement. In the following examples, the affectees are nonspecific, as indicated by the subjunctive in the relative clause. Although the affectees can only be interpreted as nonspecific, they cannot be unmarked objects.

(68) Juan no considera honrado **a/*Ø** un hombre que acepte sobornos.
    Juan NEG considers honest   a man   that accepts.SUBJ bribes
    'Juan does not consider honest a man that accepts bribes.'

(69) María hace quedarse en clase **a/*Ø** un niño que no haya terminado
    María does stay.INF in class   a boy that no has.SUBJ finished
    los deberes.
    the duties
    'María makes a boy that has not finished the assignment stay in class.'

(70) María no dejaría salir **a/*Ø** ningún niño que no haya
    María NEG let.COND leave.INF   no boy that NEG has.SUBJ
    terminado los deberes.
    finished the duties
    'María would not let any boy who has not finished the assignment go out.'

The same holds of a controlling object.

(71) María forzaría **a/*Ø** una empleada que tuviera depresion a
    María force.COND   an employee that had.SUBJ depression to
    venir al trabajo.
    come.INF to.the work
    'María would force an employee who was depressed to come to work.'

1.2.7 Obligatory Contexts: *Wh*-Phrases

Object *wh*-phrases also require accusative A.

(72) ¿**A/*Ø** quién has   llamado?
          who   have.2SG called
   'Who did you call?'

This is the case whether they front to Spec,C or stay in situ in a multiple-*wh* sentence.

(73) ¿Quién dijiste   que llamó   **a/*Ø** quién?
      who   said.1SG that called.3SG   who
   'Who did you say called who?'

Non-D-linked *wh*-phrases are commonly regarded as indefinite nominal phrases and therefore one would expect optional accusative A. It is puzzling that non-D-linked *wh*-phrases are not allowed with unmarked objects.

1.2.8 The Definiteness Scale

Some of the facts presented in this section are well-known, and every student of Spanish linguistics or DOM is familiar with them. Others have never, to my knowledge, been described before (such as the phenomena in sections 1.2.6 and 1.2.7). Even those facts that have previously been described have not, in my opinion, received the attention they deserve: for instance, the optionality of the specific readings for marked objects or the impossibility of marked objects with existential and possessor predicates. It is worth pausing to consider the significance of these data with regard to received wisdom about DOM.

The current mainstream approach to the distribution of DOM phenomena involves scales. Consider the following definiteness scale (copied from Aissen 2003, 437, which draws on work that goes back to Silverstein 1976):

(74) *Definiteness scale*
   Personal pronoun > Proper name > Definite NP > Indefinite specific NP > Nonspecific NP

This scale expresses an implication: if a language has DOM on an item in the scale, it will also have DOM on all the items to the left (Silverstein 1976). The Spanish data presented in sections 1.2.1 and 1.2.3 suggest that this language draws the line at "indefinite specific NP," since everything to the left of, and including, indefinite specific NPs is marked. Other languages draw the line at different points on the scale.

The scale makes very direct predictions. If a language marked, say, personal pronouns and indefinite specific NPs while leaving proper names unmarked, the scale would be falsified. I am not aware of any such language. Thus, it would seem, at least at first sight, that the scale does embody a real generalization that should be incorporated into any analysis.

Aissen (2003, 447–448) formalizes the scale by means of two conflicting constraints.

(75) *$\emptyset_c$ 'STARZERO': Penalizes the absence of a value for the feature CASE.

(76) *STRUC$_c$: Penalizes the presence of a value for the feature CASE.

*$\emptyset_c$ is associated with the different types of DPs, which are themselves placed in a hierarchy tied to the definiteness scale. For instance, a language in which only personal pronouns are marked would correspond to the hierarchy in (77a), while a language in which personal pronouns and proper names are marked would correspond to the hierarchy in (77b).

(77) a. *PRON & *$\emptyset_c$ ≫ *STRUC$_c$ ≫ *PROPERNAME & *$\emptyset_c$ ≫ ...
     b. *PRON & *$\emptyset_c$ ≫ *PROPERNAME & *$\emptyset_c$ ≫ *STRUC$_c$ ≫ ...

That is, in language (77a), leaving a pronoun unmarked is a worse violation than marking it. However, marking a proper name, a definite DP, and so on, is worse than avoiding the mark. In language (77b), leaving a pronoun or a proper name unmarked is worse than marking it.

In Spanish, *STRUC$_c$ would be situated quite low in the hierarchy, since several different types of objects are marked and only nonspecific objects are unmarked.

(78) *Definiteness scale for Spanish (1)*
    *PRON & *$\emptyset_c$ ≫ *NAME & *$\emptyset_c$ ≫ *DEFDP & *$\emptyset_c$ ≫ *SPECIFICDP & *$\emptyset_c$ ≫ *STRUC$_c$ ≫ *NONSPECIFICDP & *$\emptyset_c$

Now let us see whether this approach offers insight into the phenomena of concern in this monograph.

One of the surprising findings of this chapter is the scope facts that revolve around marked objects. Indefinite marked objects can take wide scope while indefinite unmarked objects *and* marked strong quantifiers cannot. I surmise that the definiteness scale has nothing to say about this.

Next, consider optionality. As we have seen, marked indefinite objects in Spanish do not have to be specific; they are only optionally so. The only way to account for this fact within Aissen's framework is to allow the constraint

*STRUC$_c$ to fluctuate, so that both (78) and (79) exist as part of the mental grammar of Spanish speakers.

(79) *Definiteness scale for Spanish (2)*
  *P$_{RON}$ & *Ø$_c$ ≫ *N$_{AME}$ & *Ø$_c$ ≫ *D$_{EF}$DP & *Ø$_c$ ≫ *S$_{PECIFIC}$DP & *Ø$_c$ ≫ *N$_{ONSPECIFIC}$DP & *Ø$_c$ ≫ *STRUC$_c$

This is reasonable, since diachronic linguistics shows that DOM expands over time along the definiteness scale (see von Heusinger and Kaiser 2005) and it is plausible to suppose there would be periods in which two different positions for *STRUC$_c$ could coexist in a language community and in the mental grammars of individual speakers.

But fluctuation does not help us with the problems described above. Fluctuation predicts that *any* indefinite nonspecific object can be marked, but this is not the case: as I showed in section 1.2.4, the pivot of the existential verb *haber* and the complement of *tener* 'have' *cannot* be marked, other types of nonspecific indefinites *can* be marked, and *wh*-phrases *must* be marked. Thus, for *haber* we would need to create a new constraint *P$_{IVOT}$DP & *Ø$_c$ and place it at the bottom of the constraint hierarchy, while allowing the constraint *STRUC$_c$ to be unordered with respect to *N$_{ONSPECIFIC}$DP & *Ø$_c$. Possible, but arguably nothing but a technical solution.

More problematic still are the data discussed in sections 1.2.6 and 1.2.7. How do we integrate the obligatoriness of accusative A in small clauses, clause union, and object control? The constraint ranking in (78) would have to be complicated with further subdivisions such as *S$_{MALL}$C$_{LAUSE}$DP & *Ø$_c$, and these constraints would be ordered high in the hierarchy. However, it is clear that the hierarchy is now mixing definiteness with a completely different type of constraint.

Thus, in Spanish—and in other languages, as I show in chapter 4—certain types of morphosyntactic objects require DOM, regardless of their position on the scale, as I showed in sections 1.2.6 and 1.2.7. The data presented in those sections cannot be easily brushed aside: they are systematic, and they do not concern boundaries between items in the scale. What is missing from the scales approach is syntax.

In chapter 2, I argue that an understanding of DOM must pass through syntax. In the view that I will advocate, DOM is the morphological expression of a syntactic configuration. A syntactic configuration for x is defined as the position that x finds itself in together with the feature structure of the immediately surrounding environment, as defined in chapter 2. That is, a subset of the objects that find themselves in a certain syntactic position π are subject to a rule of Vocabulary insertion (see Halle and Marantz 1993 and chapter 2) that results in DOM. Moreover, processes of semantic composition that can apply to a DP in position π but not to a DP in situ lead to the optional specific interpretations for the DPs in π.[12] Those predicates with obligatory DOM are the predicates whose argument needs to raise to position π.

1.3 Conclusions

In this chapter, I have outlined some of the theoretical and empirical challenges that indefinite objects present as well as the three traditions that have approached (at least some of) these challenges in one way or another. I have presented a hypothesis according to which one subset of indefinite objects scrambles while another subset does not. The indefinite objects that scramble are interpreted by means of choice functions; those that do not are interpreted by Restrict. A subset of scrambled objects may bear a special type of morphology, referred to as DOM. I have not yet presented empirical evidence for scrambling of marked objects or for the correlation among scrambling, DOM, and choice functions.

In the second half of this section, I have discussed Spanish indefinite objects and shown that they present several empirical puzzles. Marked objects can be specific and take wide scope over other sentential operators. Unmarked objects cannot. Noting the parallelism with Maori indefinites, I hinted that a parallel solution might be available. The existential verb and the possessor verb in Spanish do not allow a marked complement, while *wh*-phrases and the arguments of small clauses, clause union, and control objects must be marked. These empirical facts have yet to receive an analysis. The scales approach to DOM, best represented in Aissen 2003, was shown to be inadequate to account for any of the phenomena of interest here.

2 Scrambling and Differential Object Marking

The purpose of this chapter is to argue for a particular syntax for indefinite objects. I argue that some indefinite objects scramble to a low position. A subset of those scrambling objects (the ones that appear in the right environmental conditions, animacy of the noun in particular) bear accusative A. Other objects remain in situ and are unmarked. Case requirements are crucial: accusative Case originates in v (see Chomsky 1995 et seq.). Objects that remain in situ can only satisfy their Case requirement by incorporation into the lexical verb and by incorporation of the latter into v. Scrambled objects move to a specifier position that is governed by v. Two of the empirical problems discussed in chapter 1 receive an analysis in this chapter: the impossibility of accusative A with bare plurals, and the obligatoriness of accusative A with small clauses, clause union, and object controllers.

In section 2.1, I introduce my syntactic assumptions. In section 2.2, I argue that marked objects in Spanish undergo scrambling regardless of whether they are interpreted as specific or not. In section 2.3, I examine the distribution of DOM, taking into consideration the syntactic conclusions reached in section 2.2.

2.1 Theoretical Assumptions

2.1.1 Transitive Configurations

I subscribe to the basic tenets of generative grammar in its minimalist version (see especially Chomsky 2000). In particular, I adopt the assumption that the structure of transitive predicates involves an abstract light verb that introduces the external argument (EA).

Additionally, I assume there is a functional category between vP and VP, which I call α.

(1)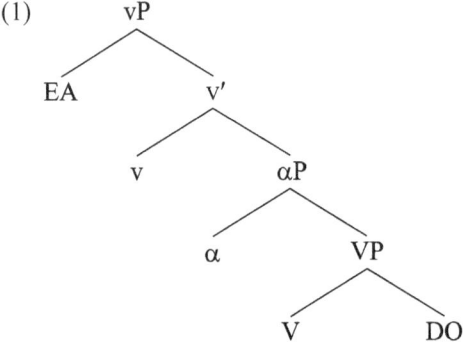

Numerous authors have proposed that a functional category exists between v and V (see, e.g., Travis 1992, 2010; Koizumi 1995; Baker and Collins 2006). As for the nature of this category, there are two trends. One trend identifies α with the applicative function; α is thus characterized as a category that introduces affected indirect objects (IOs) and may in some languages (and analyses!) assign Case to the DO (see, e.g., Marantz 1993; Cuervo 2003; Pylkkänen 2006; Bruening 2010). The second trend takes α to be a head related to inner aspect—in particular, telicity and/or boundedness (if they are the same thing; see Depraetere 1995). Travis (2010) offers the most articulated proposal along these lines. I take it that the α that I discuss in this monograph is a conglomerate of both types of properties. I will not attempt to investigate this hypothesis in depth, but simply point out that there are two reasons to think it would be useful in an analysis of DOM: (i) in many languages, DOM is morphologically identical to dative; and (ii) in many languages, DOM affects DOs in telic configurations. Elaborating a little further, there is no particular reason why the applicative function and the inner aspect function should be encapsulated in one category. In fact, in chapter 4 I will argue that in Kiswahili the two types of functions head their own phrases.

I take it that, in the same way that v may introduce an EA or may not introduce an argument at all, there is a type of α—call it $α_{[appl]}$—that introduces an argument and a type of α that does not. The structure of double object constructions (DOCs) is shown in (2).

(2)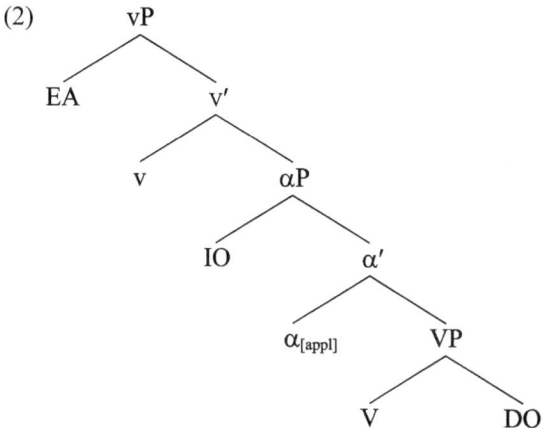

Prepositional IOs play no role in this monograph, so I will not elaborate on their properties. Following Basilico (1998), I assume that prepositional IOs are merged in a specifier position while DOs are merged in Compl,V. This ensures that the theme remains the lowest argument in the structure and therefore that the Uniformity of Theta Assignment Hypothesis is respected (following Baker 1997). A direct consequence of my assumptions is that the DO c-commands the IO only if it scrambles.

It is worthwhile lingering on the properties of ditransitives in Spanish. There are two versions of ditransitives in Spanish: one with the dative clitic *le* and one without.

(3) Juan le   envió el paquete a   un niño.
    Juan CL.DAT sent the package DAT a boy
    'Juan sent a boy the package.'

(4) Juan envió el paquete a un niño.
    'Juan sent the package to a boy.' or 'Juan sent a boy the package.'

My translation of example (3) reflects Demonte's (1995) and Bleam's (2003) finding that the Spanish ditransitives with *le* are equivalent to DOCs in English and other languages. They base this conclusion on the usual c-command tests. My translation of (4) reflects a departure from the previous authors. Both Demonte and Bleam argue that ditransitives without *le* are equivalent to ditransitives with a prepositional indirect object. Bleam (2003) in particular argues for the following structures:

(5) DOC: EA $le+v$ [$_{vP}$ DP$_{IO}$ V DP$_{DO}$]
    Prepositional ditransitives: EA v [$_{vP}$ DP$_{DO}$ V PP$_{IO}$]

I agree with Demonte and Bleam that ditransitives with *le* are DOCs. However, there are many instances of ditransitives without *le* in which the c-command relations between the DO and the IO qualify them as DOCs. I have administered acceptability tests to Spanish speakers several times over the years and found that ditransitives without *le* seem to have shifting properties.

Consider for instance Bleam's (2003) idiom test. She correctly points out that (6a) has the idiomatic meaning while (6b) does not.

(6) a. María le   ha dado la lata   a   Juan.
 María CL.DAT has given the tin.can DAT Juan
 'María has annoyed Juan.'
 b. María ha dado la lata a Juan.
 'María has given the tin can to Juan.'
 c. María ha dado la lata a mucha gente.
 'María has annoyed many people.'

She argues that the idiomatic meaning of (6a) is possible because the lower predicate forms a constituent with *la lata* that leaves *a Juan* outside (see Marantz 1984 for observations along these lines regarding the external argument and the internal argument). In (6b), the lower predicate forms a constituent with *a Juan*, leaving *la lata* outside and thus precluding the idiomatic meaning. I agree with Bleam's judgment and conclusion. However, I would like to add that if we change the example a little, the idiomatic meaning is possible even in the absence of *le*; see (6c). In this example, the indefiniteness of the IO makes the DOC structure possible without *le*. Thus, I conclude that a DOC with the structure in (2) is possible even in the absence of *le*—and I leave a detailed analysis of ditransitive predicates in Spanish for future research. As a working tool, I use c-command tests to find out if a ditransitive predicate is a DOC or not. If it is a DOC, it is possible for the IO to c-command the DO.

2.1.2 Syntactic Dependencies

I assume that there are two kinds of syntactic dependencies. The first is selection dependencies, in which a head requires a constituent of a certain category. Selection dependencies are necessary to account for the presence of expletives in natural language, as well as the selecting properties of the expletives themselves (see López 2007). I take all other syntactic dependencies to be based on *feature sharing* (see also Frampton and Gutmann 2002). Feature sharing can be the output of the *Agree* operation, which has the following form (where *uf* stands for *unvalued feature*):

(7) Agree ($a_{[f]}, b_{[uf]}$) → ($a_{[f]}, b_{[f]}$)

That is, an operation called *Agree* values or covalues all the features of the two items involved in the operation. Additionally, I assume that Agree (a,b) is strictly local, reaching only to the specifier of the complement of the probe (López 2002, 2007).

(8) X [$_{YP}$ ZP [$_{Y'}$ Y WP]]

In (8), X can have dependencies with YP and ZP, but not WP. In order to refer to the closeness of the relationship that YP and ZP have with X, I use the somewhat old-fashioned term *government*. Thus, I say that X *governs* YP and ZP and that all syntactic dependencies take place in a government configuration.

Further, I assume that movement is triggered by an unvalued feature in the moving item (López 2002, 2007; Bošković 2007). When an unvalued feature is introduced into the tree and cannot be satisfied, it must move at once. Assuming that structure is built incrementally by *Merge* and *Move*, the unvalued feature has only one place to go: the next specifier. Move stops when the unvalued feature finds itself governed by a probe with the appropriate feature. The links of a movement chain are joined together by feature sharing, formally no different than a dependency created by Agree.

A sample derivation is given in (9). Take every argumental DP to be the carrier of an unvalued Case feature ([uC]) that needs to be valued by a probe that carries a valued Case feature (Chomsky 2000; Pesetsky and Torrego 2001; López 2007). The DP is an argument of X, which has no [C] feature. Y does not have a [C] feature either, so DP must move to Spec,Y at once. Z is merged, and Z does have a [C]. Z probes and finds the DP, valuing its [C]. By virtue of feature sharing, all the links of the DP chain have their Case valued. Probing must be triggered by some unvalued feature of Z (not represented in (9)).

(9) a. [$_{XP}$ DP$_{[uC]}$ X]   Merge (Y,XP) →
 b. Y [$_{XP}$ DP$_{[uC]}$ X]   Move (DP)   →
 c. [$_{YP}$ DP$_{[uC]}$ Y [$_{XP}$ t(DP$_{[uC]}$) X]]   Merge (Z,YP) →
 d. Z$_{[C]}$ [$_{YP}$ DP$_{[uC]}$ Y [$_{XP}$ t(DP$_{[uC]}$) X]] Agree (Z,DP) →
 e. Z$_{[C]}$ [$_{YP}$ DP$_{[C]}$ Y [$_{XP}$ t(DP$_{[C]}$) X]]

Notice that the theory of syntax proposed here allows for the possibility that two or more dependencies will converge on one position. Consider the tree in (10).

(10)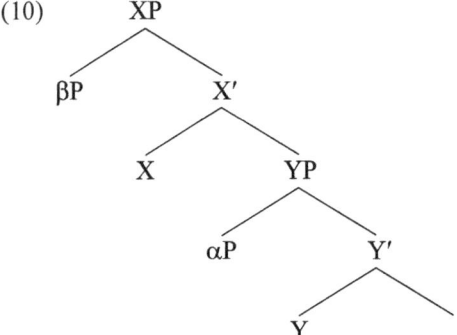

We can note the following potential dependencies:

- αP is governed by X, so they can be in a dependency together.
- αP is also the second term merged with Y. If Y selects for two terms (e.g., because it is a two-place predicate), αP is in a dependency with Y.
- βP is the second term merged with X. Therefore, βP can be in a selection dependency with X.
- Thus, βP and αP can both be in dependencies with X.

2.1.3 Order and Structure

Since Kayne 1994, it has commonly been assumed that the left-to-right linear order of constituents faithfully reflects the c-command hierarchy. Following common practice, I assume that in many languages, especially the Germanic languages (but also Persian and Hindi-Urdu (hereafter Hindi)), one can take the relative positions of adverbs and the DO as indicative of scrambling, Likewise, the relative positions of IO and DO can be taken as evidence of the presence or absence of scrambling in many languages.

(11) a. [AdvP DP] → DP [AdvP [e]]
　　 b. [IO DO] → DO [IO [e]]

However, word order does not always reflect structure in some languages with flexible order such as Spanish (see López 2009b for an approach to linearization). In fact, c-command tests sometimes suggest that a constituent X can follow *and* c-command another constituent Y. Example (12) illustrates.

(12) Juan le entregó　su$_i$ regalo a　 cada$_i$ niño.
　　 Juan CL delivered his gift　　DAT every boy
　　 'Juan gave every$_i$ boy his$_i$ gift.'

Scrambling and Differential Object Marking

This example accepts a reading in which Juan gave every boy a different gift, which entails that the IO c-commands the DO to its left. Compare (12) with (13). In (13), the quantifier in object position cannot bind a variable in the postverbal subject.

(13) Ayer vio su*$_i$ padre a cada$_i$ niño.
      yesterday saw his father every boy
      'Yesterday his father saw every boy.'

Thus, I conclude that in Spanish DOCs, word order is not a reliable indicator of structure. However, the relative order of subject and object does seem to reflect structure, as revealed by the c-command test. When discussing Spanish structure, particularly ditransitive predicates, I will rely on classic c-command tests rather than linear order. My trees will all be drawn conventionally, with the specifier to the left of the head and the complement to the right, without any commitment as to what the base order—if there is such a thing—actually is.

2.1.4 Postsyntactic Morphology

I assume a realizational theory of morphology such as the one developed under the banner *Distributed Morphology* (see Halle and Marantz 1993 for the foundational paper). Within this framework, the Lexicon consists of a set of abstract features without a phonetic matrix (see List 1 in (14)). These abstract features are combined, giving rise to syntactic configurations that are fed to the conceptual-intensional (C-I) systems and the sensorimotor (SM) interface. The process that turns syntactic structures into SM instructions involves endowing the tree terminals with phonetic matrices. To this effect, there is a *Vocabulary* (see List 2), which consists of phonetic matrices—*Vocabulary items*—associated with rules of *Vocabulary insertion* that define the types of terminals into which the Vocabulary items can be introduced. The information included in the rules of Vocabulary insertion involves exclusively the contexts of insertion. The resulting grammatical architecture is shown in (14).

(14)   C-I

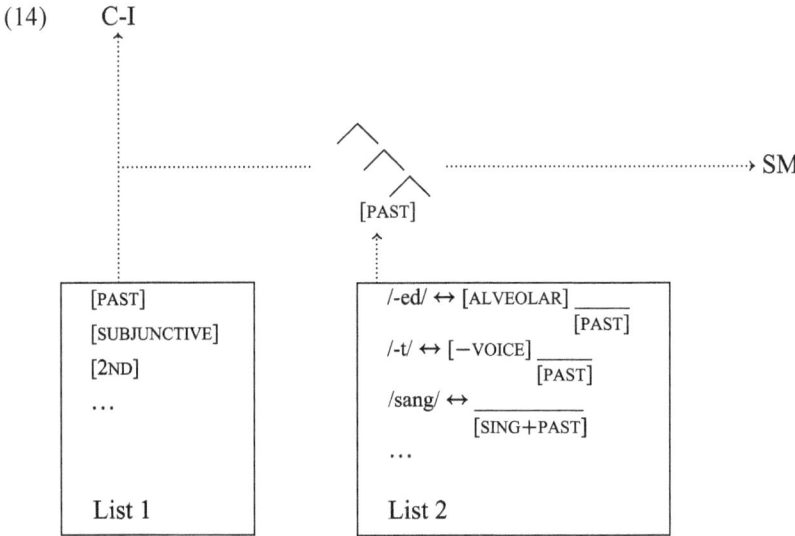

A realizational approach to marked objects seems to me to be particularly suitable because the distribution of the prefix *a* clearly depends on its syntactic context, as shown in chapter 1. Of course, another analysis is always possible: free generation of the prefix *a* in a presyntactic lexicon coupled with a filter that throws out (or filters that throw out) the instances of *a* that do not fulfill certain properties. The reader is free to consider my choice of realizational morphology a matter of taste.

Within a realizational framework, there is no "accusative A" in the lexicon or in the syntactic representation. Instead, List 1 includes a functional category F with an array of abstract features. If these features take certain values, and F appears in a certain environment, a rule from List 2 will assign F a Vocabulary item. Thus, we can provisionally define the appearance of accusative A as follows:

(15)   /a/ ↔ [___ [context]]
              [F]

(15) tells us that a functional category F in a certain context will receive the phonological matrix /a/. In order to begin thinking about this context, consider tree (16). F is the head that can undergo the rule of Vocabulary insertion (15). H is the lexical head of the extended projection of F (in the sense of Grimshaw 1991). FP is in Spec,X and is governed by the head G.

(16)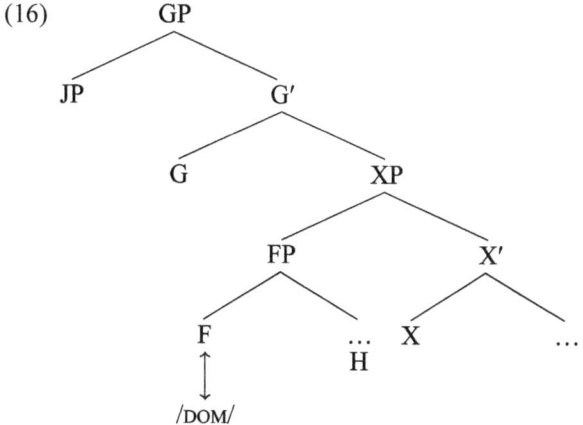

The [context] for rule (15) will be a factor of three elements: (i) properties of H, the head selected by F; (ii) properties of G and JP, since both govern FP and therefore can be in a dependency with F; and (iii) X, if FP has moved from a position that X governs.

I do not assume that any constituent outside of this local domain can have an influence on the appearance of accusative A, and therefore no "global properties" (as in García 2007 and de Swart 2007) play a role. This is consistent with my theoretical commitment to making all dependencies strictly local, as defined above. The challenging part is, of course, defining the context. This is discussed in section 2.3. First, I need to delineate the syntactic configuration of accusative A.

2.2 Short Scrambling and A-Dependencies

2.2.1 The Configuration

The goal of this section is to argue that the marked object undergoes short scrambling to Spec,α (for earlier analyses of short scrambling, see Johnson 1991 and Koizumi 1995). Tree (17) shows a case where this scrambling has taken place with an α of the applicative type (*DO.DOM* is the accusative A object; *DO* is the unmarked object).

(17)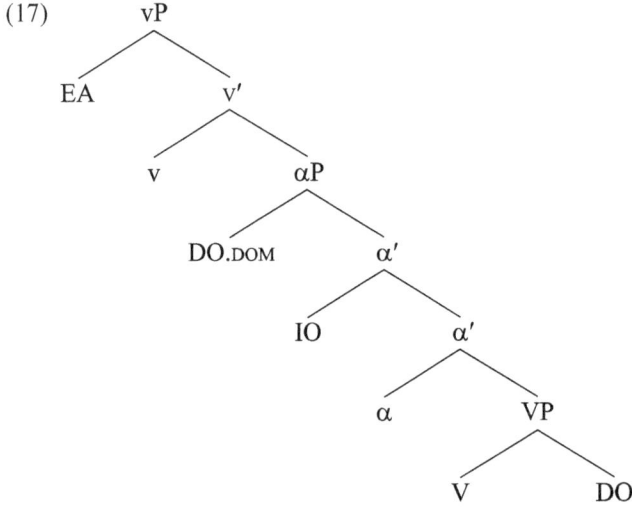

Notice that in (17), v is the locus for both accusative and dative Case assignment, as in Anagnostopoulou 2003. I should clarify that I do not take this to be universal. Ditransitives show too much apparent crosslinguistic variation to make universal claims at this point; in fact, in chapter 4 I will argue that in Kiswahili both v and α assign Case. Additional details on how accusative Case is assigned are given in sections 2.2.5 and 2.2.6.

Crucial for my argument is the evidence that a marked object is higher in the structure than an IO, regardless of whether the IO is merged with an applicative head or as an argument of V. The unmarked object stays in situ. In fact, the structure in (17) makes the following claims:

- DO.DOM c-commands IO.
- DO.DOM does not c-command EA.
- DO does not c-command IO.

These three properties make specific predictions concerning quantifier-variable relations and the binding possibilities of anaphors, which are tested in the following section.

2.2.2 Good Old C-Command Tests

Let's now discuss the evidence for short scrambling of the marked object. Consider (18) (adapted from similar examples found in Leonetti 2004).

(18) [Context: What did the enemies do? The enemies delivered X to Y and Z to W, but ...]
Los enemigos no entregaron a su$_i$ hijo **a/Ø** ningún$_i$ prisionero.
the enemies NEG delivered.PL DAT his son   no   prisoner
'The enemies did not deliver any prisoner to his son.'

The DP *ningún prisionero* 'no prisoner' can bear accusative A. Interestingly, the range of possible interpretations varies with the appearance of accusative A. When the object is marked, it is possible to read this sentence with a quantifier-variable interpretation, that is, as a pairing of prisoners and sons. This reading is absent in the version without accusative A. This difference in interpretation between the marked and the unmarked object follows directly from the structure in (17). The unmarked object stays in situ, so it cannot c-command the IO and therefore it cannot bind the variable. The marked object moves to Spec,α, from which position it can c-command the IO.

One could argue that it is unclear whether the pairing reading comes from the accusative A marker or from a specific reading of *ningún prisionero* (indeed, this is how Leonetti (2004) interprets these facts). This account is not likely because the specific reading is very weak or (to my ear) nonexistent for this DP (as compared with *ninguno de los prisioneros* 'none of the prisoners', where at least a partitive specific reading is prominent). But, to be on the safe side, I supply the same test with a noun that cannot have a specific reading and can (actually must) take accusative A. This noun is *nadie* 'no one'.

(19) Los enemigos no entregaron a su$_i$ hijo **a** nadie$_i$.
the enemies NEG delivered.PL DAT his son   no.one
'The enemies delivered no one to his son.'

As in (18), the bound reading is available.

A marked object can bind a dative reflexive. An unmarked object cannot.

(20) a. María le   entregó a   Juan un hombre.
       María CL.DAT delivered DAT Juan a   man
       'María delivered a man to Juan.'
   b. *María le   entregó a   sí mismo un hombre.
       María CL.DAT delivered DAT himself   a   man
   c. María le   entregó a   sí mismo **a** un hombre.
       María CL.DAT delivered DAT himself   a   man
       (cualquiera).
       (doesn't matter who)
       'María delivered a man to himself.'

(20a) acts as a baseline example. (20b), where the IO is a masculine reflexive and the DO is unmarked, is ungrammatical. (20c), where the DO is marked, is grammatical. The difference in acceptability between (20b) and (20c) can be accounted for if the marked object c-commands the IO, thus binding the reflexive, while the unmarked object stays in situ. The binding shown in (20c) holds even if the DO *a un hombre* 'a man' is interpreted as nonspecific, as shown by the modifier *cualquiera*.

Recall from chapter 1 that Diesing (1992) claims that indefinite nonspecific nominal phrases that appear to be high in the structure (e.g., subjects in English) must be subject to LF lowering. One could plausibly try this sort of approach for the Spanish data: in the face of optional specificity for scrambled objects in Spanish, one could claim that LF lowering takes place in Spanish and that is the reason why nonspecific indefinites can be marked. But this solution is not correct: if nonspecific indefinites underwent LF lowering, *a nadie* 'no one' would never be able to bind *a su hijo* 'to his son' in (19). Likewise, (20c) would not be grammatical. I conclude there is no such LF lowering, at least not in Spanish. There must be some other solution to the puzzle of scrambled nonspecific objects, one that makes the connection between syntax and semantics more indirect than Diesing's approach does. This solution is provided in chapter 3.

2.2.3 What about Spec,v?

The previous discussion shows that a marked object c-commands an IO. However, various types of object movement have been argued (or claimed) to target a higher position, a specifier of little v, as shown in (21).

(21)

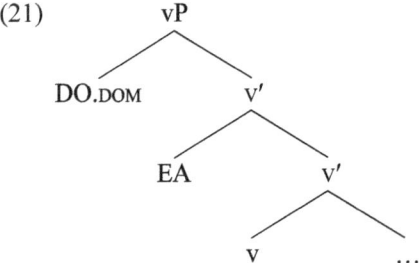

This is the configuration usually assumed for Germanic scrambling and object shift (see in particular the influential analysis in Bobaljik and Jonas 1996). It is also the configuration for marked objects assumed by Torrego (1998) and Rodríguez-Mondoñedo (2007). It is worth investigating whether (21) is a possibility.[1]

Notice that (17) and (21) make distinct predictions. According to my proposal, the marked object does not c-command the EA in situ. According to Torrego's and Rodríguez-Mondoñedo's proposals, it does.

The usual tests show that a marked object does not c-command the EA in situ. As is standard in Spanish linguistics, I take the postverbal subject to be in situ. In the following sentence, there is no quantifier-variable reading:

(22) [Context: So, what happened yesterday?]
Ayer no atacó su$_{*i}$ propio padre a ningún$_i$ niño.
yesterday NEG attacked his own father no boy
'His own father attacked no boy yesterday.'

If the marked object *a ningún niño* 'no boy' were in Spec,v, it should c-command *su propio padre* 'his own father' and therefore the quantifier-variable reading should be available.

For contrast, it is worth introducing at this point two other constructions in Spanish that trigger displacement and alteration of c-command relations: clitic right-dislocation and p-movement/scrambling.

In Spanish, any constituent can be right-dislocated. If the dislocated constituent is an object, it is doubled by a clitic. Clitic-right-dislocated DOs do c-command the EA. The bound reading is possible in the following sentence (as was discovered for Catalan by Villalba (2000)):

(23) [Context: What happened yesterday to every boy?]
Ayer lo atacó su$_i$ propio padre, a cada$_i$ niño.
yesterday CL.ACC attacked his own father each boy
'His own father attacked every boy yesterday.'

The alteration in c-command relations can also be perceived in reverse.

(24) [Context: What happened yesterday in the restaurant?]
Ayer no se limpió ningún$_i$ camarero su$_i$ chaqueta.
yesterday NEG REFL cleaned no waiter his jacket
'Yesterday no waiter cleaned his jacket.'

(25) [Context: What happened yesterday in the restaurant?]
Ayer no se la limpió ningún$_i$ camarero, su$_{*i}$ chaqueta.
yesterday NEG REFL CL.ACC cleaned no waiter his jacket
'Yesterday no waiter cleaned his jacket.'

(26) [Context: What happened yesterday in the restaurant?]
Ayer   ningún_i camarero se   la   limpió, su_i chaqueta.
yesterday no   waiter   REFL CL.ACC cleaned his jacket
'Yesterday no waiter cleaned his jacket.'

In (24), *ningún camarero* 'no waiter' can bind *su chaqueta* 'his jacket'. This reading disappears in (25), with *su chaqueta* right-dislocated. In (26), with a preverbal subject—presumably, in Spec,T or higher—the bound reading reappears. I take these judgments to provide evidence that right-dislocated objects in Spanish move to a position intermediate between the in-situ and ex-situ positions of the EA. Thus, I conclude that the grammar of Spanish indeed allows displacement of an object to Spec,v (or higher). However, marked objects do not necessarily undergo this displacement.

Spanish can also rearrange the constituent order so that the DO appears to the left of the subject; this is called *scrambling* by Ordóñez (1998) and *p-movement* by Zubizarreta (1998). The p-moved/scrambled DO c-commands the EA (Ordóñez 1998). In (27), a quantifier-variable reading is possible.

(27) [Context: What happened yesterday to every boy?]
Ayer   atacó   a cada_i niño su_i propio padre.
yesterday attacked   each boy his own   father
'His own father attacked every boy yesterday.'

This quantifier-variable reading disappears again if the EA is preverbal.

(28) [Context: What happened yesterday to every boy?]
Su*_i propio padre ayer   atacó   a cada_i niño.
his own father yesterday attacked   each boy
'His own father attacked every boy yesterday.'

2.2.4 Two Ex-Situ Positions for Objects

On the basis of these data, in López 2009a I propose that there are two ex-situ positions for objects in Spanish. The analysis is presented in (29).

(29)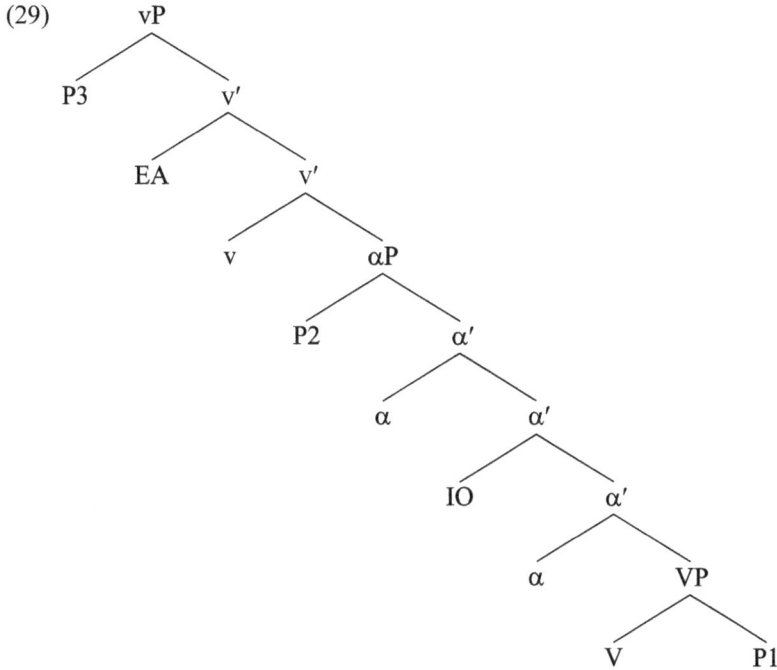

P1 is the position of unmarked objects. Given the empirical evidence presented above, unmarked objects seem to stay in situ. Marked objects move to P2, a position from which they c-command the IO but not the EA. Finally, P3 is the landing site of p-movement and clitic right-dislocation.

Interpretively, each position is distinct. As shown in chapter 1, unmarked objects—that is, objects in P1—are necessarily nonspecific, take narrow scope with respect to any sentential operators, and are compatible with existential *haber* and possessor/relator *tener*. Marked objects—now redefined as a subset of those in position P2—may or may not be specific, can take narrow or wide scope, and are incompatible with existential *haber* and possessor/relator *tener*.

Position P3 is different in character from the other two because it is connected with information structure. As I argue in López 2009a, constituents that occupy P3 and establish a dependency with v are subject to an interpretive rule that turns them into discourse anaphors. The same rule leaves the complement of v as a focus. This analysis of P3 has a broad crosslinguistic support.

The detailed examination of the different types of objects reveals that the approach taken by Torrego (1998) needs revisiting. Torrego locates Spanish marked objects in Spec,v and seeks to derive their properties—in particular, specificity—from this position. Her arguments are not empirical but are made mostly by analogy with constructions in other languages, such as Icelandic object shift: since object shift in Icelandic is specific and targets Spec,v, then marked objects in Spanish, which are also specific (so the reasoning goes), must also target Spec,v, even if there is no evidence for movement to Spec,v for marked objects in Spanish. However, the analogy is based on mistaken semantic assumptions: shifted objects in Icelandic are obligatorily specific and are obligatorily discourse anaphors, while accusative A is optionally specific and can be a focus as well as a discourse anaphor—in fact, accusative A is insensitive to information structure. Moreover, the empirical evidence presented in sections 2.2.2 and 2.2.3 clearly indicates that marked objects in Spanish do not target Spec,v (unless they are subject to subsequent p-movement or dislocation), while Icelandic shifted objects do (see Bobaljik and Jonas 1996 and much subsequent work). Thus, the difference in interpretation between Icelandic object shift and Spanish accusative A finds a correlate in the syntax.

2.2.5 The Mechanics of A-Movement: Unmarked Objects

I follow the tradition begun by Chomsky (1981) that attributes movement of nominals to the workings of Case theory. Some discussion is needed here concerning (i) the size of nominal phrases, (ii) what needs Case, and (iii) what strategies are adopted by nominal phrases to satisfy their Case requirement.

Research on the structure of nominals reveals that they do not always project a full structure but can easily project only as NP or #P (see, for instance, Cardinaletti and Starke 1999 and Déchaine and Wiltschko 2002 for pronouns, as well as the detailed discussion in Ghomeshi 2008 for regular nominal phrases). In particular, different authors have argued that bare plurals only project up to #P (Farkas and de Swart 2003; Martí 2008). Marked nominals seem to be bigger at the surface, since they include an extra functional head. I take marked nominals to be KPs that immediately dominate DPs. (For analyses of marked nominals as headed by K, see Bittner and Hale 1996 and Bayer, Bader, and Meng 2001, among many other works that propose K. See also Brugè and Brugger 1996, Brugè 2000, Kornfilt 2003, and Ghomeshi 2008 for analyses of DOM that include a K head.) Unmarked nominal phrases form a smaller structure: a DP, a #P, or an NP.[2]

This assumption leads to the next questions: What structure needs Case? Do smaller nominal phrases need Case? I claim that the whole nominal projection is subject to Case, which means that every nominal head has a [uC] feature. Let us take it that some nominals only project a #P. If Case theory were only concerned with the highest nominal category (say, DP), then #P would be free from Case theory and its distribution would reflect this—it could be the subject of a nonfinite Tense, the complement of a passive verb, and so on. Yet, as far as I know, the distribution of #P is as sensitive to the Case Filter as that of full-fledged nominals. I conclude that the need to value a Case feature spreads throughout the entire nominal projection, as shown in (30).

(30)

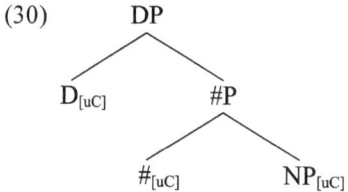

If the nominal structure is a DP, satisfaction of the [uC] of D triggers immediate satisfaction of the [uC] of the subordinate categories, since they are all in a sequence of selection dependencies. Likewise, if the nominal structure is a #P, then satisfaction of the [uC] of # spreads downward.

Next, let us turn to the strategies for Case valuation. As argued above, direct objects sometimes stay in situ and sometimes move, which leads to the conclusion that there are two strategies for Case assignment.

I start with unmarked nominal phrases. These nominal phrases stay in situ. Within my assumptions, they are too far from v to establish a dependency with it. Let us take it that nominals that we identify as unmarked objects incorporate into V (see also Bleam 2005). Some languages allow for full and visible incorporation of a noun into the verbal structure. Inspired by Van Geenhoven (1998), Dayal (1999, 2011), and Massam (2001), among others, I claim that many languages have a form or forms of "incorporation" that do not involve the actual morphological integration of a noun into the verbal structure. I suggest that one possible form of incorporation consists of copying the highest nominal head onto the lexical verb (I take the highest nominal head in unmarked nominal phrases to be D or #), as shown in (31a). Under the assumption that all Case assignment emanates from v or T/C, the Case feature of an incorporated D/# will be valued when the lexical verb incorporates into v with a valued [accusative] feature or into T/C, with [nominative]. (31b) shows a configuration in which v is the Case assigner. With D/# contained within the nucleus of a Case-assigning head, the Case requirement of D/# is satisfied (see Baker 1988 for evidence that incorporation satisfies the Case Filter).

(31)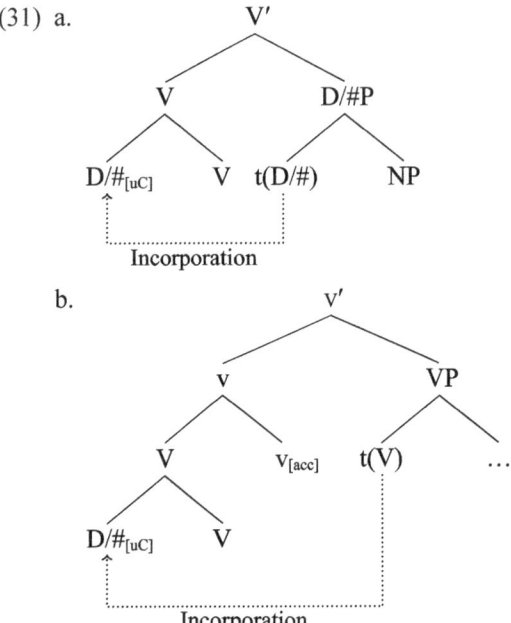

Since the incorporated D/# is in a syntactic dependency that involves feature sharing with its own copy, the whole DP satisfies the Case Filter. Usually, the copy of D that is spelled out is the unincorporated one, but Uriagereka (1995) shows that in Galician the incorporated D can be spelled out (for additional remarks on incorporation, see the appendix to this chapter).

Let me now propose a possible simplification of the analysis. Let us assume that KPs are phases but smaller nominal phrases are not (as assumed in much work influenced by Svenonius 2004). If they are not phases, they will be *transferred* (in the sense of Chomsky 2001) to the interpretive systems together with the lexical verb. I suggest that this yields the syntactic and semantic effect of incorporation. The assumption that small nominal phrases are not phases leads to another consequence. Chomsky (2001) argues that phases are different from nonphasal chunks of structure in that they are relatively self-contained and therefore able to move (but see Boeckx and Grohmann 2007 for a different view). If smaller nominal phrases are not phases, then it follows that they are not able to move and can only satisfy their unvalued Case feature by means of incorporation; raising to Spec,α is not a possibility for them.

2.2.6 The Mechanics of A-Movement: Marked Objects

Marked objects raise to Spec,α. Raising to Spec,α must be triggered by the Case Filter: the [uC] of the marked nominal phrase is not satisfied in situ and

Scrambling and Differential Object Marking

must move to be governed by a head that can satisfy it. This means that there is a class of nominals whose internal structure prevents incorporation. As suggested in the previous section, I adopt the assumption that the nonincorporated nominal is a KP, as in (32).

(32)
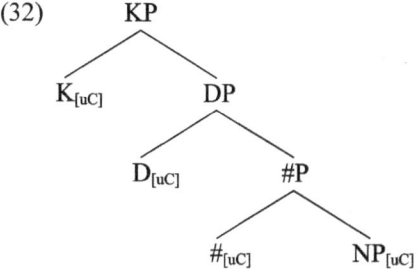

The head K is expressed morphologically in Spanish as the accusative A (Brugè and Brugger 1996; Brugè 2000), provided that the environment has the requisite features (animacy, etc.), as mentioned above. K may not have any spell-out if there is no Vocabulary item that matches its properties (e.g., if the NP refers to an inanimate object). Additionally, in chapter 3, I claim that K plays a role in the semantic interpretation of indefinites.

To account for lack of incorporation, let us assume that K is morphologically specified as a prefix of D.[3] Further, any copy of K will have this property. Thus, K cannot incorporate into V because the copy of K in V could not prefix to D. Moreover, the Head Movement Constraint (Travis 1984) ensures that D cannot incorporate into V across K. Since the path of incorporation is closed, KP cannot receive Case from v or any other higher Case assigner, given the strict locality on syntactic dependencies proposed in section 2.1. KP must move to the closest available specifier, Spec,α. In that position, the marked object can be probed by v and receive [accusative], as shown in (33).

(33)
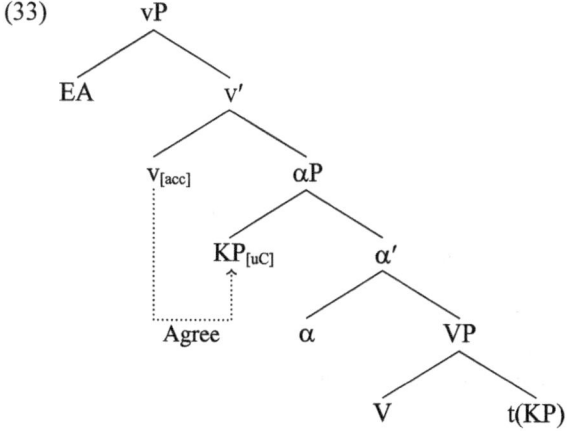

Here and henceforth, I take it that only arguments merged in the complement position of a predicate can incorporate: EAs and IOs do not incorporate. This generalization is based on a broad body of work on incorporation (e.g., Mithun 1984; Baker 1988; Baker, Aranovich, and Golluscio 2005), and it becomes a central assumption in my analyses.

Let us now return to a property of Maori indefinites mentioned briefly in section 1.2.5. Recall that the Maori indefinite determiner *he* has the properties of a Spanish unmarked object, while the indefinite determiner *tētahi* has the properties of a marked object. Additionally, I have argued that Spanish unmarked objects are incorporated into V. It follows that *he* is an incorporating determiner and therefore that it cannot be an EA. In fact, Chung and Ladusaw (2004, 56) show that only *tētahi* can be found in EA position.

(34) I   whiu tētahi/*he wahine i   tāna mōkai ki te moana.
     PAST throw a   a woman DO her pet   into the ocean
     'A woman threw her youngest child into the ocean.'

Chung and Ladusaw (2004, 59) account for this by positing that EAs in Maori must be specific. However, notice that in (34), *tētahi wahine* could more easily be interpreted as nonspecific than as specific. Let me suggest an alternative or perhaps complementary reason why *he* cannot head an EA: if *he* is an incorporating determiner, it can never be an EA.

As an alternative to the present approach, we could regard K not as a separate functional category but as a feature of D. Rodríguez-Mondoñedo (2007) makes a proposal along these lines. He claims that there are two subclasses of D: D and D*, the latter being the marked one. Because he does not elaborate further on the properties of D*, his proposal is difficult to evaluate. For instance, he makes no connection between the two types of D and Case theory, as I have done here. Nonetheless, for the sake of argument, we can adapt Rodríguez-Mondoñedo's analysis and take D* to include K, along the lines represented in (35).

(35)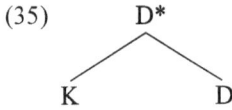

However, there is some empirical evidence, from coordination, that K must be a distinct syntactic head. Consider (36a–d).

(36) a.   Juan encontró **a** un hombre y una mujer.
         'Juan found a man and a woman,'
     b. *Juan encontró un hombre y **a** una mujer.

c. Juan encontró una casa y la fuente de la eterna juventud.
'Juan found a house and the fountain of eternal youth.'
d. Juan encontró **a** un hombre y **a** una mujer.

The contrast between (36a) and (36b) can easily be accounted for if K is a functional category that selects a D. In (36a), K selects for two coordinated DPs. The ungrammaticality of (36b) comes about because we are trying to coordinate two different syntactic phrases, a KP and a DP. If K is not a separate category, there is no particular reason why (36b) should be ungrammatical, since two DPs can be coordinated. One could counterargue that D and D* are distinct types of determiners and that this suffices to make coordination ungrammatical. But this counterargument is incorrect: (36c) shows that two DPs with clearly distinct Ds can be coordinated. (36d) is grammatical, but its meaning is slightly different from that of (36a). While (36a) can only refer to one single event of finding two individuals, (36d) can refer to two different events of finding one individual. Although I am not able to provide a full analysis of this fact here, it does lend some empirical weight to Torrego's (1998) claim that Spanish DOM is linked to telicity—and it suggests that the assumption that α involves an aspectual feature is on the right track.

Moreover, as pointed out above, there is good evidence that nominal phrases may have different sizes (Cardinaletti and Starke 1999; Déchaine and Wiltschko 2002; Ghomeshi 2008; Martí 2008). An approach that takes K as a separate head rather than as a feature of D allows me to integrate my analyses into a well-founded tradition.

In the present analysis, there is only one type of accusative Case, and there are two alternative pathways to satisfy it, each coming into play depending on the composition of the nominal phrase. By contrast, Belletti (1988) and de Hoop (1996) argue that objects receive two types of Case assigned by two different heads or configurations: partitive and accusative (Belletti), weak and strong (de Hoop). There are some advantages to my approach. Assuming two types of Case for objects entails adding some complications to the theory: there should be a mechanism to ensure that only one type of Case is present in the structure; there should be another related mechanism that inhibits assigning the wrong Case or a filter that throws out incorrect matches of nominal phrases to Case, and so on. In fact, neither Belletti nor de Hoop is very explicit about the mechanics of Case assignment. In my approach, there is one type of Case, which is assigned by incorporation unless the structure of the nominal phrase makes it impossible, in which case XP-movement takes place.

With this much apparatus in place, we are ready to tackle two of the empirical problems pointed out in chapter 1: the impossibility of accusative A with bare plurals and the obligatoriness of accusative A with small clauses, clause union, and object control.

2.2.7 Bare Plurals

As noticed by Brugè and Brugger (1996) and Brugè (2000), bare plurals do not accept accusative A.

(37) Ayer   vimos   *a/Ø mujeres.
     yesterday saw.1PL   women
     'Yesterday we saw women.'

Martí (2008) has argued that bare plurals in Spanish project only to #P; in particular, they do not have a DP and, by implication, no other functional category beyond D, including K. It follows that bare plurals cannot have accusative A. It also follows that their Case requirement is satisfied by incorporation.

Brugè and Brugger (1996) remark that bare plurals are subject to another well-known restriction. Bare plural unaccusative and passive subjects can only be found in postverbal position (Contreras 1976). The contrast between (38a) and (38b) shows that bare plurals must remain postverbal. (38c) and (38d) show that any modification suffices to lift the restriction.[4]

(38) a. Llegaron hombres de   todas partes.
         arrived men   from all   parts
         'Men arrived from everywhere.'
     b. *Hombres llegaron de todas partes.
     c. Muchos hombres llegaron de todas partes.
         'Many men arrived from everywhere.'
     d. Hombres implacables llegaron de todas partes.
         'Implacable men arrived from everywhere.'

Since we have concluded that marked objects scramble, we can unify both sets of data under one generalization.

(39) Bare plurals cannot move.

The reason for (39) involves how Case requirements are satisfied: bare plurals are of category #P and therefore their Case requirement must be satisfied by incorporation. Thus, with (39) one analysis accounts for two apparently dissimilar properties of bare plurals.

To add one more complication to the bare plurals puzzle: As mentioned in note 9 of chapter 1, a plural without a determiner can be modified or can be subject to contrastive focus. In such a case, accusative A is possible.

(40) Yo contrato solo **a/Ø** traductores cualificados.
    I hire only translators qualified
    'I only hire qualified translators.'

(41) Yo contrato **a/Ø** TRADUCTORES, no **a/Ø** REDACTORES.
    'I hire translators, not editors.'

I would like to propose that the addition of a modifier or of contrastive focus turns the nominal phrase into a bigger type of constituent that can be selected by K.

2.2.8 Small Clauses, Clause Union, and Object Control

Now let us now address the second puzzle introduced in section 1.2: the obligatoriness of accusative A and the absence of bare plurals with small clauses, clause union, and object control. Recall that these arguments are marked accusative even if they are nonspecific.

Small clauses

(42) El profesor considera **a/*Ø** un estudiante inteligente.
    'The professor considers a student intelligent.'

(43) *El profesor considera **a/Ø** estudiantes inteligentes.
    'The professor considers students intelligent.'

Causatives

(44) María hizo llegar tarde **a/*Ø** un niño.
    María made arrive.INF late a boy
    'María made a boy be late.'

(45) *María hizo llegar tarde **a/Ø** niños.
    'María made boys be late.'

Permissives

(46) María dejó llegar tarde **a/*Ø** un niño.
    María let arrive.INF late a boy
    'María allowed a boy to be late.'

(47) *María dejó llegar tarde **a/Ø** niños.
    'María allowed boys to be late.'

Perceptual predicates

(48) María vio llegar tarde **a/*Ø** un niño.
    María saw arrive.INF late a boy
    'María saw a boy be late.'

(49) *María vio **a/Ø** niños llegar tarde.
    'María saw boys be late.'

Object control
(50) Juan forzó **a/*Ø** un niño a hacer los deberes.
    Juan forced   a boy to do.INF the homework
    'Juan forced a boy to do his homework.'

(51) *Juan forzó **a/Ø** niños a hacer los deberes.
    'Juan forced boys to do their homework.'

Let us begin with small clauses. Their structure would be something like (52) (where *NomP = nominal phrase*, an expression I use to refer to an extended projection headed by a noun while remaining neutral as to whether the whole projection is a KP or a DP).

(52)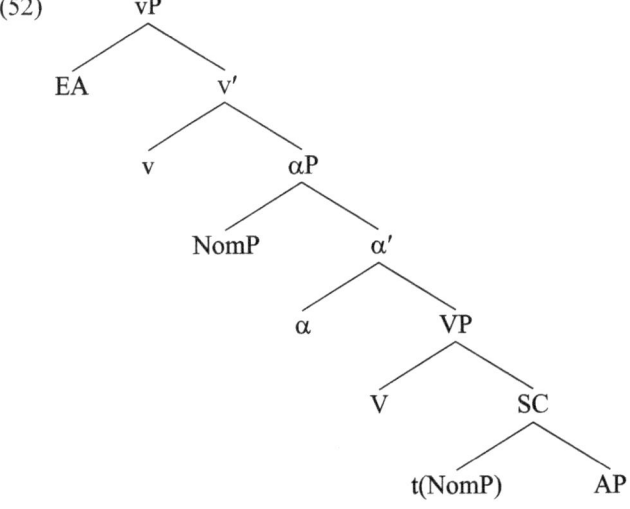

The NomP in the small clause needs Case, but the path of incorporation is closed because only an internal argument of V can incorporate into V. Further, it is safe to assume that the adjective cannot assign Case to the NomP either. Thus, the nominal phrase has to raise to Spec,α. Under the assumption that smaller NomPs are not movable, the NomP will have to be a KP. The head K may spell out as accusative A under the conditions specified above.

Recall that the argument of a small clause cannot be a bare plural.

(53) *El profesor considera **a/Ø** estudiantes inteligentes.
    'The professor considers students intelligent.'

This fact is to be expected. Since the arguments of small clauses require accusative A and bare plurals reject accusative A, it should follow that bare plurals cannot be found in small clauses. My analysis follows directly from what we have seen so far. Since bare plurals are headed by # and not K, they can only be licensed by incorporation. But incorporation can only take place from complement to head; the argument of a small clause cannot incorporate, and hence it cannot be a bare plural.

Belletti (1988) and de Hoop (1996, 89) provide alternative analyses of the absence of bare plurals in small clauses. Belletti (1988) argues that bare plurals can only receive partitive Case, which is assigned under θ-assignment. Since the argument of a small clause does not receive a θ-role from the verb, partitive Case cannot be assigned. Belletti's approach and mine make the same predictions with respect to bare plurals in small clauses. However, the restriction against bare plurals extends beyond small clauses, reaching clause union and object controllers, as seen in (42)–(51). Take object controllers. An object that controls a PRO presumably receives a θ-role from the verb and should receive partitive Case. But object controllers cannot be bare plurals. Thus, Belletti's account is insufficiently general.

De Hoop's (1996) proposal relies instead on the semantic properties of the predicates of small clauses. De Hoop starts by arguing that small clause predicates are individual-level predicates. Then she argues (building on Milsark 1974) that individual-level predicates are only compatible with strong determiners. Since bare plurals are by definition not strong determiners, it follows that they cannot occur in small clause predicates.

Regardless of the validity of Milsark's (1974) claims, weak determiners are comfortable as arguments of small clause predicates, as (54) and (55) show. In (54), the argument of the small clause includes a relative clause in subjunctive mood. As mentioned above, the subjunctive in the relative clause forces the noun to be nonspecific. In (55), the argument of the small clause is *nadie* 'no one', which is inherently nonspecific.

(54) Yo no considero inteligente a una persona que no sepa ruso.
     I NEG consider intelligent a person that NEG knows.SUBJ Russian
     'I don't consider intelligent a person who does not speak.SUBJ Russian.'

(55) Yo no considero inteligente a nadie.
     I NEG consider intelligent no.one
     'I consider no one intelligent.'

Therefore, I conclude, contra de Hoop (1996), that the absence of bare plurals in small clauses does not follow from an individual-level semantics for small clauses.

My approach to clause union follows the same lines as my approach to small clauses. Let us assume that clause union involves the selection of a type of small clause: a predicate without any functional structure above vP (Li 1990; Guasti 1992; López 2001). I take the causative construction as an example and assume that the structure of a causative with an unaccusative complement is as shown in (56) (see López 2001). I take it that unaccusative predicates do not project a vP (although projecting a vP without an EA and without accusative Case would make no difference to my analyses.

(56)

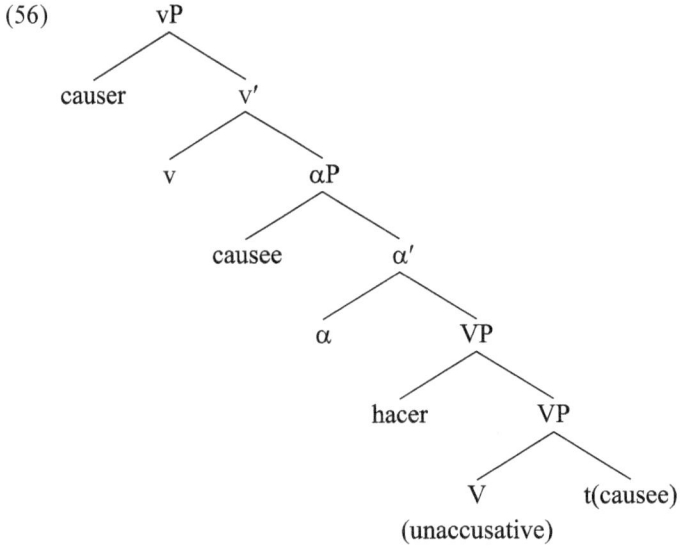

Here, I crucially assume that the causative construction in Spanish does not involve incorporation of the lower verb into *hacer* (Guasti 1992). Since the causative verb is not an affix, there is no apparent motivation for incorporation. Moreover, material can freely stand between the causative verb and *hacer*. In (57), the causee itself stands between the two verbs.

(57) Juan le   hizo a   Pedro configurar el   ordenador de nuevo.
      Juan CL.DAT made DAT Pedro configure the computer of new
      'Juan made Pedro configure the computer again.'

Just by inspecting the configuration in (56) we can see that the causee cannot satisfy its Case requirement by means of incorporation. The D/# of the causee might incorporate into V—but V does not incorporate into *hacer*, and D/#

Scrambling and Differential Object Marking

remains stranded far from the domain of a Case assigner. The Case requirement of the causee can only be satisfied if the causee raises until it finds itself in Spec,α, where it is governed by v. Since the causee must raise for Case reasons, it must be a KP.

If instead of an unaccusative predicate we have an unergative one, the result is the same: the verb *hacer* selects a vP with an EA, and this EA must raise to satisfy its Case requirement. This can be seen in tree (58).

(58)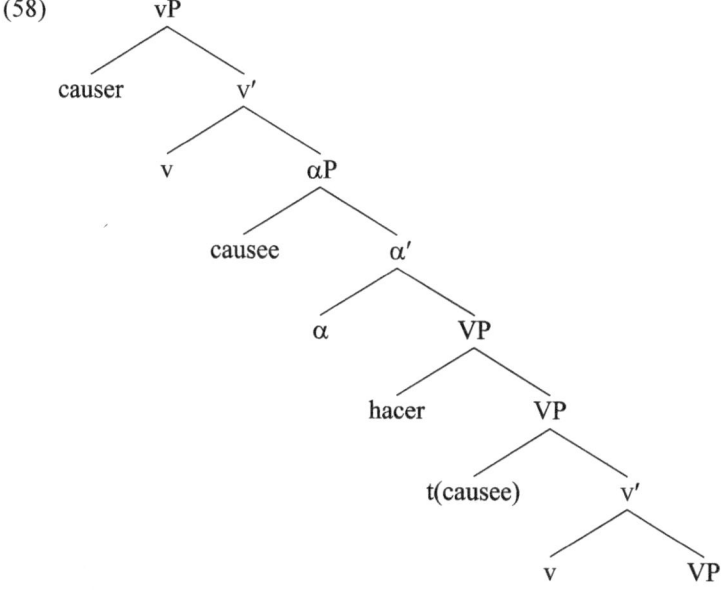

Let us now consider transitive predicates. With transitive predicates, the causee is dative.[5] The complement of the subordinate verb does not need to be a marked object.

(59) María hizo visitar **a/Ø** un enfermo a un empleado.
María made visit.INF a sick DAT an employee
'María made an employee visit a sick person.'

Again, this follows directly from my structural assumptions. The subordinate predicate 'an employee visit a sick person' is a full vP and therefore the object can receive Case from v by incorporation into V. The causee 'an employee', on the other hand, will receive Case from the matrix predicate. This is exemplified in (60).

(60)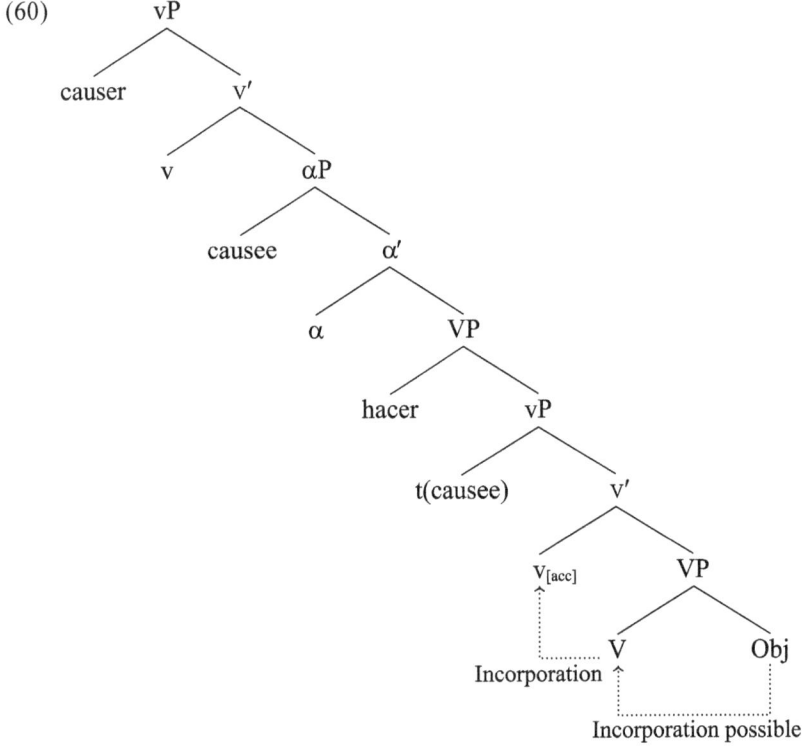

Object control receives the same kind of analysis. The object should c-command the subordinate clause; if it did not, it would not be able to control PRO. This is captured in the structure in (61).

(61)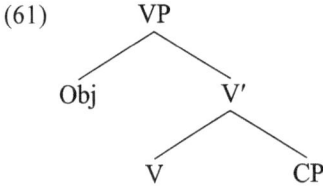

The object occupies a specifier position and therefore cannot incorporate. In order to satisfy its Case requirement, it must raise to Spec,α.

2.2.9 Conclusions

In this section, I have argued that marked objects in Spanish scramble to a position intermediate between the initial Merge position of the IO and that of the EA. I have sketched an approach to A-dependencies in which smaller nominal phrases must incorporate to satisfy their Case requirement while full KPs raise to Spec,α. These assumptions enabled me to account for the fact that bare plurals cannot be marked objects. The assumption that only nominal phrases in Compl,V can incorporate leads to the prediction that arguments of small clauses, affectees in clause union structures, and object controllers must be KPs and therefore are marked.

2.3 The [Context] of Accusative A

In this section, I outline my view of the distribution of DOM generally and accusative A in Spanish more particularly. I present just the general framework of analysis, omitting many language-particular details. However, I believe this presentation suffices to give an idea of how the system would work for any given language with DOM.

Recall that I subscribe here to the basic tenets of Distributed Morphology, a realizational approach to morphology. Within this framework, there is no "accusative A" in the Lexicon (List 1), but only a functional category with an array of features. The phonetic matrix that this functional category receives—a Vocabulary item from List 2—depends on the context in which it appears.

The contexts of DOM are represented in (62). DOM is the Vocabulary item inserted in the K terminal when v governs K (Spanish, Hindi, Persian), or a piece of morphology that attaches to v when v governs K (Kiswahili), or a Vocabulary item inserted in K accompanied by a clitic attached to the verb (Romanian). (62a) represents the rule of Vocabulary insertion for those languages in which DOM is expressed on the nominal, and (62b) represents the rule for those in which it is expressed in the verbal morphology.

(62)
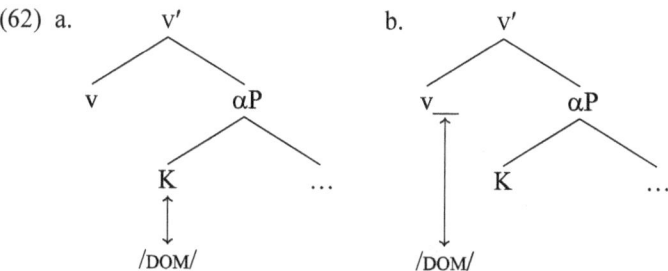

Notice that rule (62) says nothing about specificity or wide scope. Since neither specificity nor wide scope of DOM is obligatory in Spanish, this is a good result. In fact, as I articulate in chapter 3, specificity and wide scope of indefinite objects depend on the syntactic configuration, not on a piece of morphology. In other words, both DOM and specificity are keyed to the syntactic configuration, thus giving rise to the impression that a certain morphological case embodies a semantic feature like specificity or wide scope. The approaches to DOM that treat it as a marker of specificity are, I hope to demonstrate, incorrect.

(62) represents only the skeleton of how DOM works. Language-specific properties may further constrain the appearance of DOM. These properties are in effect features that can be found in the immediate local environment of K. Thus, the spell-out of K can be influenced by (i) features of the nominal phrase selected by K, as well as by (ii) features of α, (iii) features of v, and even (iv) features of the EA selected by v. In fact, all the elements in the local configuration represented in (16) may play a part.

Let us start with (i). The conditions on the complement of K are the best-known. For instance, in Spanish, Romanian, Kiswahili, and Hindi, animacy plays a role in DOM. In Spanish, for a large class of predicates, only animate objects can be headed by accusative A (there is a small class of predicates for which the rule is more complex, as I explain shortly). For the other languages that are sensitive to animacy, the actual conditions vary in intriguing ways that I cannot explore in depth in this monograph.

Thus, the rule that inserts accusative A needs to include some information about the properties of the noun that heads the extended projection. The representation in (63) is a skeleton that stands for a class of possible language-specific solutions.

(63)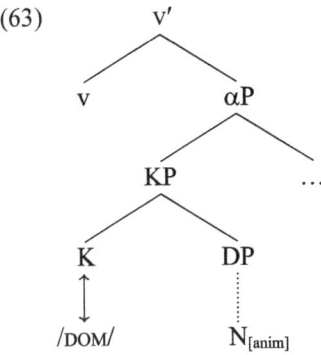

In some other languages, the DOM rule places additional restrictions on K, following the definiteness scale, repeated here.

(64) *Definiteness scale*
Personal pronoun > Proper name > Definite NP > Indefinite specific NP > Nonspecific NP

Scrambling and Differential Object Marking

In these languages, only a subset of instances of K are spelled out. I suggest that this phenomenon can be captured by adding an extra condition on K. For instance, in a language in which only pronouns are marked, the rule that spells out K specifies that K is spelled out only if it selects for a pronoun. Catalan is such a language. (65a,b), for example, show that object pronouns require accusative A while proper names reject it. The Vocabulary insertion rule is given in (66).

(65) a. Jo la   vaig veure **a/*Ø** ella.
       I CL.ACC.F.SG PAST.1 see.INF   her
       'I saw her.'
    b. Jo vaig   veure   ***a/Ø** la Maria.
       I PAST.1 see.INF   the Maria
       'I saw Maria.'

(66)

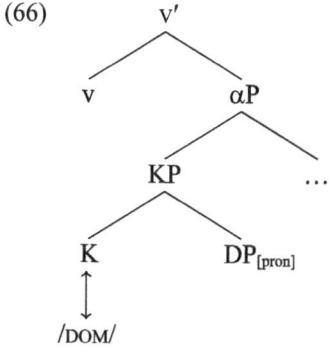

The feature on K can also have wider scope, thus embracing the different values of the definiteness scale.

Next, let us consider factor (ii), features of α. A clear example in which DOM depends on features of α is Finnish. In this language, objects can appear in accusative or partitive case (which I take to be the default case). According to the literature, objects in Finnish appear in accusative case if they are specific and the predicate itself is telic (Vainikka 1989; Kiparsky 1998; Ritter and Rosen 2001). Consider (67). With its object in accusative case, (67a) must be interpreted as definite/specific and the predicate is telic (and perfective, I would add). With the object in partitive case, the predicate in (67b) can be telic, in which case the object is interpreted as nonspecific, or the predicate can be atelic, in which case the object can be interpreted as specific or nonspecific. Accusative case correlates with the intersection of telicity and specificity.

(67) a. Hän   kirjoitt-i kirjee-t.
         she/he wrote   letters-ACC
         'She/He wrote the letters.'
    b. Hän   kirjoitt-i kirje-i-tä.
         she/he wrote   letters-PART
         'She/He wrote letters.'
         'She/He was writing letters.'
         'She/He was writing the letters.'
         (Kiparsky 1998, 267–272; Ritter and Rosen 2001, 435)

Following in particular Ritter and Rosen (2001), one can take the functional head α to be or to contain a feature concerning the telicity of the predication (see also Travis's (2010) extended research into the properties of inner aspect as well as my own brief remarks at the beginning of this chapter). If so, the Vocabulary insertion configuration that regulates DOM (= accusative) in this language is as shown in (68).

(68)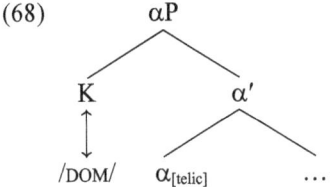

Finally, we can consider factors (iii) and (iv). Spanish DOM with inanimate objects provides an example of how v and the EA can influence DOM on the object. Consider the following contrasts (from López 2011):

(69) a. El cambio climático siguió   a/*Ø la sequía.
         the change climatic   followed   the drought
         'Climate change followed the drought.'
    b. El cambio climático provocó   *a/Ø la sequía.
         the change climatic   provoked   the drought
         'Climate change provoked the drought.'
    c. El cazador siguió   *a/Ø el rastro de la perdiz.
         the hunter   followed   the trail of the partridge
         'The hunter followed the partridge's trail.'

In (69a), accusative A is obligatory, although the DO is inanimate. The configuration that yields accusative A on an inanimate DO is a combination of a v that assigns a theme θ-role to its EA and an EA that has to be inanimate. In (69b), v assigns a cause θ-role to an inanimate EA and accusative A is ungrammatical. In (69c), v assigns a theme θ-role but the EA is animate and accusative A is again ungrammatical. Thus, we can see that the features of v and the EA can also play a role in DOM (for a different take on the role of the EA in DOM, see García 2007). However, no items beyond this domain play a role: neither tense, modality, nor properties related to the C domain play any role at all, in keeping with the hypothesis that only the local network defined in (16) does.

Thus, the problem of trying to define when DOM will show up consists of specifying the appropriate context for the rule of /DOM/ insertion. Although it is expected that languages tend to simplify this sort of rule, thus opening the field for the sort of broad generalizations that linguists like (formalized by means of hierarchies, scales, and so on), there is no a priori reason why that should be the case. Hence the fact that many languages with DOM end up with broadly applicable rules, while other languages end up with narrower rules; not surprisingly, one can even find lexically specified contexts. In this view, the problem of DOM is likened to any other morphological problem.

Take English past tense inflection as an example. English has the general [PAST] rule that adds an alveolar stop to a verbal root, unless that verbal root consists of an irregular verb like *bend*, in which case a lexically specified rule ensures that *bend*+[PAST] is spelled out as *bent* and not as **bended*. Similarly, in Spanish, the verbs *llamar* 'call' and *sustituir* 'take the place of' obligatorily govern accusative A.

(70) a. Juan llamó **a/*Ø** un médico.
     'Juan called a doctor.'
   b. Juan sustituyó **a/*Ø** un médico.
     'Juan took the place of a doctor.'

Consider now the Spanish words *nadie* 'no one' and *alguien* 'someone'. The basic fact about these two words is that they require accusative A. Similar words such as *ningun-* 'no' and *algun-* 'some' bear DOM optionally, like any other nominal. Thus, the rule that spells out [a] for *alguien* and *nadie* must be a rule of Vocabulary insertion so tightly defined that it affects only these two lexical items. According to many linguists who have written about *nadie* and *alguien*, the obligatoriness of accusative A with these words is a consequence of their animacy feature, which somehow trumps their lack of specificity. However, it is not the case that animate nominals in object position require accusative A; thus, a "trumping" analysis alone cannot account for this phenomenon. I think the solution involves looking at the structure of these words in more detail.

The feature that makes these words distinctive is indeed animacy. While in regular nominal phrases the noun is [±animate] and the D is neutral with respect to animacy (i.e., the determiners are the same for animate and inanimate nouns), *alguien* and *nadie* arguably include a [+animate] D, inherently or by incorporation of an animate noun (as noted by Rodríguez-Mondoñedo (2007)). This feature makes *alguien* and *nadie* different from *ningún-* and *algún-*, which are not inherently animate. I would like to propose that another DOM rule, (71), inserts *a* into K if the determiner bears the feature [animate].

(71)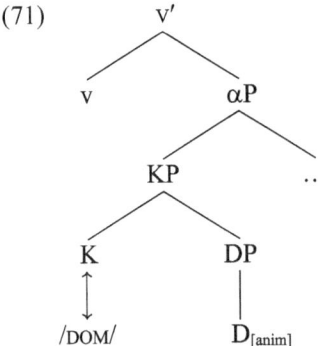

To conclude, the morphology of all languages includes very specific rules of Vocabulary insertion acting on top of more general ones. If we adopt the view that DOM distribution is a matter of defining a context for Vocabulary insertion, we should not be surprised to find very specific contexts for DOM alongside very general ones. The scales approach successfully identified those factors related to the noun while leaving out other factors of the syntactic environment. Ultimately, whether an object bears DOM or not depends on whether it has scrambled from its in-situ position, another important factor left out of mainstream approaches.

2.4 Conclusions

In this chapter, I have argued that marked objects in Spanish scramble to an intermediate position while unmarked objects stay in situ and satisfy their Case requirement by means of incorporation.

I have argued that an indefinite object may be merged as a KP or may involve a smaller nominal structure. If the structure is smaller than K, the highest functional head incorporates into V. After V incorporates into v, the Case requirement of the in-situ nominal phrase is satisfied. A KP needs to raise to Spec,α, where it receives Case under government by v. Given appropriate contextual conditions, K is spelled out in Spanish as accusative A. The obligatory nature of accusative A with small clause arguments, arguments of clause union, and

PRO-controlling objects is accounted for because these nominal phrases are never merged in a position from which they can incorporate into V. They have to raise to Spec,α for Case reasons and therefore have to have a full KP structure. My analyses are also able to account for the impossibility of accusative A with bare plurals and the general ungrammaticality of bare plurals as affectees or object controllers. Thus, I have resolved two of the puzzles discussed in chapter 1, both of which I showed to be completely outside the scope of the mainstream scale-based approach, while demonstrating that any analysis of DOM must involve syntax.

Finally, I have sketched an approach to DOM distribution based on the syntactic findings of this chapter and the morphological theory called Distributed Morphology. Although I have not attempted to provide a complete set of rules for inserting DOM in any language, I have presented a framework of analysis in which irregular instances of DOM that were intractable in previous approaches become unsurprising and almost expected, since Morphology includes rules that affect only one lexical item or a small set of lexical items together with more general rules that affect natural classes of items. I submit that this change in perspective constitutes a substantial advantage of the present approach.

Appendix: On Incorporation of Indefinite Objects

I have proposed in this chapter that Spanish unmarked objects incorporate into V, incorporation being reduced in this instance to head movement of a functional category of the nominal phrase. The reader may rightly wonder what sense of the term *incorporation* I am using or whether I am just making up a new syntactic operation and disguising it by using a venerable term—not to mention the fact that I am bundling together all nonspecific indefinites in one syntactic operation, while at least some researchers would prefer to make distinctions among them. Some words on this matter are in order.

Indeed, the term *noun incorporation* was originally reserved to refer to the phenomenon whereby a noun surfaces as part of the morphological structure of a verb. This is the sense of the term as used by Sapir (1911), Mithun (1984), and Baker (1988), among others. But recent work has extended the term to apply to V+DO structures that have at least some of the same properties as incorporation proper. I would like my proposal to be regarded within this tradition, and I hope that the remarks in this appendix will be found to justify my use of the term *incorporation*.

I start with Niuean. Massam (2001) proposes that this language makes use of a structure that she calls "pseudo-incorporation." Niuean is normally a VSO language, as shown in (72a). Notice that the subject is prefixed by an ergative case morpheme and the object is absolutive. As (72b) shows, VOS order is possible if accompanied by some changes in the structure. First, the object appears as a bare noun, without case and number marking. Second, the subject changes its case morphology from ergative to absolutive, indicating that (72b) is morphosyntactically an intransitive sentence. This is what Massam calls pseudo-incorporation.

(72) a. Takafaga tūmau nī   e   ia e   tau ika.
        hunt   always EMPH ERG he ABS PL fish
        'He is always fishing.'
    b. Takafaga ika tūmau nī   a   ia.
        hunt   fish always EMPH ABS he
        'He is always fishing.'
        (Massam 2001, 157)

How are the VOS and VSO orders obtained? Massam argues that VPs are always fronted in Niuean. The VOS order is the result of two movements: first, the subject moves to Spec,T; then, the VP moves to a higher category. This is shown in (73a). The VSO order comes about when the object raises out of the VP before VP-fronting. VP-fronting does not pied-pipe the DO, which is outside the VP and therefore ends up stranded. This is shown in (73b).

(73) a. 1. S [$_{VP}$ V O] →
        2. [$_{VP}$ V O] S t(VP)   (72b)
    b. 1. S [$_{VP}$ V O] →
        2. S O [$_{VP}$ V t(O)] →
        3. [$_{VP}$ V t(O)] S O   (72a)

The parallelism with my own approach to Spanish DOM is obvious, once the distracting variable of VP-movement is controlled for. Consider the VSO structure. One can take the Niuean nonincorporated object to be a KP, as suggested by its explicit case morphology. Like the Spanish KP, it raises to a position lower than the initial Merge position of the EA. Thus, stage (73b2) represents movement of the DO to Spec,α.

Now consider the VOS structure. The Niuean incorporated object is equivalent to the Spanish unmarked object. The difference between Spanish and Niuean lies only in the size of the nominal phrase: the Niuean incorporated object is stripped to an NP without any functional categories, while the Spanish unmarked object includes a #P and (possibly) a DP. Another difference is that Spanish is not an ergative-absolutive language. Other languages that exhibit forms of pseudo-incorporation are Hungarian (Farkas and de Swart 2003) and Hindi (Dayal 1999, 2011).

Apart from these surface similarities, do we have objective criteria that allow us to draw a line between phenomena that are clearly cases of "incorporation" and phenomena that clearly are not? In an abstract sense, the answer to this question is always no. If we have phenomena X, Y, and Z with both common and distinguishing properties, classifying X and Y together while leaving Z out is as arbitrary and prescriptive as classifying Y and Z together while leaving X out—be they phenomena in languages of the same family, animal species with a common ancestor, or any other continuum.

However, there are related properties that Inuit incorporation (Van Geenhoven 1998), Niuean and Hindi pseudo-incorporation, and Spanish unmarked objects have in common: they are nonspecific indefinites that must take narrow scope.[6] If a language that otherwise allows for wide scope of nominal phrases (i.e., a language whose grammar includes QR and/or choice functions) singles out a subclass of nominal phrases as not amenable to taking wide scope, we must conclude that there is some grammatical operation affecting those nominal phrases that places them out of the range of QR and/or choice functions. The construct of noun incorporation, with its consequence that the Case requirement of the nominal is satisfied in situ, provides a plausible account: those indefinite nominal phrases that scramble are subject to choice functions; those that do not scramble cannot be type-shifted and must be interpreted by means of Restrict. The details are articulated in the next chapter.

In an influential paper, Carlson (2006) proposes additional "meaningful bounds" to incorporation: number neutrality and "typicality."

Number neutrality is a complex issue, and it may separate Spanish from at least some other languages with incorporation or pseudo-incorporation (Hindi and Hungarian, as described in Dayal 2011 and in Farkas and de Swart 2003, respectively). The idea is this: in at least some of the languages discussed in the literature, an object can be a bare singular count noun, which can be interpreted as singular or plural. The following example is from Hindi:

(74) Anu botal ikaTThaa kartii hai.
Anu bottle collects
'Anu collects bottles.'
(Dayal 2011, 141)

The sentence corresponding to (74) is ungrammatical in Spanish. One approach to this difference between Hindi or Hungarian and Spanish is to posit that in Spanish the #P is always projected with count nouns while in Hungarian and Hindi such projection is not required if the noun itself is incorporated. It is interesting to note that Dayal (2011) argues that the incorporated verb is only number-neutral if the verb is conjugated in the imperfect aspect (more details on Hindi are given in chapter 4).

Let us now turn to the second of Carlson's bounds, typicality. Typicality does not seem to be a necessary property of unmarked nouns in Spanish, although it is a property of bare singulars. Consider the following examples:

(75) María por fin encontró gestora.
 María finally found   manager
 'María finally found a manager.'

(76) #María por fin encontró jugador de fútbol.
  María finally found   player of soccer

(77) María por fin encontró un jugador de fútbol.
 María finally found   a player of soccer
 'María finally found a soccer player.'

(78) Guardiola por fin encontró delantero centro. Se llama Ibrahimovic.
 Guardiola finally found   forward center SE calls Ibrahimovic
 '[Head soccer coach] Guardiola finally found a center forward. His name is Ibrahimovic.'

In a business context, sentence (75), with a bare DO, is grammatical and felicitous. Sentence (76), also with a bare DO, is very odd; I assume this is because it is atypical for a regular person to go around looking for a soccer player. By contrast, (77) is grammatical because the object includes an indefinite determiner. (78) is also grammatical, because it is typical for a soccer coach to go around looking for a suitable center forward. However, (78) would not work if instead of 'center forward', the object were simply 'soccer player', presumably because coaches go around looking for specific types of soccer players, not just any soccer player.

Carlson's (2006) proposal would lead us to classify the bare nouns in (75) and (78) as incorporated nominals, while the indefinite determiner in (77) would not be incorporated. One initial difficulty is how to integrate the feature [+typical] as part of a morphosyntactic analysis in a rigorous manner that prevents circularity. Until such an analysis is developed, I prefer to keep all non-specific, narrow scope indefinite objects under the same syntactic umbrella. This should not be taken as denying the interest of Carlson's findings and the reality of the contrasts illustrated above, which I hope future research will clarify.

3 Scrambling and Semantic Composition

3.1 Introduction

In this chapter, I argue that short scrambling is a precondition for the application of a choice function to an indefinite object. Conversely, I also argue that all and only those indefinite objects that stay in situ remain of type $\langle e,t \rangle$ and therefore need to compose with the verb in a manner different from plain Function Application. Sticking to the theoretical assumptions laid out in chapter 1, I take it that in-situ indefinite objects combine by means of Restrict. Thus, the interface between syntax and semantics is not resolved by direct mapping between position and interpretation; rather, a syntactic position makes available a mode of semantic composition, which provides a range of possible semantic representations.

Let's recall some of the empirical puzzles in Spanish discussed in section 1.2:

• Unmarked objects can only take narrow scope with respect to other quantifiers and sentential operators. Marked objects can take wide scope even outside islands.
• Unmarked objects can only be nonspecific. Marked objects can be specific.
• Marked objects are impossible with existential *haber*, relational *tener*, and bare plurals.
• Object *wh*-phrases require accusative A even when they do not raise to Spec,C.
• Maori EAs cannot bear the determiner *he*, but they can be nonspecific.

As we move on to consider the semantic composition of indefinite objects, I take Diesing 1992, Reinhart 1997, and Chung and Ladusaw 2004 as my points of reference (see also section 1.1).

Diesing (1992) develops an articulated theory of the syntax-semantics interface with particular emphasis on indefinite nominal phrases. Recall that

Diesing (1992) argues for the Mapping Hypothesis, according to which material within the VP is mapped onto the nuclear scope while material outside the VP is mapped onto the restrictor. Further, she claims that there are two varieties of indefinites: weak determiners without a quantificational force of their own, which stay in situ (the nuclear scope); and strong quantifiers, which raise into the IP area and are mapped onto the restrictor. (Recall that at the time Diesing was writing, she assumed a clause structure that consisted only of a VP (where both EA and IA were merged), an IP, and a CP.)

The Spanish DOM data that I presented in chapter 1 partially confirm the Mapping Hypothesis. We have seen that marked objects in Spanish scramble. All strong quantifiers, including indefinite strong quantifiers, are marked objects. Since marked objects scramble, the Mapping Hypothesis would seem to be confirmed. However, the scrambling undergone by Spanish marked objects does not move them into the TP area, which is unexpected under the Mapping Hypothesis. We know that the scrambling of marked objects is very short because marked objects c-command only the IO, not the EA in situ.

Moreover, scrambled indefinites do not need to have a strong interpretation. Rather, such an interpretation is a possibility open to them. Diesing argues that there is a direct link between syntactic position and semantic interpretation, but the Spanish data do not support such a direct link. Thus, we retain from Diesing's work the idea that there is a connection between scrambling and nominal phrase interpretation as well as the claim that indefinites that remain in situ can only be interpreted as weak noun phrases. However, the data lead us to reject the Mapping Hypothesis as formulated by Diesing.

I sketchily introduced choice functions and Restrict in chapter 1. I showed that the definition of choice function proposed by Reinhart (1997) and Chung and Ladusaw (2004) (and many others) makes the wide scope of indefinites independent of their syntax. In particular, Reinhart argues that wide scope can be obtained by means of QR or choice functions. QR is a syntactic operation; it places a quantifier in a position from which it c-commands other scope-taking elements. A choice function allows an indefinite nominal to take wide scope regardless of its syntactic position.

But the syntactic position of indefinite objects seems to be important for wide scope, even in examples in which a choice function and not QR plays a role. In Spanish, only those objects that scramble, even if the scrambling is very short, can take wide scope, while objects that do not scramble can only take the narrowest scope. Notice that the scrambling argued for in chapter 2 is not a form of QR. Under the assumption that syntactic c-command maps onto semantic scope, QR enlarges the scope of a QP insofar as it extends its c-command domain. However, the scrambling described in chapter 2 is very short and does not place the marked objects in a position where they c-command sentential operators—nonetheless, indefinite objects that undergo this short scrambling are able to take wide scope over operators that they do not c-command. Short scrambling seems to be a precondition for the application of the semantic rule that allows object indefinites to take wide scope: choice function.

I have also shown that there is a telling parallelism between the behavior of marked and unmarked objects in Spanish and the behavior of the determiners *tētahi* and *he* in Maori. This parallelism invites an analysis of Spanish objects in which the mechanisms of semantic composition that Chung and Ladusaw propose for the Maori data should be useful for the Spanish data.

Finally, I would like to point out that Chung and Ladusaw do not present an articulated analysis of transitive predicates. I will try to do so, using Chomsky's (1995) vP construct and Kratzer's (1996) mechanisms of semantic composition. I will show that putting together (i) Kratzer's theory of transitive semantics, (ii) Chung and Ladusaw's theory of argument composition, and (iii) the role of scrambling provides an illuminating perspective on the syntax-semantics interface.

The analyses that I provide in this chapter have points of contact and divergence with some earlier approaches. A quick summary is in order to help situate my proposal.

De Hoop (1996) discusses the semantics of marked objects in Turkish, arguing that Turkish marked objects are generalized quantifiers of type $\langle\langle e,t\rangle,t\rangle$. Bleam (2005) borrows this idea for her analysis of the semantics of accusative A. She takes marked objects to be uniformly strong quantifiers of type $\langle\langle e,t\rangle,t\rangle$ and unmarked objects to be of type $\langle e,t\rangle$. In her account, the latter are interpreted by means of semantic incorporation as in Van Geenhoven 1998. As for the former, although Bleam is not specific about them, presumably they should be interpreted by regular Function Application after they undergo QR.

Bleam's approach and mine are parallel in our conception of unmarked nominal phrases, but we part company in the way we see marked nominal phrases. Bleam's analysis of accusative A does not take into account that strong quantifiers are scope-rigid in Spanish (at least in object position), as I discussed in section 1.2.2. In other words, *Un hombre ama a toda mujer* 'A man loves every woman' does not evoke an inverse scope reading. If marked indefinite objects are indeed of type $\langle\langle e,t\rangle,t\rangle$, they would be the only quantifiers of this type in Spanish with the ability to take wide scope. Moreover, since indefinites can take scope over islands, the possibility of a QR-based analysis does not present itself. I conclude that an analysis of marked objects in terms of strong quantifiers is empirically inadequate. That is why we need choice functions.

In fact, other researchers have thought of using choice functions in analyzing DOM. Von Heusinger (2002) was probably the first linguist to propose the connection between DOM and choice functions, and the work presented here is heavily indebted to his. However, von Heusinger does not mention scrambling in his work. Lidz (2006) presents an account of Kannada DOM in which the marked objects are interpreted by means of choice functions. The Kannada data, as described by Lidz, are subtly different from the data discussed in this monograph, and so are Lidz's conclusions. By contrast to my argument that scrambling is a necessary condition for indefinite objects to be composed by choice functions, Lidz argues that in Kannada, choice functions and Diesing-style scrambling are alternative ways for an indefinite object to achieve wide scope. (Unfortunately, I am not able to investigate the properties of Kannada objects in this monograph.) Neither von Heusinger nor Lidz presents a detailed syntax-semantics mapping like the one I develop in this chapter, nor do they discuss existential and possessor verbs or *wh*-phrases.

This chapter is organized as follows. In section 3.2, I present the general framework and the initial analysis. In section 3.2.1, I begin by discussing Kratzer's (1996) semantics for transitive predicates. In section 3.2.2, I present Restrict and Satisfy within a Kratzer-style framework, with the result that some weaknesses of Chung and Ladusaw's (2004) proposals are foregrounded. In section 3.2.3, I show how incorporating scrambling into the picture overcomes these weaknesses. In section 3.3, I discuss the empirical puzzles from chapter 1 (*haber* and *tener*, bare plurals, and *wh*-phrases); I also briefly discuss IOs and EAs. In section 3.4, I present conclusions.

3.2 Restriction, Saturation, and the Structure of Transitive Predicates

3.2.1 Kratzer's Semantics for vP

Recall the basic structure of transitive sentences that we are assuming in this monograph.

(1) [$_{vP}$ EA v [$_{VP}$ V DO]]

Kratzer's (1996) semantics for transitivity provides a compositional semantics for a syntactic theory in which an EA is introduced by a head distinct from the lexical verb. The combinatorics is based on *Event Identification*. Assume that a little v and the lexical verb both include an event argument as part of their predicate structure. Event Identification is the hypothesis that v and the VP

Scrambling and Semantic Composition

conjoin if their event arguments are compatible. The result of the conjunction is a semantic structure in which their event arguments are bound by the same lambda operator.

The general framework of Kratzer's theory is presented in (2). Consider line 1 of (2). The input to the rule of Event Identification consists of two functions, represented as **f** and **g**. Syntactically, **g** corresponds to the lexical VP, and **f** is the little v. Semantically, **g** is a function from events (s) to truth values (t), and **f** is a function that takes entities (e) as input to yield a function from events to truth values as output. The output of Event Identification is again a function that takes entities to yield functions from events to truth values. Line 2 of (2) uses the lambda format. I take the little v to denote *initiation* (Ramchand 2008), shortened to *Init*. *V'* and *a'* signify respectively *denotation of V* and *denotation of a*.[1]

(2) 1.   **f**   **g**   →   **h**
      ⟨e,⟨s,t⟩⟩   ⟨s,t⟩   ⟨e,⟨s,t⟩⟩
  2. λxλe Init(x)(e)   λe V'(a')(e)   λxλe Init(x)(e) ∧ V'(a')(e)

The following is an example:

(3) a. John called Mary.

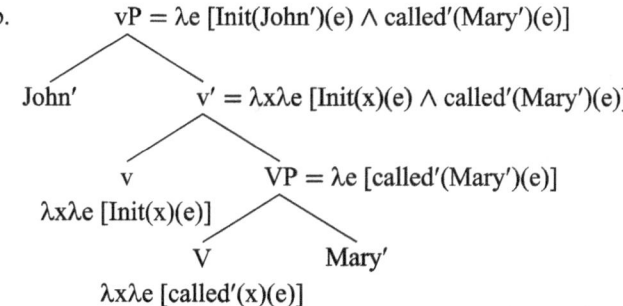

    b.   vP = λe [Init(John')(e) ∧ called'(Mary')(e)]

John'   v' = λxλe [Init(x)(e) ∧ called'(Mary')(e)]

v   VP = λe [called'(Mary')(e)]
λxλe [Init(x)(e)]

V   Mary'
λxλe [called'(x)(e)]

Finally, the event argument must be bound by an existential quantifier. Let us assume, following Travis (2010), that the event variable is bound immediately after the vP has been constructed, as in (4).

(4)   ∃e [Init(John')(e) ∧ called'(Mary')(e)] = John called Mary

∃   λe [Init(John')(e) ∧ called'(Mary')(e)]

3.2.2 Restrict and Satisfy

In this section, I discuss Chung and Ladusaw's (2004) proposals in more detail while inserting their approach into the Kratzer-style transitive structure that I introduced in section 3.2.1. By articulating the compositional semantics of transitive structure in detail, I highlight the advantages as well as the unclarities of Chung and Ladusaw's approach. In particular, it is not certain that Chung and Ladusaw are successful in ensuring that Restrict yields narrow scope for unmarked objects (and presumably Maori *he* nominals). It is also not certain that the prohibition against *tētahi* (and marked objects) in Maori existential and possessive predicates follows directly from their system. These concerns can only be fully addressed after we take scrambling into consideration. Thus, this section lays the groundwork for the solutions to these problems developed in the following sections.

Chung and Ladusaw (2004) argue that the two Maori determiners reflect two different modes of semantic composition of indefinite DPs. *He* is an instruction to the semantic component that the DP must be interpreted by means of Restrict. *Tētahi* is an instruction to the effect that the DP must be interpreted by means of Satisfy (essentially, a choice function).

Let us begin with Restrict. Take an indefinite DP to be of type $\langle e,t \rangle$, denoting a property p.[2] If a DP combines with a predicate by means of Restrict, the DP does not saturate the predicate: instead, the DP is conjoined with it. If a predicate is a function **f** that ranges over a domain of elements, the outcome of Restrict is that the domain of **f** is limited to a subdomain of the original domain. This subdomain is made up of those objects that have the property p.

(5) illustrates the workings of Restrict in combination with the assumptions on the semantics of transitive predicates that I have just introduced.

(5) Mary called a man.

Lexical array:
V: $\lambda x \lambda e$ [called'(x)(e)]
NomP: man'[3]
v: $\lambda y \lambda e$ [Init(y)(e)]
NomP: Mary'

Derivation of VP:
Merge ($\lambda x \lambda e$ [called'(x)(e)], man')
Restrict: $\lambda x \lambda e$ [called'(x)(e) $\wedge$ man'(x)]
Existential closure(x): $\lambda x \lambda e$ [called'(x)(e) $\wedge$ man'(x)] = $\lambda e\ \exists x$ [called'(x)(e) $\wedge$ man'(x)]

Derivation of vP:
Merge ($\lambda y \lambda e$ [Init(y)(e)], $\lambda e\ \exists x$ [called'(x)(e) $\wedge$ man'(x)])
Event Identification: $\lambda y \lambda e$ [Init(y)(e) $\wedge\ \exists x$ [called'(x)(e) $\wedge$ man'(x)]]
Merge (Mary', $\lambda y \lambda e$ [Init(y)(e) $\wedge\ \exists x$ [called'(x)(e) $\wedge$ man'(x)]])

Function Application: λe [Init(Mary')(e) ∧ ∃x [called'(x)(e) ∧ man'(x)]]
Existential closure(e): ∃e [Init(Mary')(e) ∧ ∃x [called'(x)(e) ∧ man'(x)]]

Now let us turn to Satisfy. We continue with the assumption that an indefinite nominal phrase is of type ⟨e,t⟩. A choice function **f** picks an individual from the set, thus type-shifting the indefinite nominal from ⟨e,t⟩ to ⟨e⟩. The type-shifted nominal combines with the predicate by regular Function Application. Following Reinhart (1997), I take it that **f** must be existentially closed.

(6) Mary called a man.
 Lexical array:
  V: λxλe [called'(x)(e)]
  NomP: man'
  v: λyλe [Init(y)(e)]
  NomP: Mary'
 Derivation of VP:
  Satisfy: 1. Type-shift: man' → **f**(man')
      2. Merge (λxλe [called'(x)(e)], **f**(man'))
      3. Function Application: λe [called'(e) (**f**(man'))]
 Derivation of vP:
  Merge (λyλe [Init(y)(e)], λe [called'(e) (**f**(man'))])
  Event Identification: λyλe [Init(y)(e) ∧ called'(e) (**f**(man'))]
  Merge (Mary, λyλe [Init(y)(e) ∧ called'(e) (**f**(man'))])
  Function Application: λe [Init(Mary')(e) ∧ called'(e) (**f**(man'))]
  Existential closure(e): ∃e [Init(Mary')(e) ∧ called'(e) (**f**(man'))]
  Existential closure(**f**): ∃**f** ∃e [Init(Mary')(e) ∧ called'(e) (**f**(man'))]

Chung and Ladusaw (2004) argue that the two forms of semantic composition give rise to different interpretive possibilities. Indefinite objects like *tētahi* combined by means of choice functions can take wide scope. Those like *he* combined by means of Restrict can only take the narrowest scope. Let's see how.

Reinhart (1997) argues that the wide and intermediate scopes of indefinites hinge on the point of existential closure (see my discussion in section 1.1.2, and the dissenting opinion expressed in Kratzer 1998). Consider (7). In (7a), the existential quantifier that closes the choice function variable is c-commanded by the universal quantifier, obtaining linear scope. In (7b), the existential quantifier c-commands the universal quantifier, yielding inverse scope.

(7) Every woman saw a man.
  a. $\forall y$ [woman(y)] $\exists f\, \exists e$ [[Init(y)(e)] $\wedge$ [seen' (**f**(man'))(e)]]
     'For every woman y there is a choice function **f** that picks out a man and there is an event e such that y saw the man picked out by **f** in e.'
  b. $\exists f\, \forall y$ [woman(y)] $\exists e$ [[Init(y)(e)] $\wedge$ [seen' (**f**(man'))(e)]]
     'There is a choice function **f** that picks out a man and for every woman y there is an event e such that y saw the man picked out by **f** in e.'

If an indefinite nominal is subject to Restrict, the predicate remains unsaturated. Adopting the assumption that the predicate must be saturated before the event argument is existentially closed (Chung and Ladusaw 2004, 11, 51), an existential quantifier must be merged to bind the indefinite DP at once. Example (8) is well-formed and interpretable because the predicate *seen* has been saturated before the event variable is existentially closed. The formula in (9) is not well-formed because the event has been existentially closed before the predicate has been saturated.

(8) $\lambda e\, \exists x$ [seen'(x)(e) $\wedge$ man'(x)] $\rightarrow$ $\exists e\, \exists x$ [seen'(x)(e) $\wedge$ man'(x)]

(9) *$\lambda x\, \exists e$ [seen'(x)(e) $\wedge$ man'(x)]

Thus, an indefinite DP that is composed by Restrict will necessarily take narrow scope with respect to other clausal operators—negation, quantifiers, and so on.

Now, does Chung and Ladusaw's system indeed derive narrow scopes for Restrict? In answering this question, I would like to bring back to the fore Kratzer's approach to transitivity. Within this tradition, Chung and Ladusaw's assumption that the predicate is saturated before the event argument is existentially closed does not suffice to ensure that Restrict forces the narrowest scope on the indefinite object. Consider the following structure:

(10) $\exists e\, \exists x$ [$_{vP}$ EA v [. . . IO DO(x)]]

In (10), the event variable is closed after the object variable is closed, respecting the condition that Chung and Ladusaw assume. However, the existential quantifier that binds the DO variable c-commands the entire vP. Consequently, this existential quantifier takes scope over the EA and the IO. Therefore, the condition that the variable of the DO be existentially closed before the event variable is closed does not ensure that the indefinite object takes narrow scope with respect to the IO or the EA. Chung and Ladusaw's system does not ensure that indefinites composed by Restrict take narrow scope; hence, it does not fully account for the narrow scope of Maori *he* indefinites.

Unmarked indefinites in Spanish are also left out of the loop. Let me briefly review the facts. Consider the examples in (11). In (11a), the EA is in postverbal position, probably in situ. The unmarked object cannot take scope over the EA. The marked object can. Likewise, in (11b), the unmarked object cannot take scope over the IO, in contrast to the marked object.

(11) a. Ayer   vieron la mayoría de los hombres **a/Ø** un niño.
        yesterday saw   the most   of the men   a boy
        'Yesterday most of the men saw a boy.'
        ∃ > MOST only with accusative A
    b. Ayer   entregaron **a/Ø** un niño a   la mayoría de las madres.
        yesterday delivered   a boy DAT the majority of the mothers
        'Yesterday they delivered a boy to most of the mothers.'
        ∃ > MOST only with accusative A

Thus, we need an analysis of unmarked objects with a mechanism that ensures that they have the narrowest scope possible. Let us assume that unmarked objects are composed by means of Restrict. Then, we need existential closure of the object to take place before any other arguments are merged.

(12) ∃e [$_{vP}$ EA v [... IO ... ∃x [DO(x)]]]

I agree with Chung and Ladusaw that existential closure of the variable of the DO must take place at once. The problem is that the condition that they impose does not accomplish this within what I consider to be a fairly standard hypothesis about transitivity. In section 3.3, I add scrambling to the mix and suggest a way to force narrow scope of unmarked objects.

3.2.3 Syntax and Choice Functions

According to what we saw in chapter 2, a KP raises to Spec,α in search of a Case assigner, while a DP or smaller nominal incorporates into V. Once in position Spec,α, KP can be probed and be assigned accusative Case. Given the appropriate contextual conditions (most prominently, animacy of the noun), this Case is realized in Morphology as *a* in the K position.

Here, I would like to suggest that K can be associated to a semantic function. Provided that the complement of K is of type ⟨e,t⟩, K translates in the semantics as a *choice function variable*.[4] K triggers type-shifting of the indefinite DP from type ⟨e,t⟩ to type ⟨e⟩.[5]

(13)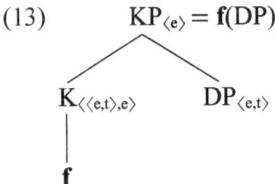
    KP$_{\langle e \rangle}$ = **f(DP)**
    K$_{\langle \langle e,t \rangle, e \rangle}$ DP$_{\langle e,t \rangle}$
    |
    f

Thus, an indefinite KP is a **f**(DP). A KP needs to move for Case reasons to Spec,α, leaving a trace behind. The assumption that K introduces a choice function allows us to ensure that we have a direct connection among choice functions, short scrambling, and DOM.

The structure resulting from movement is represented as in (14).

(14) a. Mary saw a man. / María vio **a** un hombre.
    b.

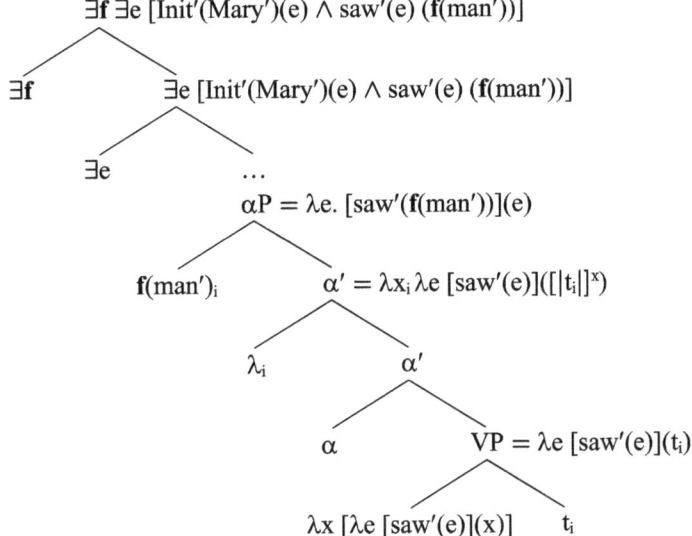

Let us consider this tree from the bottom up. The complement of *saw'* is a KP and, as such, it moves to Spec,α, where its [uC] can be valued by v. KP leaves a trace behind. Traces are of type ⟨e⟩, so they can combine with the verb by Function Application and lambda conversion, yielding the VP indicated. The VP combines with α, whose semantic contribution I take the liberty of ignoring for the present.[6] The next step reflects the assumption (see Heim and Kratzer 1998) that any moved item introduces a lambda operator. Lambda conversion places *f(man)* as an argument of *saw'*. The rest is routine and repeats (6).

To facilitate comparison, I show a tree structure, (15b), without scrambling of the object and application of Restrict.

(15) a. Mary saw a man. / María vio un hombre.

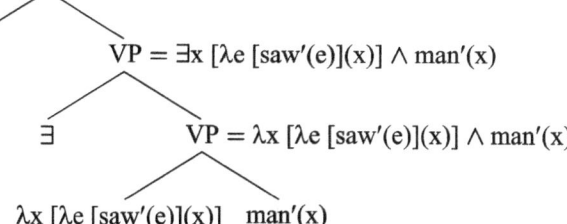

We have seen that indefinite objects subject to choice functions can take wide scopes. How do we make sure that indefinite objects composed by Restrict do not take scope over an IO or the EA? Or, to put it more precisely, how do we make sure that the variable of the indefinite is bound by an existential quantifier before any other argument is introduced?

Recall that Chung and Ladusaw (2004) propose that the predicate must be saturated before the existential closure of the event variable, but that would be too late for our purposes. I propose instead that leaving the output of Restrict unresolved creates a structure that Event Identification cannot recognize. Recall that the general structure of Event Identification is as follows:

(16)   f   g   →   h
     ⟨e,⟨s,t⟩⟩   ⟨s,t⟩   ⟨e,⟨s,t⟩⟩
     λxλe Init(x)(e)   λe V'(a')(e)   λxλe Init(x)(e) ∧ V'(a')(e)

Notice that if there is an unsaturated predicate in **g**, **g** is of type ⟨e,⟨s,t⟩⟩. Thus, Event Identification cannot apply. But if existential closure applies immediately, **g** must be of type ⟨s,t⟩, as desired and as shown in (16). The same reasoning ensures that existential closure takes place before the IO is introduced, under today's fairly mainstream assumption that IOs are introduced by separate heads (see Marantz 1993 and Bobaljik 1995 for the classic references), in effect becoming configurationally nondistinct from external arguments.[7]

3.2.4 Discussion

We can now understand the scrambling discussed in chapter 2—and the many examples to be presented in chapter 4—as a mechanism built into C$_{HL}$ (the computational system for human language) designed to place objects in a position where semantics can work on them. In this section, I discuss the syntax-semantics interface in more detail.

For the analyses presented in section 3.2.3 to go through, we need to ensure that marked and unmarked objects not only *can* be composed by different semantic mechanisms but in fact *must* be, so that the empirical results follow from the system and not the other way around. In practice, this entails answering four separate questions. The answers to the first three questions involve the assumptions developed so far; the answer to the fourth opens up a new theoretical consideration.

• *Question 1:* I have to make sure that no marked objects in Spanish (and, presumably, no *tētahi* nominals in Maori) can be composed by means of Restrict. If a subclass of marked objects could be interpreted by Restrict, they would take obligatory narrow scope.

Answer: Marked objects are KPs, as revealed by their case morphology. Therefore, by (13) they must be of type $\langle e \rangle$ (or $\langle\langle e,t\rangle,t\rangle$ if the complement of K is a strong quantifier). Restrict involves the conjunction of a constituent of type $\langle e,\langle s,t\rangle\rangle$ with a constituent of type $\langle e,t\rangle$.[8]

• *Question 2:* I have to make sure that unmarked indefinites cannot be interpreted by means of choice functions. If they could be, then Maori *he* and Spanish unmarked objects could take wide scope.

Answer: A choice function variable entails the presence of a head K in charge of type-shifting. An unmarked indefinite does not involve a head K.

• *Question 3:* I have to make sure that an unmarked object cannot move to Spec,α and be interpreted by Restrict (in which case, we would have a scrambled object that could only take narrow scope).

Answer: The syntax does not allow for this: unmarked objects are nominals smaller than a KP. Unmarked objects can only satisfy Case requirements by means of (pseudo-)incorporation (as argued in section 2.2.6).

• *Question 4:* I have to make sure that a marked object (a KP) cannot stay in situ *and* be interpreted by means of choice functions followed by regular Function Application.

There is an easy answer to this question: K cannot incorporate, so it must move (see section 2.2.5). But let's make things a bit harder and imagine a scenario in which nothing prevents K from incorporating. In this scenario, what prevents Function Application from applying to a KP in Compl,V? To answer this question, I draw on a proposal presented by Carlson (2003) (and ultimately, the findings in Diesing 1992).

But first, let me review the types of nominal phrases that require accusative A. Strong quantifiers, proper names, definite DPs, and strong pronouns all bear accusative A.

(17) Juan vio **a/*Ø** . . .
  'Juan saw . . .
  a. todos.
     all.'
  b. cada primo.
     each cousin.'
  c. la mayoría de sus primos.
     most of his cousins.'
  d. Pedro.
  e. el futbolista.
     the soccer player.'
  f. ella.
     her.'

If my analyses in chapter 2 are correct, all of these nominal phrases are headed by K and therefore have scrambled out of Compl,V. Thus, when we take all the types of nominal phrases into consideration, we get the following picture:

Weak indefinites
Type: $\langle e,t \rangle$ Position: within VP

Strong indefinites, quantified noun phrases, definite DPs, proper names, pronouns
Types: $\langle e \rangle$ or $\langle \langle e,t \rangle, t \rangle$ Positions: outside VP

I conclude that what is special about the position Compl,V is that it can be occupied only by nominal phrases of the $\langle e,t \rangle$ type—which means there must be something about the semantics of lexical verbs that makes them select properties.

Following Carlson (2003), let us take it that the denotation of V is an eventuality (Bach 1986). Thus, we assume that our model includes a set **E** of eventualities and that each lexical verb denotes a member of the set. All the verbs together denote a subset of **E**. Anything that composes with the verb at this level yields another member of **E**, a more specific event type than that of the verb in isolation. The denotation of a weak indefinite is a property, and the set **P** is the domain of nominal meanings. Thus, weak indefinites can stay within VP and be interpreted in their initial Merge position (by means of Restrict, if my analyses are correct). In contrast, nominal phrases denoting individuals or generalized quantifiers cannot be found in Compl,V when syntax maps onto semantics because they have no denotation in **E** or **P**.[9]

At the αP and vP levels, the heads α and v introduce individuals or, rather, property instantiations (the reason that Carlson (2003) chooses this term is that individuals may change their properties over time—the boy becomes a man and so on). Thus, we posit a set **U** of property instantiations. The denotation of αP and vP is a token event. The set of token events instantiating an event type is a set called **Σ**. The extension of any event type is included in **Σ**. As we merge arguments, we produce event types that are a subset of the input event type. TP meanings (and beyond) involve traditional propositional semantics, beyond our purview.

Carlson's (2003) proposal derives the fact that any nominal phrase to be found in Compl,V by the interface with semantics must be a weak DP; anything else is uninterpretable in this position. Carlson's proposal does not require indefinite DPs with narrow scope and a nonspecific reading to be in Compl,V (correctly, given the possible readings of marked objects in Spanish). But given the syntactic considerations mentioned above, anything smaller than a KP will have to stay in situ. If nominal phrases smaller than a KP exist in the grammar of natural languages, it follows that an appropriate mode of semantic composition that allows us to combine a lexical verb with a weak indefinite must exist. If Chung and Ladusaw (2004) are correct, we need a distinct mode of semantic composition—what they call Restrict.

Before we move on, I would like to say a few words about Van Geenhoven's (1998) *Semantic Incorporation*. This is a type-shifting operation that applies to lexical verbs, allowing them to combine with properties of type $\langle e,t \rangle$ by means of Function Application. This is shown in (18) and illustrated in (19) for *(Mary) saw a man*.

(18) a. $\lambda y \, \lambda x \, [V'(x,y)] \rightarrow$
 b. $\lambda P \, \lambda x \, \exists y \, [V'(x,y) \wedge P(y)]$

(19) $\lambda x \, \exists y \, [see'(x,y) \wedge man'(y)]$

```
            V                        DP
λP λx ∃y [see'(x,y) ∧ P(y)]    λz man'(z)
```

Van Geenhoven's system would seem to work for our purposes just as well as Chung and Ladusaw's Restrict. In fact, it would seem to work even better, since existential closure is built into the lexical representation of the verb and therefore the narrow scope for the incorporated object follows without further ado. Why not use Van Geenhoven's system in my analyses? One of the main themes of this monograph is the correlation between syntax and modes of semantic interpretation, such that indefinites that have been type-shifted need to raise out of the VP for Case purposes and, ultimately, so they can find themselves in a configuration where they can have a denotation. In Van Geenhoven's system, the way the object is interpreted depends exclusively on the lexical structure of the verb and there is no reason why a subset of nominal phrases would need to scramble. Scrambling is left without a raison d'être. However, as I have shown and as I will show more extensively in chapter 4, scrambling plays a crucial role in the interpretation of indefinites, since only those that scramble can be interpreted by means of choice funcions.[10]

3.2.5 Specificity

As I pointed out in chapter 1, Spanish marked objects can be specific but unmarked objects cannot (for references, see Torrego 1998, 1999). I also pointed out—following Farkas (1997) and von Heusinger (2002)—that specificity is a property distinct from scope.

However, it cannot be an accident that marked objects can take wide scope *and* be specific, while unmarked objects have the opposite properties. This state of affairs calls for an analysis: the operation that allows indefinite KPs to take wide scope must be related to the operation that allows for specific readings. Following Reinhart (1997), Chung and Ladusaw (2004), and many others, I claimed earlier that the wide scope readings of indefinites can be analyzed by means of choice functions. Following von Heusinger (2002 et seq.), I claim that specificity also hangs on the presence of a choice function. As von Heusinger argues, specificity can be construed as "anchoring" the indefinite to the speaker or to the referent of the subject of the sentence (see section 3.1). Technically, this can be implemented by subscripting the choice function as shown in (20).

(20) $KP_{\langle e \rangle} = f_{speaker/subject}(DP)$

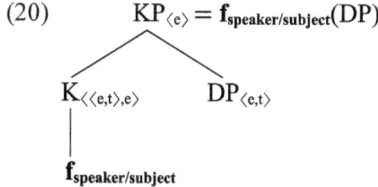

(21) a. Juan vio **a** una cierta mujer.
       'Juan saw a certain woman.'
   b. $\exists f\, CH(f) \wedge$ Juan saw $f_{speaker}$(woman)
       'There is choice function **f**, which picks out a woman, known to the speaker, and Juan saw the individual picked out by **f**.'

Although this approach looks a bit like diacritic linguistics, it does make some clear predictions. It predicts that indefinites that can take wide scope can also be specific and vice versa. It predicts that there is no language in which a subset of indefinites can take wide scope but cannot be specific or in which a subset of indefinites can be specific but cannot take wide scope.

3.3 Empirical Consequences

3.3.1 *Haber* and *Tener*

Recall from section 3.2.2 that Maori *tētahi* is incompatible with existential sentences. Chung and Ladusaw (2004, 53) claim that this indicates that the existential verb can be satisfied only by means of Restrict, not by means of Satisfy. However, as far as I can tell, they do not provide an argument that this fact follows from their system.

Likewise, Spanish *haber* 'have (existential)' and *tener* 'have (possession)' do not allow accusative A. This is a puzzling fact because accusative A is compatible with narrow scope, nonspecific meanings, and the introduction of new discourse referents. To complicate matters a little more, the stage-level versions of *tener* do allow for marked objects. I repeat the relevant chapter 1 data here:

(22) En el patio hay   *a/Ø un niño.
    in the yard HABER   a boy
    'There is a boy in the yard.'

(23) María tiene *a/Ø tres hijos.
    'María has three children.'

(24) ¡Ya   tengo   a/Ø uno!
    already have.1SG   one
    'I got one!'

(25) María tiene a/Ø un hijo en el ejército.
    'María has a son in the army.'

This prohibition on *haber* and *tener* should be a consequence of the feature structure of these verbs: they only combine by means of Restrict. This restriction should not extend to (24) and (25).

Let us start with *haber*. I adopt the simplest possible semantics for *haber* sentences: they consist of an existential quantifier binding two variables in two semantically conjoined predicates (the so-called *pivot* and *coda*). The coda is a form of locative.[11]

(26) ∃x Loc(x) ∧ Q(x)

There are of course many precedents for this way of treating existentials. See McNally 1997 for arguments that the pivot is a property of type ⟨e,t⟩.

A conclusion immediately follows. Since indefinite marked objects are individuals of type ⟨e⟩, a marked object cannot be the complement of *haber*.

Let us explore the properties of *haber* in more detail. If one of the two conjuncts is missing, the sentence becomes ungrammatical.[12]

(27) a. Hay un libro en la tienda.
HABER a book in the store
'There is a book in the store.'
b. Allí hay un señor que regala caramelos.
there HABER un gentleman that gives candy
'There there is a gentleman that gives candy away.'
c. *Hay un libro.
HABER a book
(ungrammatical if the locative cannot be reconstructed from the context)

Haber contrasts with *existir*, which does not require a coda.

(28) Dios existe.
'God exists.'

Haber also contrasts with another similar verb, *estar* 'be (locative)', more interesting for our purposes.[13] *Estar* also relates a pivot with a locative coda. However, the set of DPs that can be pivots with *estar* is in complementary distribution with the set that can be pivots with *haber*: with *estar*, weak quantifiers are banned; instead, the pivot consists of strong quantifiers, proper names, and pronouns.

(29) a. El niño está en la tienda.
'The boy is in the store.'
b. *Hay el niño en la tienda.

(30) [What happened?]
a. #Un niño está en la tienda.
a boy is in the store
(pragmatically acceptable with a context that forces a specific reading on *un niño*)

b. Hay un niño en la tienda.
   HABER a boy in the store
   'A boy is in the store.'

Morphosyntactically, *haber* and *estar* are also different. The pivot of *haber* is an object (see note 8, chapter 1). The pivot of *estar* is clearly a subject.

Let me articulate the analysis of *haber* and *estar* in more detail. Continuing within the Distributed Morphology framework (chapter 2), I propose that *haber* and *estar* are both spell-out variations of the same lexical head from List 1, which I will refer to as $BE_{(p,c)}$. The role of $BE_{(p,c)}$ is to link a pivot and a coda; $BE_{(p,c)}$ does not participate in compositional semantics (here I find inspiration in Den Dikken's (2006) notion of *Relator*).

Recall that I assume that the pivot of the existential predicate is of type $\langle e,t \rangle$. I propose that the head of the pivot incorporates into $BE_{(p,c)}$. $BE_{(p,c)}$ eventually raises to v, and the complex $[v + BE_{(p,c)}]$ raises to T. The pivot receives accusative Case as a by-product of incorporation, in conjunction with the properties of v. Thus, the pivot of the existential behaves in relevant respects like an indefinite unmarked DO.

(31) a. Hay un hombre en el jardín.
        HABER a man in the garden
        'There is a man in the garden.'
     b.

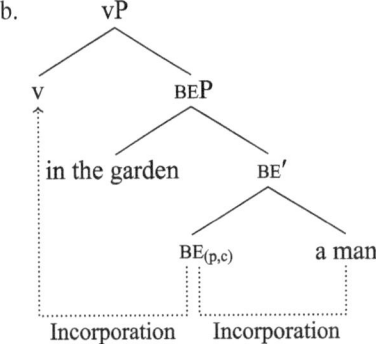

The pivot and the coda compose by means of Restrict (see also Chung and Ladusaw 2004, 53, for the claim that the pivot of a Maori existential is composed by Restrict). This is shown in (32).

(32)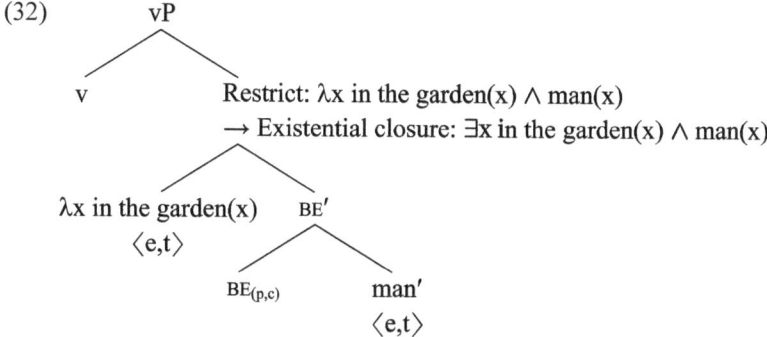

Under this view, *haber* is nothing but the spell-out of [BE$_{(p,c)}$ + N] (where N is a stand-in for whatever is the highest functional category within the coda).

I surmise that this approach might also be applicable to Maori *he/tētahi*. Recall that *tētahi* is associated with a choice function, while *he* is associated with Restrict. Nominals that are interpreted by Restrict stay in situ, which means that they incorporate to satisfy their Case requirement. If the Maori existential is like the Spanish one, with a nominal category incorporated into it, it follows that *tētahi* cannot be found in existential sentences in Maori.

Before we move on, let us consider the alternative syntax of existentials articulated by Freeze (1992). Freeze places the pivot and the coda in the opposite configuration: the pivot as specifier and the coda as complement. Additionally, Freeze argues that the head of the construction is the locative preposition. Freeze's proposal is exemplified in (33).

(33)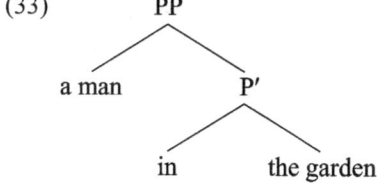

Is it the case that the theme c-commands the locative? Evidence concerning structure usually comes from c-command tests involving anaphors and quantifier-variable dependencies. However, these tests are unworkable in existential constructions because they require that the constituents involved be specific or strong quantifiers. Fortunately, the locative-theme tandem appears in other constructions that do not require nonspecific arguments, such as certain unaccusatives like *arrive*. Yatsushiro (1999) studied the counterparts of such verbs in Japanese, a language in which QR appears to be absent and scope is directly reflected in surface structure. The result of her tests is very clear: the locative argument c-commands the theme. Consider this example:

(34) a. Dokoka-ni   daremo-ga   tuita.
        somewhere-LOC everyone-NOM arrived
        = somewhere > everyone
        ≠ everyone > somewhere
    b. Daremo-ga   dokoka-ni   tuita.
        everyone-NOM somewhere-LOC arrived
        = somewhere > everyone
        = everyone > somewhere
        (Yatsushiro 1999, 35–36)

The locative argument can take scope over the theme argument in either order. The theme argument can take scope over the locative argument only when it raises above it. These facts can be easily accommodated if the locative argument c-commands the theme argument in its base position and the nominative argument c-commands the locative argument only after scrambling. Assuming a higher initial Merge position for the theme argument would leave these facts unaccounted for.

One could assume that the locative c-commands the theme in unaccusative predicates whereas the opposite is true in existentials. However, the null hypothesis is that at least their relative hierarchies should remain constant throughout and that constructional variation is what needs to be argued for.[14]

Moving on to the other locative predicate in Spanish, *estar*, I suggest that it has the same lower structure as *haber*, but that its DP is of type $\langle e \rangle$ or $\langle\langle e,t \rangle, t\rangle$ rather than of type $\langle e,t \rangle$ (unless everything in Compl,V except weak indefinites always moves, as I claim above, in which case the complement of *estar* is always a trace of type $\langle e \rangle$; for simplicity, I abstract away from this in the following discussion). This assumption has two consequences. First, the pivot does not incorporate. Second, Restrict does not apply; instead, regular Function Application applies.

(35) a. El hombre está en el jardín.
        'The man is in the garden.'
    b.   in the garden'(man')
           ╱────────────╲
      λx in the garden(x)   man'
          $\langle e,t \rangle$ ╱────╲
                          BE$_{(p,c)}$ man'
                                    $\langle e \rangle$

Scrambling and Semantic Composition

The Spanish Vocabulary item *estar* is, along these lines, the spell-out of $\text{BE}_{(p,c)}$ without an incorporated nominal category. The pivot enters a dependency with T, resulting in the expected agreement and case morphologies.

Turning now to *tener*, I suggest that the plain possessor *tener* (the individual-level *tener* of Bleam 2005) is another form of existential predicate and takes a property of type $\langle e,t \rangle$ as a complement (see Keenan 1987). Marked objects are not properties (of type $\langle e,t \rangle$) but individuals (of type $\langle e \rangle$), and therefore a marked object cannot be a complement of individual-level *tener*.

Further, I take it that the expression of possession found in Hindi, Latin, and Celtic more closely reflects the lexical structure of possession. In these languages, the proposition "I have a brother" is expressed by a sentence that looks more like "to me is a brother," with a locative copula as head (see Freeze 1992). Thus, I take the semantics of possessive *tener* to have the following form (see (26)):

(36) $\exists x \, \text{AFF}(x) \wedge Q(x)$

That is, one of the two predicates of the conjunct—the coda—must be a predicate of "affectedness," expressed by a dative DP in Hindi, Latin, and Celtic. In Spanish, possessive *tener* diachronically lost its inherent case, and the coda surfaces as a regular nominative. The pivot receives accusative from v. Otherwise, the syntax of *tener* is identical to that of *haber*, with the affected predicate in the place of the coda.

(37) a. Yo tengo un hermano.
    'I have a brother.'
  b.

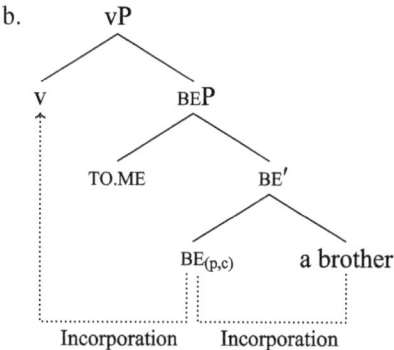

The argument composition of individual-level *tener* is also identical to the semantics of *haber*: the coda and the pivot are composed by Restrict, as shown in (38).

(38)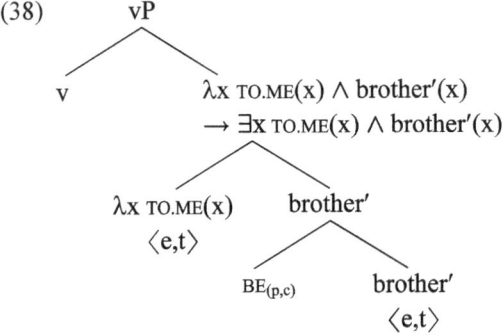

Under this view, individual-level *tener* is the spell-out of $BE_{(p,c)}$ when the latter includes an affected rather than a locative argument. I (provisionally) suggest the following environment:

(39) [[AFF] _____] ↔ *tener*
          [$BE_{(p,c)}$+N]

Let us now turn to stage-level *tener*. Consider the following example:

(40) ¡Ya   tengo **a/Ø** uno!
     already have.1   one
     'I got one!'

The complement of stage-level *tener* can be presupposed: a strong quantifier, a definite DP, a name, and so on.

(41) ¡Ya tengo **a** todos / **a** la reina / **a** María!
     'I got all / the queen / María!'

Thus, it is clear that existential quantification is not part of the lexical semantics of stage-level *tener*. Instead, we can take it to be composed of a $BE_{(p,c)}$ with an affected argument and a pivot of type ⟨e⟩ or ⟨⟨e,t⟩,t⟩, as shown in (42).

(42) a. Tengo a María.
       'I got María.'
    b.

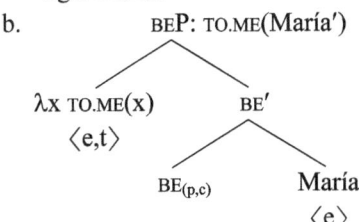

It is worth noticing the parallelism between the two versions of *tener*, and between *haber* and *estar*, which this analysis reflects.

The same analysis holds for (43).

(43) María tiene **a/Ø** un hijo enfermo / en el ejército.
'María has a son sick / in the army.'

The object here does not need to be newly introduced into the discourse; it can be a strong quantifier, a definite DP, a name, or the like.

(44) María tiene **a** su hijo / **a** todos los hijos / **a** Juanito enfermo / en el ejército.
'María has her son / all her children / Juanito sick / in the army.'

Thus, in this instance *tener* does not include an existential structure either.

Before we are done with stage-level *tener*, there is one more wrinkle to iron out. The question is how to analyze *enfermo* 'sick' or *en el ejército* 'in the army' in (43). Bleam (2005) assumes a small clause structure for this sort of example. But as I argued in chapter 2, the argument of a small clause predicate requires accusative A. I reasoned that the structural position of the small clause argument prevents incorporation, and therefore it must raise to Spec,α for Case reasons. Thus, if *enfermo* or *en el ejército* formed a small clause with *a un hijo*, we would expect obligatory accusative A.

(45)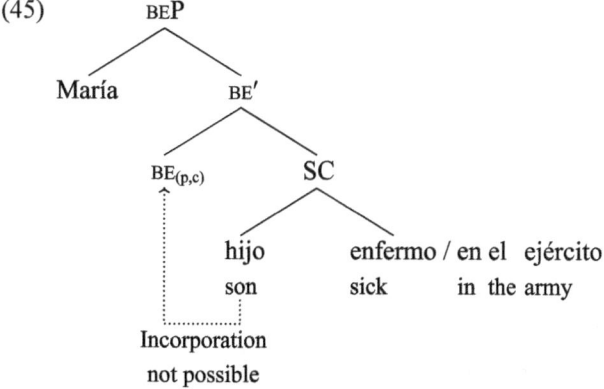

Since accusative A is not obligatory, the complement of stage-level *tener* cannot be a small clause. Consequently, the theme argument is the complement of the verb and the locative is an adjunct.

A piece of empirical evidence suggests that *enfermo* and *en el ejército* are indeed secondary predicates and therefore adjuncts. A well-known restriction on secondary predicates is that they must be stage-level (Déchaine 1994), as shown in (46). Small clauses do not have this restriction, as shown in (47). The Spanish construction of interest does have the restriction, as shown in (48).

(46) a. I saw John angry.
b. *I saw John intelligent.

(47) a. I consider John angry.
b. I consider John intelligent.

(48) a. María tiene **a/Ø** un hijo enfermo / en el ejército.
'María has a son sick / in the army.'
b. *María tiene **a/Ø** un hijo inteligente.
'*María has a son intelligent.'

If *a un hijo* is not part of a small clause, it must be the complement of stage-level *tener*. Nothing in the syntactic environment prevents incorporation. It follows that the complement of stage-level *tener* can be a marked or an unmarked object. This is shown in example (49).

(49) a. María tiene **a/Ø** un hijo enfermo / en el ejército.
b.

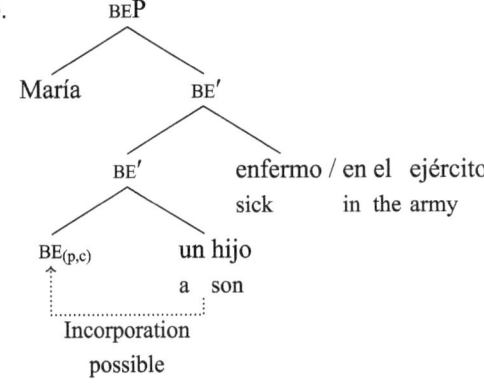

Finally, let me present a summary of the spell-out rules of $BE_{(p,c)}$. We know that the three Vocabulary items under discussion have the following properties:

(50) *estar:* $BE_{(p,c)}$ does not incorporate N
    haber: $BE_{(p,c)}$ incorporates N
    tener: $BE_{(p,c)}$ has an [AFF] argument (and optionally incorporates N)

The lexical items from List 1 that participate are just three: $BE_{(p,c)}$, N, and [AFF]. The spell-out rules in (51) provide the environment for the Vocabulary items from List 2 that flesh out the items from List 1. I present these rules in an underspecified format.

(51) 1. [[AFF] ____] ↔ *tener*
       BE$_{(p,c)}$
   2. [_____] ↔ *haber*
       BE$_{(p,c)}$ + N
   3. [_____] ↔ *estar*
       BE$_{(p,c)}$

The rule with the most specific environment applies first. Thus, if BE$_{(p,c)}$ appears in a context in which Spec,BE$_{(p,c)}$ contains an affected argument, it spells out as *tener*. If there is no affected argument and BE$_{(p,c)}$ has a nominal head incorporated into it, it spells out as *haber*. Otherwise, BE$_{(p,c)}$ spells out as *estar*.

To summarize what we have seen in this section: The initial question was why the complements of *haber* and individual-level *tener* cannot take accusative A and can only take an unmarked complement (the pivot). The answer is that these verbs spell out a conjunction of two predicates. Accusative A is not a predicate and therefore cannot be part of this construction. I surmised that Maori *tētahi* is unable to occur with existentials for the same reason. In this section, I also compared *haber*, *estar*, and the two versions of *tener*. Using the semantic tools introduced in this chapter and the Distributed Morphology approach introduced in chapter 2, I showed that *tener*, *haber*, and *estar* form a tight network.

3.3.2 Bare Plurals

As noted in chapter 1, bare plurals cannot combine with accusative A (Brugè and Brugger 1996; Brugè 2000).

(52) a. Juan vio hombres.
        'Juan saw men.'
    b. *Juan vio **a** hombres.
    c. Juan vio **a** muchos hombres.
        'Juan saw many men.'
    d. Juan vio **a** hombres implacables.
        'Juan saw implacable men.'

Bare plurals are acceptable with *haber*, and they always take narrow scope with respect to sentential operators (see McNally 2004). Thus, bare plurals have all the properties of nominals that compose only by means of Restrict.

(53) Hay bomberos en el jardín.
    'There are firemen in the garden.'

(54) Todos los bomberos aceptan propinas.
'All the firemen accept tips.'
= ∀ > ∃
≠ ∃ > ∀

(55) No hay bomberos en el jardín.
'There are no firemen in the garden.'
= ¬ > ∃
≠ ∃ > ¬

The question then is why a bare plural cannot be type-shifted and become the argument of a choice function.

As shown in chapter 2, I take it that bare plurals in Spanish are nominals of category #P; all higher functional categories are absent from the structure, as argued by Martí (2008). The properties of bare plurals follow from this assumption: since they are nominals, they have a [uC] feature that needs to be satisfied. Since the structure does not include a K, a marked object is not possible. In order to value its [uC], the head # needs to incorporate into V. Given the incorporating syntax of #P, it follows that bare plurals can only compose by Restrict. Restrict only allows for narrow scopes.

3.3.3 *Wh*-Phrases

Wh-phrases are indefinite nominal phrases. Consequently, one would expect them to take accusative A optionally. Unexpectedly, accusative A is obligatory.

(56) a. Busqué   un gestor.
        sought.1SG a   manager
     b. Busqué **a** un gestor.
        'I looked for a manager.'

(57) a. *¿Quién buscaste?
         who   sought.2SG
     b. ¿**A** quién buscaste?
        'Who did you look for?'

One possible account for this contrast builds on the fact that the *wh*-phrases in (57) move, in combination with the assumption that semantic composition takes place after all syntactic movement is finished (within a domain such as a sentence or a phrase). If a *wh*-phrase is not in the position of complement of V at the time semantic composition takes place, it follows that the *wh*-phrase cannot combine by means of Restrict. *Wh*-phrases necessarily value their Case feature in Spec,α and exhibit accusative A.

Next, let us consider so-called *wh*-in-situ. In a multiple *wh*-question, accusative A is obligatory on the in-situ *wh*-phrase.

(58) a. ¿Quién dices   que buscó   **a** quién?
         who   say.2SG that sought.3SG who
         'Who do you say looked for whom?'
   b. *¿Quién dices que buscó quién?

If we take as a basic assumption that accusative A is a sign of scrambling, I conclude that *wh*-in situ is not really in situ—it is in Spec,α. The question is why.

An account of the obligatory presence of accusative A with (animate) *wh*-phrases could go along these lines. Let us adopt the approach to *wh*-in-situ that follows Baker (1970) in that *wh*-phrases that do not raise to Spec,C are bound by a [Q] operator in C (see also Reinhart 1997, 2006, where binding by [Q] is taken to be simply existential closure of the choice function variable). This binding is required for the interpretability of the *wh*-phrase.

Keeping this in mind, let us see what would happen if *wh*-phrases stayed in situ. If they stayed in Compl,V, they would be treated like any other indefinite in that position (see section 3.2.3): they would be composed by means of Restrict and bound by existential closure at the VP level.

At this point, there are two scenarios to consider. Let us assume that there is a [Q] in C. Let us further assume that Full Interpretation forbids vacuous quantification (see different empirical arguments that a ban against vacuous quantification is part of the grammar in de Hoop 1996, Koopman and Sportiche 1982, and Kratzer 1988). If so, the [Q] operator would not be able to bind the *wh*-phrase because the latter would have already been bound by the existential quantifier. [Q] would in fact have nothing to bind, and the resulting LF would turn out to be uninterpretable. This is what is represented in (59a).

If, instead, there is no [Q] in the structure, the *wh*-phrase is not interpreted as a *wh*-phrase; it is interpreted as a plain indefinite and is spelled out accordingly (in fact, in many languages the words for 'what' and 'something' spell out identically). This is what is shown in (59b).

(59c) represents the structure of *wh*-in-situ. Short scrambling of the *wh*-phrase ensures that it will not be closed by existential closure at the VP level. Instead, it becomes available to be bound by [Q].

(59) a. *[Q]$_i$ ... $\exists_i$ [$_{VP}$ ... wh_i]
   b. *$\exists_i$ [$_{VP}$ ... wh_i]
   c. [Q]$_i$ ... [$_{\alpha P}$ wh_i ... t$_i$]

3.3.4 External Arguments and Indirect Objects

The proposal I am developing here has consequences for the grammar of the other sentential arguments. In effect, my framework leads to the conclusion that neither EAs nor IOs can be composed by means of Restrict, since they are merged in specifier positions and do not incorporate (Baker 1988). If they are composed by choice functions, their scope should always be ambiguous. Consider the following triplet:

(60) No trajo   malas notas   **un niño / uno de los niños**.
     NEG brought bad   grades a   boy /   one of the boys
     'A boy / One of the boys did not bring home bad grades.'
         Possible reading: $\exists > \neg$

(61) María no trajo   **a un niño / a   uno de los niños** una manzana
     María NEG brought DAT a   boy / DAT one of the boys   an apple
     podrida.
     rotten
     'María did not bring a boy a rotten apple.'
         Possible reading: $\exists > \neg$

(62) María no trajo   **un novio**   decente / *uno de los novios
     María NEG brought a boyfriend decent /   one of the boyfriends
     decentes a esta casa.
     decent   to this house
     'María didn't bring home a decent boyfriend / one of the decent boyfriends.'
         *$\exists > \neg$

The constituent order in (60) is VOS. With this order, the EA *un niño* is most likely in situ. It is possible for this EA to be specific and to take wide scope over negation. The wide scope reading is more salient if the DP is partitive. The same is true for the IO in (61): it can take narrow or wide scope. Thus, indefinite EAs in situ and IOs behave like marked objects, and we can conclude that they are interpreted by means of choice functions. Of course, I cannot prove that EAs and IOs *cannot* be interpreted by Restrict. An indefinite EA in situ can always take narrow scope with respect to other sentential operators, and there is no evidence that Restrict could not be involved. It could be argued that (60) and (61) are only consistent with my analyses. In (62), I present an unmarked object for contrast. As we know, unmarked objects cannot take scope over negation, an impossibility I have attributed to the assumption that unmarked objects can only be interpreted by Restrict. The ungrammaticality of *uno de los novios* 'one of the boyfriends' arises precisely because of the contradictory requirements of the partitive (which seeks wide scope) and the unmarked morphology of the object (which rejects it). The contrast between DOs and the other clausal arguments should be taken as evidence that there is indeed something different in the way unmarked DOs are interpreted.

The subject of an unaccusative predicate is also scopally ambiguous, even in postverbal position.

(63) Ayer no llegó un niño.
 yesterday NEG arrived a boy
 'A boy didn't arrive yesterday.'
 Possible reading: ∃ > ¬

This is consistent with my analysis. If the verb is in T, there are a number of positions in which the postverbal unaccusative subject could find itself, including Spec,α.

3.4 Conclusions

It has long been known that movement has consequences for semantic interpretation. In the 1980s and 1990s, it became standard to assume that distinct positions in the tree were mapped directly onto distinct semantic interpretations. The most famous of these models is, I believe, Diesing's (1992) Mapping Hypothesis: an object moved out of the VP is mapped onto the restrictive clause of a quantifier (audible or inaudible) and interpreted as specific, strong, and so on; an object that stays in situ is mapped onto the nuclear scope and interpreted as existential, weak, and so on.

(64) *Mapping Hypothesis*
 a. Material from VP is mapped into the nuclear scope.
 b. Material from IP is mapped into a restrictive clause.
 (Diesing 1992, 10)

The Mapping Hypothesis offered some valuable insights into the syntax-semantics interface. But, as we have seen, it does not provide a realistic picture. Accusative A scrambles (to the position that I have named Spec,α) but it does not take an obligatory wide scope or a specific reading.

The theory presented here hypothesizes that the connection between displacement and meaning is indirect, at least for indefinite DPs. The movement / in situ choice leads to different modes of semantic composition for indefinite nominal phrases: indefinite objects that stay in situ are composed by Restrict; those that scramble are type-shifted by a choice function variable and undergo Function Application. These differences in composition may have consequences for meaning because choice functions allow for wide scope. Thus, accusative A may take scope over other quantifiers, negation, or the conditional operator.

In Montagovian semantics, the only operation of semantic composition that is acknowledged is Function Application. Contemporary semantic theory entertains the possibility that other modes of semantic composition are possible: Kratzer's (1996) Event Identification, Heim and Kratzer's (1998) Modification Rule, and Chung and Ladusaw's (2004) Restrict. One might wonder whether this multiplication of modes of semantic composition could lead to an unrestricted theory.

Chung and Ladusaw's (2004) theory of the semantics of indefinites would seem to take us a step in the wrong direction. Indefinite nominal phrases can be composed by means of Satisfy or Restrict, and both possibilities seem to be available whenever an indefinite nominal phrase is merged in the structure. Moreover, the effects of Restrict are properly contained within the effects of Satisfy, to the extent that Restrict only allows for narrow scopes while Satisfy allows for both narrow and wide scopes. At any given point, we can combine an indefinite nominal phrase in either mode, and the choice, at least some of the time, yields indistinguishable interpretations.

My proposals in this chapter help put Chung and Ladusaw's theory on a firmer footing. There is one particular environment where Restrict applies: Compl,V. A nominal phrase outside of the VP must compose by Function Application. Moreover, the environment in which Restrict applies is an environment in which Restrict must apply, and there is no other environment in which Restrict may apply. The range of semantic interpretations is predictable from the configuration in which the indefinites are found. The system that maps syntactic structures to semantic composition does not have to make any choices and can apply blindly. I surmise this is a desirable result.

The model presented here makes several correct empirical predictions: (i) that marked objects are incompatible with existential and possessor/relator predicates; (ii) that bare nouns cannot be marked; and (iii) that *wh*-phrases "in situ" are marked and are not truly in situ, but are subject to short scrambling.

At the same time, this approach cleans up problems left over from Chung and Ladusaw 2004: namely, how to ensure that the output of Restrict is subject to existential closure immediately and how to make restrictions on existentials follow from the theory. Additionally, we saw in chapter 2 that this model correctly predicts that the arguments of small clauses, clause union, and an object that controls the subject of an infinitive require accusative A.

My claims can be summarized as follows. An indefinite nominal phrase can come into the derivation as a KP or can constitute a smaller structure.

Smaller indefinite nominal phrases
• Smaller indefinite nominal phrases are of type $\langle e,t \rangle$.
• If merged in Compl,V position, smaller indefinite nominal phrases incorporate into V.
• The complements of existentials and individual-level possessors must be of type $\langle e,t \rangle$ and incorporate into V.
• Incorporated nominal phrases are interpreted by means of Restrict.
• Existential closure of incorporated nominal clauses must take place at once so that the VP can serve as input to Kratzer's (1996) Event Identification rule.
• As a consequence, nominal phrases interpreted by Restrict must take narrow scope with respect to any other quantifiers, the IO, or the EA.

KPs
• K is associated with a choice function variable **f** that shifts the type of the indefinite DP. The resulting KP is of type $\langle e \rangle$. The properties of choice functions allow for wide and intermediate scopes.
• If merged in Compl,V, KP raises out of VP for Case reasons.
• Given appropriate environmental conditions (most specially, an animate noun), an object K spells out audibly (e.g., in Spanish as accusative A).
• Specificity is a feature parasitic on **f**, so only type-shifted indefinite nominals can be specific.
• Indefinite nominal phrases not merged in Compl,V cannot incorporate into V—in particular, (i) arguments of small clauses, (ii) affectee arguments of clause union, (iii) objects that control into infinitivals. Therefore, these nominal phrases must be KPs. Thus, given appropriate contextual conditions, these arguments will show up morphologically as marked objects.

I would like to end this chapter by mentioning a question raised by von Fintel and Matthewson (2008, 177–178): "why, if Restrict is universally available, few phenomena in few languages show strong evidence for its existence." The analysis in this chapter extends the scope of Restrict to at least one extra domain: unmarked objects in Spanish. The possibility presents itself that the workings of Restrict can be detected more generally in many DOM languages: those in which the interpretive difference between the marked and the unmarked object relates to scope and specificity. And this possibility segues quite naturally into the next chapter.

4 Crosslinguistic Predictions

4.1 Introduction

The analyses that I presented in chapters 2 and 3 have so far been substantiated only for Spanish data (apart from my brief remarks on Maori and Niuean). But in fact, they constitute a hypothesis about how the computational system of human language (C_{HL}) interacts with the conceptual-intensional (C-I) module. This hypothesis makes predictions for any language in which marked objects are or can be specific while unmarked objects are not. It also makes predictions for languages without overt marked objects but with scrambling. The goal of this chapter is to test these predictions with regard to five languages: Persian, Hindi, Kiswahili, Romanian, and German. I show that the results largely support the framework developed in chapters 2 and 3.

Survey work has shown that literally hundreds of languages exhibit some form of DOM (see Bossong 1985 for the seminal research). As Bossong and others have shown, DOM can split objects in two classes according to a variety of criteria. Here, we are interested in languages in which DOM divides indefinite objects into two classes such that the marked one can be characterized as specific and wide-scope-taking.

Consider the structure in (1). According to my analyses in chapters 2 and 3, marked objects in Spanish move to P2, while unmarked objects stay in P1. P3 is a higher scrambling position.

Indefinite objects in P1 are incorporated into V and composed by Restrict, the result being bound by existential closure right after the VP has been built (see chapter 3 for details). As a consequence of immediate existential closure, such objects can only take narrow scope with respect to any other scope-taking constituent in the clause and they can only be nonspecific.

Indefinite objects in P2 are type-shifted to type $\langle e \rangle$ by choice function variables and (according to Reinhart's (1997) view) are bound by existential closure. The point in the tree where the existential quantifier is merged defines the scope of the indefinite. Indefinite objects in P2 can also be specific because, as argued by von Heusinger (2002), specificity is a feature parasitic on choice functions. If the environment is conducive, they show up morphologically as marked objects.

(1)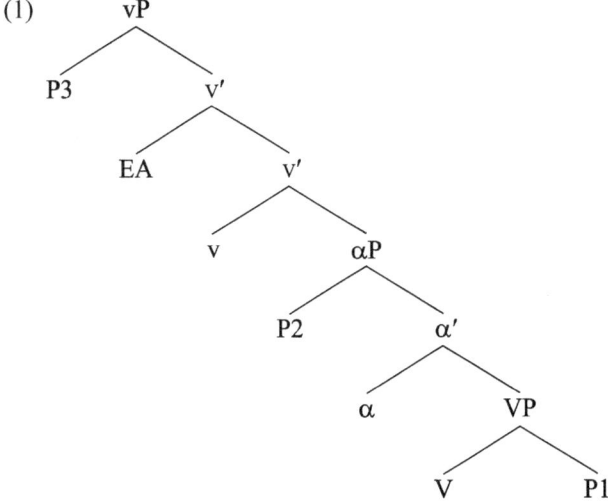

Accusative arguments not merged in P1—small clause arguments, clause union arguments, object control arguments—must be marked in Spanish. This derives from their configuration, which I represent, somewhat abstractly, in (2) and (3) (where NomP is a nominal phrase of any size).

(2)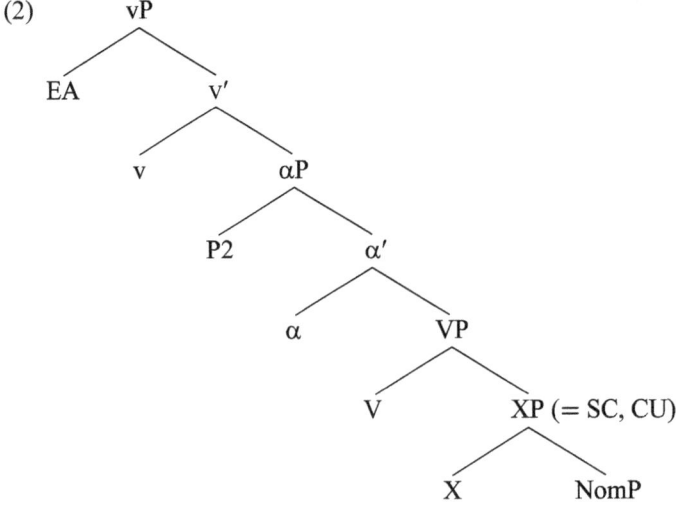

(3)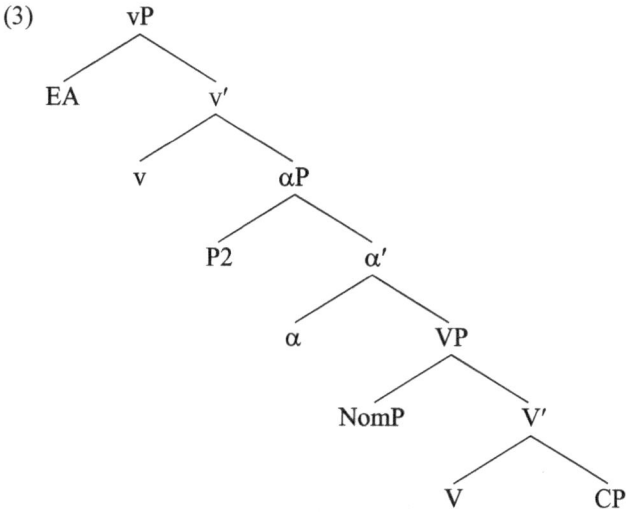

First, consider (2). Take X to be the head of a small clause or a clause union. Assume that X does not incorporate into V (as is the case in Spanish). Under these circumstances, the nominal phrase in (2) cannot satisfy its Case requirement by means of incorporation even if the nominal phrase itself could incorporate into X. In order to satisfy its Case requirement, the nominal phrase needs to raise to Spec,α: this accounts for obligatory accusative A with small clauses and clause union. Next, consider (3). The nominal phrase in (3) cannot incorporate into V because it is merged in a specifier position and only objects merged in complement position can incorporate (Baker 1988). We saw that this analysis makes the correct prediction that in Spanish, the nominal phrase of object control must be marked. We are going to see that these assumptions make good predictions for Persian and Romanian, languages in which DOM is extended to these syntactic configurations. Hindi and Kiswahili provide different outcomes for clause union—but in a manner that extends and deepens the framework, as I show in this chapter.

An additional prediction of my analysis is that DO *wh*-phrases need to scramble. If they stayed in P1, they would be composed by Restrict and bound by an existential quantifier, thus becoming unavailable for binding from [Q] in C. As a result, *wh*-phrases are expected to be marked. This expectation is met in some languages (Romanian, Kiswahili) but not others (Persian, Hindi). Not by chance, the latter two are languages in which the connection between DOM and specificity is categorical. A brief account is presented capitalizing on this property.

My predictions concerning existentials and possessors are complex, and the conditions relevant to check them do not exist in most languages. My model predicts that in those languages in which it leads to optional specificity, DOM will still be banned in existential and possessive structures of the individual-level type. I find that only Kiswahili fits this description, and it confirms the prediction. DOM in existential and possessor clauses is also banned when it is obligatorily specific or when the pivot of the existential becomes a subject— trivially consistent with my framework.

In extending my analyses to other languages, I must consider linguistic features absent from Spanish but present in some of the other languages being studied. The first feature to consider is that some languages allow more extensive incorporation than Spanish, including incorporation of a predicate into another predicate. Consider (2) again. There are languages in which some lexicalizations of X are incorporated into the selecting verb (e.g., if the selecting verb is a causative). In that configuration, an indefinite argument merged in Compl,X should be able to incorporate into X and piggyback its way to V and to v, as in (4).

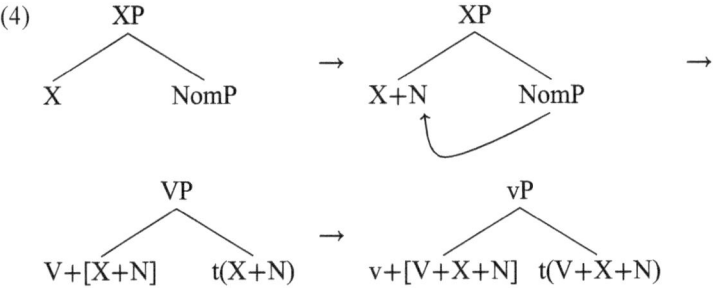

On the other hand, if the argument is not merged in Compl,X, it must be marked. Thus, in languages in which the lower predicate incorporates into the selecting verb, it should be possible to find unmarked arguments in small clauses or clause union. As I will show in this chapter, Hindi and Kiswahili are two languages where this is the case.

The second linguistic feature that I need to consider in this chapter is the cover term α. In chapter 2, α was defined as involving inner aspect and the applicative function. It should not be surprising to find that the two functions are spread across two separate functional heads in some languages. I will, somewhat speculatively, claim that this is the case in Kiswahili.

Here is a summary of the predictions generated by the hypotheses in chapters 2 and 3:

- Only marked nominal phrases can (or must) be specific and can have wide scope. Wide scope of indefinite nominal phrases does not respect islands. Unmarked nominal phrases cannot be specific or take scope outside islands. (As usual, the marked/unmarked opposition abstracts away from animacy; as we saw in chapter 3, what is crucial is the presence or absence of K in the nominal structure.)
- Marked nominal phrases scramble.
- The arguments of small clauses and clause union arguments must be marked if there is no predicate incorporation. Predicate incorporation allows for the possibility of unmarked objects if they are merged in Compl,X.
- Object control arguments must be marked.
- Object *wh*-phrases must be marked (this statement will be qualified later).
- DOM is banned in existential and possessive sentences even if the marked object is not obligatorily specific.
- Unmarked objects are incorporated into V. Although the type of incorporation that I have argued for in Spanish is fairly abstract, more transparent evidence of it should be found in at least some languages.

As mentioned, the purpose of this chapter is to test these predictions on a broader database. For this purpose, I have chosen Persian, Hindi, Kiswahili, Romanian, and German for close examination. In making this choice, I juggled scientific as well as practical reasons. I wanted to discuss enough languages to make a Universal Grammar claim convincing, but not so many that this chapter would become a tedious inventory. I wanted to include representatives of all the modalities of DOM: dependent-marked DOM (Persian, Hindi), head-marked DOM (Kiswahili), both dependent- and head-marked DOM (Romanian), and no visible DOM but visible scrambling (German).

In a typological survey, it is important to include representatives from different language families. Here, I discuss data from one Bantu language; the other languages are Indo-European. Thus, this chapter does not qualify as a typological survey, nor is it intended to be one. My goal is to investigate instances of DOM that developed independently, to ensure that their grammatical intersections cannot be the result of a genetic relationship, and this requirement is fulfilled. The genetically closest languages discussed in this monograph are Spanish and Romanian; they are only 1,500 years apart, but their different forms of DOM evolved separately and using different ingredients (see Stark 2011). Thus, even if some of the languages discussed in this chapter are genetically related, the DOM phenomena that they exhibit are not.[1]

4.2 Dependent-Marked DOM: Persian

4.2.1 Properties of -râ

DOM in Persian is expressed by means of the suffix -râ (which surfaces as -o or as -ro). Its properties are fairly well-understood thanks to the work of Ghomeshi (1997, 2008) and Karimi (1990, 2003, 2005), among others.

-râ attaches to the edge of the nominal phrase, rather than to a noun, as example (5) shows.[2]

(5) kolâh-e un   mard-e qad-boland-**o**
    hat-EZ that man-EZ height+tall-RÂ
    'the hat of the tall man'
    (Ghomeshi 1997, 136)

It is external to any indefinite or definite suffixes, when present.

(6) a. ketâb-i-**ro**
       book-INDEF-RÂ
       'a book'
    b. zan-a-**ro**
       woman-DEF-RÂ
       'the woman'

Thus, -râ spells out a nominal category structurally higher than the determiners.

Both these properties are reminiscent of Spanish accusative A, which is also external to the determiners and a phrasal affix. It is quite natural to follow Ghomeshi (1997) in assuming that -râ is the spell-out of K, as shown in (7). Thus, I commit myself to the claim that Spanish accusative A and -râ spell out the same category.

(7)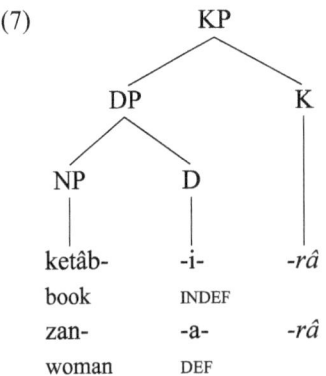

-râ is obligatory with strong quantifiers, proper names, pronouns, and definite DPs.

(8) a. Ali-**ro** did-am.
 Ali-RÂ saw-1SG
 'I saw Ali.'
 (Ghomeshi 2008, 100)
 b. To-**ro** did-am.
 you-RÂ saw-1SG
 'I saw you.'
 (Ghomeshi 2008, 100)
 c. Kimea un   zan-a-**ro**   dust=na-dār-e.
 Kimea that woman-DEF-RÂ friend=NEG-have-3SG
 'Kimea doesn't like that woman.'
 d. Kimea hame-ye ketab-ha-**ro** xund.
 Kimea every-EZ book-PL-RÂ read
 'Kimea read every book.'
 (Jila Ghomeshi, personal communication)

-râ can also attach to bare nouns, as in (9a), and nouns bearing an indefinite suffix or prefix, as in (9b).

(9) a. Sandali-**ro** did-am.
 chair-RÂ   saw-1SG
 'I saw the chair.'
 (Ghomeshi 2008, 100)
 b. Jān (yek) zan-i-**ro**   did-am.
 Jan (one) woman-INDEF-RÂ saw-1SG
 'Jan saw a woman.'
 (Jila Ghomeshi, personal communication)

In (9a), *-râ* is optional; but when it is absent, the meaning of the nominal phrase changes from definite to nonspecific indefinite. Ghomeshi (2008) argues that bare nouns in Persian can be of two types: they can be of type $\langle e,t \rangle$ with an NP syntax or they can be individuals with a DP syntax that includes a phonetically empty definite determiner (see also the discussion of Hindi nominal phrases in section 4.3). In object position, the presence of *-râ* forces a definite interpretation while a bare noun can only be read as a weak indefinite (9a). In (9b), the presence of the indefinite determiner *yek*, in conjunction with *-râ*, yields a specific interpretation. Colloquial Persian also includes the suffixes *-i* and *-a* with an indefinite and definite meaning, respectively (see (6a,b)). All these ingredients are captured in the tree in (10).

(10)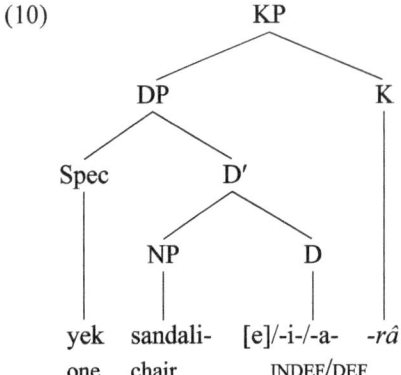

The uses of -*râ* are broader than those of Spanish accusative A. In particular, -*râ* shows up on temporal adjuncts and also on nominals extracted out of direct object DPs or out of PPs. I am not able to provide a detailed analysis of these phenomena within the limits of this monograph, but a few words are in order to orient the reader.

Marked accusative with temporal adjuncts is exemplified in (11).

(11) Shab-e pish-o aslant na-xābid-am.
night-EZ last-RÂ at.all NEG-slept-1SG
'Last night I didn't sleep at all.'
(Karimi 1990, 143)

It is not unusual for time adjuncts to bear accusative case morphology (e.g., in German). Interestingly, Ghomeshi (1997) argues that the presence of -*râ* has the semantic effect of delimiting the temporal frame of the event involved. This is of interest here because Spanish accusative A has also been argued to involve this delimiting role (see Torrego 1998), although Spanish accusative A does not attach to time adjuncts. The role of -*râ* in time adjuncts is suggestive, given that I have claimed that inner aspect is part of the feature structure of α.

The occurrence of -*râ* with extracted nominals is exemplified in (12).

(12) Mâshin-o dar-esh-o bast-am.
car-RÂ door-3SG-RÂ closed-1SG
'I closed the car's door.' / 'As for the car, I closed the door.'
(Karimi 1990, 143)

It is worth remarking that extraction out of DPs often triggers concord between the extracted constituent and the larger DP unit. For instance, floating quantifiers agree in φ-features and case with the extracted DP; for some Icelandic and

Catalan examples, see Sigurðsson 1991 and Solà 1992, respectively. Persian exemplifies the same phenomenon.

(13) Gilâs-a-**ro** Kimea be bachche-hâ goft ke hama-**ro** boxoran.
cherry-PL-RÂ Kimea to child-PL said that all-RÂ SUBJ.eat.3PL
'The cherries, Kimea told the children to eat them all.'
(Karimi 2005, 39)

I venture that (12) exemplifies a similar type of phenomenon.

Let us return to our main focus: direct objects with marked accusative case morphology. We are pursuing the hypothesis that Persian -*râ* is of the same category as Spanish accusative A. According to my analysis of Spanish DOM in the previous chapters, marked objects in Persian are expected to show the following behavior: (i) they scramble; (ii) the marked suffix is obligatory with the arguments of small clauses and object control verbs;[3] (iii) the marked object is banned with existentials and possessives; (iv) marked nominals are composed by means of choice functions and therefore must be able to take wide scope and have a specific interpretation. A fifth expectation, that DO *wh*-phrases should be marked, is not fulfilled; I will present a possible account for this failure shortly, based on the properties of the -*râ* suffix. I start with the specificity question and then I test predictions (i) through (iv).

The linguists who have worked on Persian agree that -*râ* objects are obligatorily specific. For instance, -*râ* is not possible with "looking for a manager" sentences.

(14) Jān dombāl-e monši$_i$(*-**râ**) mi-gard-e.
John search-EZ assistant CONT-look-3SG
U$_i$ bāyad ālmāni be-dun-e.
she/he must German SUBJ-know-3SG
'John is looking for an assistant. She/He must know German.'
(Jila Ghomeshi, personal communication)

Recall that the equivalent of this example in Spanish can have accusative A, as shown in (15).

(15) Juan busca **a** un ayudante. Tiene que saber alemán.
Juan seeks an assistant must that know.INF German
'Juan is looking for an assistant. She/He must know German.'

Examples such as (15) led me (and others before me) to argue that accusative A is not necessarily specific. How to account for this difference between Persian and Spanish? I argued in chapter 3 that specificity is parasitic on the choice function variable. I claim now that in Persian this association is obligatory while in Spanish it is optional. In the terms developed in chapter 3, whenever K translates as **f** in the semantics, the feature [specific] attaches to it.

This difference between Spanish and Persian has an additional consequence. Object *wh*-phrases in Persian do not need to bear the *-râ* suffix; one can easily glean examples of unmarked object *wh*-phrases in the published literature (Karimi 2005; Lotfi 2008). This raises a concern, as my analyses lead to the conclusion that object *wh*-phrases cannot stay in situ. If we assume this conclusion to be correct, then why is it that of all the indefinite objects that move out of P1, only *wh*-phrases need not bear the *-râ* suffix? My answer hinges precisely on a conflict between the properties of *wh*-phrases and *-râ*. Although *wh*-phrases need to scramble, non-D-linked *wh*-phrases *cannot* be specific. If K selects a non-D-linked [wh] determiner, the rule that associates the choice function variable to specificity is canceled.

The Morphology rule that inserts *-râ* is also sensitive to specificity, so *-râ* is inserted in the K position only if the latter bears the specificity feature. When [specific] is not part of the feature structure of K[wh], *-râ* is not inserted. This explains why *wh*-phrases in P2 do not have to exhibit *-râ* in Persian if they are not specific.

This is the more nuanced prediction that we can make with respect to DOM and object *wh*-phrases. In those languages in which the connection among **CH**, DOM, and specificity is categorical (Persian), *wh*-phrases will exhibit DOM only optionally. However, in those languages in which choice functions and specificity are not categorically connected (Spanish), the DOM Vocabulary insertion rule may be sensitive only to the position of the DO in Spec,α, regardless of specificity. If so, *wh*-phrases will be obligatorily marked. This nuanced prediction is confirmed when we look at Hindi, Kiswahili, and Romanian.

4.2.2 Scrambling

Let us now address prediction (i): scrambling of marked objects. Ghomeshi (1997) and Karimi (2003) argue that marked objects in Persian occupy a position higher than regular objects. They show that an object with *-râ* c-commands an IO while an object without this suffix does not.

(16) Man se-tā bachche-hâ-**ro** be hamdige mo'arrefi kard-am.
 I three-PART child-PL-RÂ to each.other introduction did-1SG
 'I introduced the three children to each other.'
 (Karimi 2003, 115)

(17) *Man se-tā bachche-hâ be hamdige mo'arrefi kard-am.
I three-PART child-PL to each.other introduction did-1SG
(Karimi 2003, 115)

Karimi (2003) additionally invokes word order to argue that there is a difference between marked and unmarked objects. A marked object can appear to the left of an IO or a VP adverb (but scrambling in Persian is productive enough that a marked object can also scramble to a position to the left of the subject). Unmarked objects must remain adjacent to the verb unless they are contrastively focused, a context that favors scrambling. This is exemplified in (18) and (19), where both sentences are to be pronounced with a neutral intonation. We see that the -*râ* object appears to the left of the IO while the unmarked object appears to the right. The adverb *aghlab* 'often' demarcates the vP area.

(18) Kimea aghlab barâ mâ ye she'r az Hafez mi-xun-e.
Kimea often for us a poem by Hafez HAB-read-3SG
'It is often the case that Kimea reads a poem by Hafez for us.'
(Karimi 2003, 91)

(19) Kimea aghlab ye she'r az Hafez-**ro** barâ mâ mi-xun-e.
Kimea often a poem by Hafez-RÂ for us HAB-read-3SG
'It is often the case that Kimea reads a poem by Hafez for us.'
(Karimi 2003, 91)

Karimi (2003) proposes that the marked and the unmarked objects in Persian are initially merged in different positions: marked objects in Spec,V, unmarked objects in Compl,V (see Karimi 1990, 2003 and, for a similar proposal, Ghomeshi 1997). However, it seems to me that one could plausibly argue for a movement analysis here. The evidence comes from SCs and object control—and smoothly segues into prediction (ii). In the following examples, -*râ* is obligatory:

(20) Jān ye bachche-**ro** majbur kard Nintendo bazi kone.
John one child-RÂ oblige do.3SG Nintendo play SUBJ.do.3SG
'John forces a child to play Nintendo.'

(21) Jān ye dānešju-**ro** ahmaq mi-dun-e.
John one student-RÂ stupid CONT-know-3SG
'John considers a student stupid.'

My consultants tell me that a specific reading is obligatory for these examples. As I mentioned earlier, these constructions do not inherently force the relevant argument to be specific. We saw that when we looked at the Spanish data. The following English examples make the point clear:

(22) I consider no one stupid (until I meet them).

(23) I force no one to follow me.

If we construct parallel examples in Persian that naturally lead to a nonspecific interpretation—involving imperfect tenses, negative polarity items—the Persian examples still require -*râ* and are read as specific. For instance, the consultant with whom I discussed (24) insisted that (24) should be uttered in a context in which there is a known group of people and John considers that no one in this group is stupid.

(24) Jān kasi-**ro** ahmaq ne-mi-dun-e.
John anyone-RÂ stupid NEG-CONT-know-3SG
'John doesn't consider anyone stupid.'
(Muhammad Belverdi, personal communication)

These data raise the following question: since small clauses and so on do not force a specific interpretation, why is -*râ* obligatory? The obligatoriness of -*râ* in these contexts is, of course, exactly what one would expect if my proposals in chapter 2 are on the right track. (20) exemplifies object control, and -*râ* is obligatory on the controller. (21) exemplifies a small clause, and the argument of the small clause also requires -*râ*. They are both examples of morphosyntactic dependents of the lexical verb that are not initially merged in Compl,V. As I argued in chapter 2, nominal phrases that do not merge in Compl,V need to raise to Spec,α to receive Case. In that position, they can only be interpreted by means of choice functions. Since a choice function in Persian is obligatorily associated with a specificity reading, these indefinite arguments need to have a specific reading.

Keeping this in mind, let us revisit the hypothesis that -*râ* nominal phrases are base-generated in Spec,V. I take it that a strong version of the Internal Argument Hypothesis should hold: all arguments of a predicate are merged with (a projection of) the predicate. This leads to an analysis that involves movement. Take the small clause sentence (21) as an example. According to the standard analysis of small clauses, *ye dānešju-ro* 'one student' and *ahmaq mi-dun-e* 'consider stupid' are constituents of the same category, in keeping with the Internal Argument Hypothesis. The standard analysis of small clauses can be maintained if *dānešju-ro* is indeed merged within the small clause and later raised to a higher position—Spec,α, according to my assumptions. This

Crosslinguistic Predictions

is represented in the tree in (25), which uses the assumptions laid out in chapter 2.

(25)
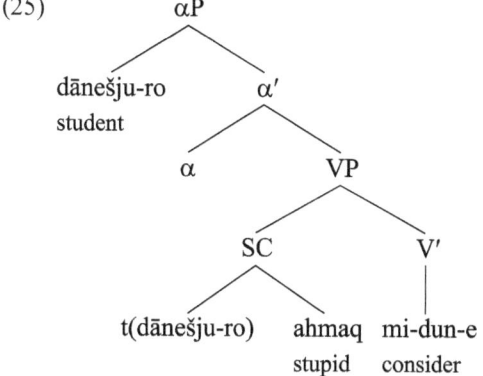

If, following Karimi (2003), all marked arguments in Persian are initially merged in Spec,V, the correct analysis of this example should be as shown in (26). (26) conflicts with the Internal Argument Hypothesis because *dānešju-ro* 'student' would never be an argument of *ahmaq* 'stupid'.

(26)
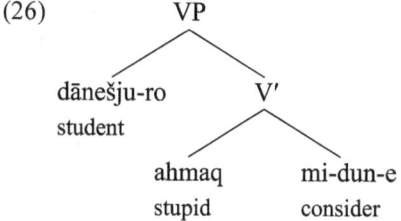

To preserve the Internal Argument Hypothesis and stick to Karimi's (2003) proposals as closely as possible, we would have to conclude that there are two types of marked arguments in Persian: those that move (small clauses, object control) and those that are initially merged in Spec,V. Alternatively (and preferably for simplicity), we could assume that *-rā* objects always scramble. This assumption affects none of Karimi's and Ghomeshi's insights.

As a matter of fact, Karimi (2005, 109) changes her earlier analysis and proposes that *-rā* objects scramble. The target of scrambling is an inner specifier of vP, as shown in (27).

(27)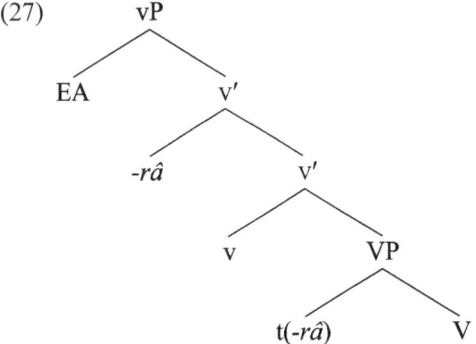

Karimi provides no details about how this structure is built. There are two possibilities: either the marked object raises to Spec,v before the EA is merged or it is "tucked in" afterward. In the first case, there is no mechanism in the theory that prevents assignment of a second θ-role to the marked object, leaving none for the EA itself (see López 2001 on this). As for "tucking in," McGinnis (1998) has argued that it should not be allowed in the vP area. Indeed, the evidence from languages in which object shift is easily detected—especially Icelandic—shows that shifted objects raise to the higher Spec,v, as theoretical considerations lead us to expect. Marked objects in Persian do not raise to a position higher than the initial Merge position of the EA, as is clear from Karimi's (2003, 2005) discussion of constituent order patterns (unless they Ā-scramble to a position in the left periphery).

So, I agree that marked objects scramble to a position lower than the initial Merge position of the EA. However, Spec,α is a much more likely target of this movement than Spec,v.

4.2.3 Existentials, Incorporation, Scope

Let us move on to prediction (iii). Marked objects in Persian are indeed prohibited as the pivots of existential constructions.

(28) a. Ruye miz   yek ketab ast.
         on   table a   book   is
         'There is a book on the table.'
   b. *Ruye miz   yek ketâb-o ast.
         on   table a   book-RÂ is

(29) a. Man yek ketab daram.
         my a   book have.1SG
         'I have a book.'

b. *Man yek ketâb-o daram.
   my a book-RÂ have.1SG
   (Jila Ghomeshi and Muhammad Belverdi, personal communications)

Since marked objects are obligatorily specific, this is not surprising (unlike what we found with Spanish marked objects, for which specificity is only optional and whose incompatibility with existential and possessor predicates is therefore surprising). It is nonetheless comforting that the data are consistent with my claims.

Finally, let us turn to prediction (iv): scope and specificity. With regard to scope, Persian behaves according to the predictions laid out in previous sections. The indefinite marked object can take scope over a subject quantifier.[4]

(30) Hame-ye mard-ā yek zan-o dust dār-an.
   all-EZ man-PL one woman-RÂ friend have-3SG
   'All men like a woman.'
   $\exists > \forall$
   $\forall > \exists$
   (Jila Ghomeshi, personal communication)

There are two reasons to suppose that the wide scope of the indefinite is caused by choice junction. First, Karimi's (2003) discussion of scope effects in Persian leads to the conclusion that there is no (covert) QR in this language. For instance, (31) is not ambiguous.

(31) Yeknafar har ketâb-i-ro mi-xun-e.
   someone every book-INDEF-RÂ HAB-read-3SG
   'Someone reads every book.'
   $\exists > \forall$
   *$\forall > \exists$
   (Karimi 2003, 115)

Second, marked objects can take scope even over strong islands. As usual, I exemplify this with a conditional sentence. In (32), *philosophiro* can take wide scope.

(32) Waghti Bert philosoph-i-ro dawat mikonati, Lud nârahat
   if Bert philosopher-INDEF-RÂ have invite Lud unhappy
   khahad shod.
   be.FUT
   'If Bert invites a philosopher, Lud will be unhappy.'
   (Muhammad Belverdi, personal communication)

The indefinite marked object can take scope over negation. In (33), only the reading where the object takes wide scope is acceptable.

(33) Jān zan-o   dust   na-dār-e.
     John woman-RÂ friend NEG-have-3SG
     'John doesn't like a woman.'
       ∃ > ¬
      *¬ > ∃
     (Jila Ghomeshi, personal communication)

But marked objects in Persian do not have to take wide scope. For instance, -râ can combine with a negative polarity item, and the result yields an obligatory narrow scope reading.

(34) Jān hich zan-i-ro   dust   na-dār-e.
     John any woman-INDEF-RÂ friend NEG-have-3SG
     'John doesn't like any woman.'
       *∃ > ¬
        ¬ > ∃
     (Jila Ghomeshi, personal communication)

Let us now turn to unmarked objects. Karimi (2003) argues that bare nouns in Persian are combined with the lexical verb by means of an operation that she calls Syntactic Word Formation (SWF; Karimi 2003, 105). The input to SWF is a V' (lexical verb + direct object). The output of SWF is a complex verb in which the object is semantically fused with the verb in such a way that the object becomes part of the event rather than a participant in the event. By contrast, the marked object is outside V' and therefore not subject to SWF. SWF leads to the prediction that unmarked objects can only take the narrowest scope. Karimi's analysis is, of course, very similar to the account I developed in chapter 2 for Spanish unmarked objects as well as to the proposals of Van Geenhoven (1998) and Carlson (2003). The narrow scope of indefinites is accounted for by means of Restrict in my account rather than by means of semantic fusion as in Karimi's.

Karimi (2003) also discusses indefinite nominal phrases introduced by *ye(k)* 'a, one'. They are different from bare nouns because they can introduce a referent that becomes available in discourse while bare nouns do not.

(35) Kimea tunest   mâhi be-gir-e.   *Un xeyli châgh-e.
     Kimea managed fish SUBJ-catch-3SG   it very fat.be-3SG
     'Kimea managed to catch fish.'   'It was very fat.'

(36) Kimea tunest   ye âpârtemân peydâ kon-e.   Un xeyli ghashang-e.
    Kimea managed an apartment find   do-3SG   it   very pretty.be-3SG
    'Kimea managed to find an apartment.'   'It was very pretty.'

But *yek* unmarked nominals also seem incorporated. In fact, they must take narrow scope with respect to (e.g.) negation.

(37) Kimea ye ketâb na-xarid.
    Kimea a   book NEG-bought
    'Kimea didn't buy a book.'
    *∃ > ¬
    ¬ > ∃
    (Karimi 2003, 111)

The bare noun in (35) bears the hallmarks of incorporation: it is adjacent to the verb and it is number neutral (more on the issue of number neutrality in section 4.3). However, the examples with *ye(k)* also suggest incorporation in the sense used here. A likely analysis could run as follows: The bare nouns are indeed NPs without additional functional heads, and they incorporate into the verb. The NP cannot introduce a discourse referent because it is incorporated, as Karimi argues. The nouns with *ye(k)* project some additional functional structure, and incorporation for these nominal phrases is of the variety described in chapter 2: it involves copying the higher functional head onto the verbal structure. This leaves the noun free to become a discourse referent.

I conclude that unmarked objects in Persian incorporate into V: either the noun itself incorporates or a higher functional head does. Consequently, they are interpreted by Restrict, which allows only narrow readings. Marked indefinite objects in Persian, on the other hand, can take wide scope over other sentential operators or even outside a strong island—but, as shown by the negative polarity item example (34), they do not have to. This strongly suggests the workings of choice functions.

4.2.4 Conclusions

To conclude this section: Marked indefinite objects in Persian scramble, as shown by binding and order facts. Marked indefinite objects are specific and may take wide scope. Unmarked (non-*wh*) indefinite objects cannot be specific or take wide scope. The arguments of small clauses and PRO-controlling objects must be marked. Existentials and possessive pivots cannot be marked. Thus, Persian confirms point by point the hypotheses laid out in chapters 2 and 3.

4.3 Dependent-Marked DOM: Hindi-Urdu

There are by now numerous studies that either focus or touch on specificity, (pseudo-)incorporation, scrambling, or agreement in Hindi-Urdu (which I continue to refer to as Hindi; see, e.g., Gair and Wali 1989; Mahajan 1990, 1992; Butt 1993, 1995; Mohanan 1994; Bhatt and Anagnostopoulou 1996; Dayal 1999, 2011; Kidwai 2000; Davison 2004; Bhatt 2005). There is unanimity among Hindi-Urdu scholars that objects marked with the suffix *-ko* are specific (Butt 1993; Mohanan 1994). Object agreement has also been argued to be a source of specificity (Mahajan 1990, 1992), but this claim is more disputed. In fact, consideration of the data presented by Butt (1993) and Mohanan (1994) leads to serious doubt that agreement is connected with specificity.

I begin by focusing on *-ko* objects in sections 4.3.1–4.3.5. In section 4.3.6, I discuss the structure of the Hindi DP and in section 4.3.7, object agreement.

4.3.1 Properties of *-ko*

The suffix *-ko* is available in any type of clause and, just like Spanish accusative A, is homophonous with the dative marker. Additionally, presence/absence of *-ko* with DOs is also connected with the animacy scale, although the environment of *-ko* is different from that of accusative A and apparently varies dialectally. I adopt the following generalizations here (based on Mohanan 1994, 74; de Swart 2007, 175; Dayal 2011):

- *-ko* is obligatory with human pronouns and personal names.
- Definite human DPs take *-ko* (but in positions other than object, they can also be bare nouns or bare plural nouns).
- *-ko* is obligatory with indefinite specific animate objects.
- *-ko* is optional with indefinite specific inanimate objects.

I understand that these generalizations are probably idealizations of the data and that they may not hold true for some speakers. In constructing my argument, I use objects that are animate but not human in order to bring about the marked/unmarked—specific/nonspecific correlation.

I give some examples in (38). Example (38a) involves a personal name; (38b) and (38c) involve an animate nonhuman object. The presence of *-ko* makes the object definite. The noun+*-ko* structure is preferably interpreted as definite unless it is accompanied by a determiner like *ek* 'one', which brings about the specific indefinite reading. (38d) and (38e) involve an inanimate noun. An inanimate noun can be specific/definite even in the absence of *-ko*. (Examples (38b,c) were constructed on the basis of data provided by language consultants.)

Crosslinguistic Predictions

(38) a. Ram Anil-**ko**/*Ø uthae-gaa.
    Ram Anil-KO   carry-FUT
    'Ram will carry Anil.'
    (Mohanan 1994, 92)
  b. Ila-ne ciRiyaa-**ko** uthay-aa.
    Ila-ERG bird-KO   carry-PERF
    'Ila carried the bird.'
  c. Ila-ne ciRiyaa uthay-aa.
    Ila-ERG bird   carry-PERF
    'Ila carried a bird.'
  d. Ila-ne haar-**ko**   uthay-aa.
    Ila-ERG necklace-KO carry-PERF
    'Ila carried the necklace.'
    (Mohanan 1994, 80)
  e. Ila-ne haar   uthay-aa.
    Ila-ERG necklace carry-PERF
    'Ila carried a/the necklace.'
    (Mohanan 1994, 80)

As shown in (39), I assume that *-ko* is another spell-out of the functional category K, just like Spanish accusative A and Persian *-râ*.

(39)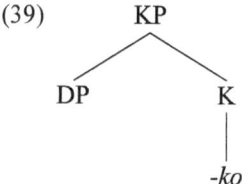

This tree leaves the internal structure of the DP opaque. This is enough for our purposes for now, but later I will articulate what hides under the label DP in more detail.

The link between *-ko* and specificity is as categorical in Hindi as it is in Persian. The "looking for a manager" test gives clear results.

(40) John ek assistant-***ko**/Ø DhuuNDh rahaa hai.
    John a assistant   search   PROG is
    'John is looking for an assistant . . .
    Us-**ko** German   aa-nii   caahiye.
    he-KO German(F) come-INF.F should
    . . . He should know German.'
    (Rajesh Bhatt, personal communication)

Since *-ko* is so categorically linked to definiteness/specificity, it should be optional on *wh*-phrases, just as it is in Persian. This is in fact the case (Koul 2008).

In the rest of my discussion of Hindi, I will take the same tack as in my discussion of Persian. The claim that accusative *-ko* is indeed the equivalent of Spanish accusative A and Persian *-râ* generates a set of predictions: (i) accusative *-ko* scrambles, and this scrambling might be very short; (ii) the arguments of small clauses, clause union, and object control verbs require *-ko*; (iii) *-ko* is unavailable with the pivot of existential and possessive predicates; (iv) *-ko* indefinite objects may take wide scope while unmarked objects cannot.

4.3.2 Scrambling

To start with prediction (i): Bhatt and Anagnostopoulou (1996) argue that *-ko* objects scramble. Using arguments similar to Karimi's (2003) regarding Persian, they use the basic order in ditransitive predicates as evidence. In Hindi, a regular SOV language, the IO normally precedes the DO, as shown in (41).

(41) Ram-ne Anita-ko chitii bhej-ii.
Ram-ERG Anita-KO letter send-PERF.F
'Ram sent a letter to Anita.'

But when the DO bears the *-ko* suffix, the order of the DO and the IO is inverted. This inversion is obligatory.

(42) Ram-ne chitthii-**ko** Anita-ko bhej-aa.
Ram-ERG letter-KO Anita-KO send-PERF
'Ram sent the letter to Anita.'

Bhatt and Anagnostopoulou (1996) conclude that the DO+IO order is the result of scrambling of the DO, and I concur.

Bhatt (2007) adds an additional test for scrambling. He shows that EAs can always control PRO in an adjunct clause. DOs with the *-ko* suffix can also do so, but DOs without the *-ko* suffix cannot.

(43) a. Mina-ne$_i$ bazaar-me ek sailani-**ko**$_j$ [PRO$_{i/j}$ naacte-hue] dekh-aa.
Mina-ERG market-in one tourist-KO dancing-while see-PERF
'Mina saw a tourist in the market dancing.' or 'Mina, while dancing, saw a tourist in the market.'
b. Mina-ne$_i$ bazaar-me ek sailani$_j$ [PRO$_{i/*j}$ naacte-hue] dekh-aa.
Mina-ERG market-in one tourist dancing-while see-PERF
'Mina, while dancing, saw a tourist in the market.'

Bhatt takes this as evidence that *-ko* DOs are in a higher position, from which they can control into the adjunct clause.

The question now is where exactly *chitthii-ko* 'letter' has landed in scrambling cases like (42). Since *Ram-ne* could have stayed in situ in Spec,v or could have raised to Spec,T, at least two analyses are possible.

(44) a. [$_{TP}$ Ram-ne chitthii-ko [$_{vP}$ t(EA) Anita-ko t(DO) bhej-aa]]
b. [$_{TP}$ [$_{vP}$ Ram-ne chitthii-ko Anita-ko t(DO) bhej-aa]]

The first analysis would be orthogonal for my argument. The second one would provide empirical evidence that my argument is on the right track. Bhatt and Anagnostopoulou (1996) claim that the *-ko* object has raised out of VP, but at the time they were writing, the split v-V structure that I assume here had not been developed yet.

Adverb placement is a time-honored tool for testing grammatical structure. For this purpose, I rely on Bhatia's (2006) study of adverb position in Hindi. Bhatia finds a class of adverbs (her class IV) that are located lower than v, and a second group of adverbs (her class V) that are located on the edge of VP (see (45a)). (45b) presents a plausible analysis of adverb position in Hindi, based on Bhatia's arguments and my own structural assumptions.

(45) a. Class IV: *aksar* 'often', *dubaaraa* 'again', *pehle se* 'already', ...
Class V: *acchi tara se* 'well', *jaldi se* 'quickly', *puuri tara se* 'completely', ...
b. [$_{vP}$ v [CLASS IV [$_{\alpha P}$ ... α [CLASS V [$_{VP}$ ... V]]]]]

If *-ko* objects raise to Spec,α and stay there, they should be able to appear between these two groups of adverbs. In this light, consider (46).

(46) Ram-ne aksar / dubaaraa / pehle se chitthii-**ko** Anita-ko acchi tara se /
Ram.ERG often / again / already letter.KO Anita.KO well /
jaldi / puuri tara se chitthii bhej-aa.
quickly / completely letter send.PERF
'Ram often/again/already sent the/a letter to Anita well/quickly/completely.'
(Rajesh Bhatt, personal communication)

To the extent that Bhatia's classification of adverbs in Hindi is correct, the grammaticality of (46) with *chitthii-ko* between the two sets of adverbs shows that the *-ko* object only needs to scramble to a position lower than v—Spec,α, by hypothesis. Notice also the postadverbial position of *chiitthii*, revealing the prescrambling position of DOs in Hindi.

Other features of Bhatt and Anagnostopoulou's (1996) description of short -*ko* scrambling cohere with my analyses in previous chapters. Bhatt and Anagnostopoulou argue that the position to which -*ko* objects move must be an A-position. Evidence for this claim is that this A-position is a reconstruction position when the -*ko* objects scramble even higher. Consider the following examples. (47a) shows the basic constituent order, (47b) shows the DO scrambled over the IO, and (47c) shows the DO scrambled over the EA.

(47) a. Unhõne$_i$ laRkiyõ-ko$_j$ ek-duusre$_{i/j}$-kii kitaabẽ d-ĩĩ.
    they   girls-KO   each-other-GEN books give-PERF
 b. Unhõne$_i$ ek-duusre$_{i/*j}$-kii kitaabẽ laRkiyõ-ko$_j$ d-ĩĩ.
    they   each-other-GEN books girls-KO   give-PERF
 c. Ek-duusre$_{i/*j}$-kii kitaabẽ unhõne$_i$ laRkiyõ-ko$_j$ d-ĩĩ.
    each-other-GEN books they   girls-KO   give-PERF
    'They gave each other's books to the girls.'

(47a) shows that the object anaphor can be bound by the IO or by the subject. The short scrambling in (47b) alters the situation, since at this point the IO can no longer bind the reciprocal. (47c) maintains the binding relations found in (47b). Bhatt and Anagnostopoulou (1996) reason that the movement that places the reciprocal at the beginning of the sentence in (47c) is of the Ā-type and therefore reconstructible. On the other hand, the short scrambling exemplified in (47b) is not reconstructible and therefore must be of the A-type. Additionally, Bhatt and Anagnostopoulou present evidence from weak crossover and Principle C that leads to the same conclusion. Since I claim that Spec,α is a position in which a KP can establish a dependency with v and satisfy its Case requirement, Bhatt and Anagnostopoulou's arguments that -*ko* DPs scramble to an A-position fall neatly into place with my analysis.

Bhatt and Anagnostopoulou also note that the IO cannot scramble to the left of the -*ko* object. This can be readily accounted for if the IO is initially merged in Spec,α. Recall that I presented in chapter 2 the assumption that the functional head α includes the feature [applicative] (see Marantz 1993 and much later work) and hence introduces an IO.

(48) IO α$_{[appl]}$ [$_{VP}$ V DO]

Short scrambling of the DO moves it to a higher Spec,α. An additional movement of the IO from Spec,α to Spec,α is unwarranted and therefore ruled out.

(49) 1. [$_{αP}$ DO [$_{α'}$ IO α t(DO) V]]
  2. *[$_{αP}$ IO [$_α$ DO [$_{α'}$ t(IO) α t(DO) V]]]

Crosslinguistic Predictions

Recall that inanimate nominal phrases may be specific/definite without *-ko*. If my analyses are on the right track, I predict that these bare object definites also scramble. As a matter of fact, they do, as de Swart (2007) shows. In (50a), the object *haar* 'necklace' is inanimate and therefore does not require a *-ko* suffix to be definite or specific (recall (38d,e)). A nonspecific noun may scramble, as (50b) shows.

(50) a. Sunaar-ne   laDkii-ko haar   bhej-aa.
        goldsmith-ERG girl-KO   necklace send-PERF
     b. Sunaar-ne   haar   laDkii-ko bhej-aa.
        goldsmith-ERG necklace girl-KO   send-PERF
        'The goldsmith sent the/a necklace to the girl.'
        (de Swart 2007, 177)

As de Swart reports, the scrambled direct object can only have a definite interpretation, while the unscrambled one is more readily interpreted as nonspecific indefinite.

4.3.3 Small Clauses, Clause Union, and Object Control

Moving on to prediction (ii), recall that my analyses predict that the arguments of small clause predicates, clause union, and object control verbs need to move for Case reasons and therefore will surface as marked objects if predicate incorporation does not take place. As (51) illustrates, *-ko* is obligatory with small clauses.

(51) Saadhu-ne   ciRiyaa-ko/*Ø raanii samjh-aa.
     holy.man-ERG bird-KO   queen consider-PERF
     'The holy man considered the/a bird to be a queen.'
     (Rajesh Bhatt, personal communication; Veneeta Dayal, personal communication)

The same effect is found with permissives.

(52) Anjum-ne   ciRiyaa-ko/*Ø jaa-ne di-yaa.
     Anjum-ERG bird-KO   go-INF give-PERF
     'Anjum let the/a bird go.'
     (Rajesh Bhatt, personal communication; Veneeta Dayal, personal communication)

I take it that the impossibility of unmarked objects with small clauses and permissive predicates confirms the analyses presented earlier in this monograph for Spanish and Persian.

Since the Hindi suffix *-ko* is a dative suffix as well as a marked accusative, one could at this point ask whether the *-ko* that we find in examples (51) and (52) is "in fact" the dative marker. This question depends, of course, on maintaining an analysis in which accusative and dative are fundamentally distinct. It might seem that this question is beside the point, since what is important is that the argument cannot be unmarked. However, it is something worth looking into, at least for completeness.

Mohanan (1994) provides a test to differentiate the dative *-ko* from the accusative *-ko*: passive sentences. In a passive sentence, the dative *-ko* keeps the morphological case suffix while the accusative *-ko* becomes nominative. This can be seen in the following examples:

(53) Raam Anil-**ko** uthae-gaa.
   Ram Anil-KO carry-FUT
   'Ram will carry Anil.'
   (Mohanan 1994, 92)

(54) Anil (Raam-se) uthaa-yaa jaae-gaa.
   Anil (by Ram) carry-PERF go-FUT
   'Anil will be carried (by Ram).'
   (Mohanan 1994, 92)

(55) Anil-ko haar   bhej-aa   ga-yaa.
   Anil-KO necklace send-PERF go-PERF
   'Anil was sent the necklace.'
   (Mohanan 1994, 93)

If we apply this test to examples (51) and (52), we obtain ambiguous results. My language consultants agree that when we passivize a small clause or a permissive predicate, the theme subject may optionally bear the *-ko* suffix.

(56) a. CiRiyaa-**ko**/Ø saadhuu-dwaaraa raanii   maan-ii   jaa-tii
      bird.F-KO   holy.man-by   queen.F consider-PERF.F go-HAB.F
      hai.
      be
      'A/The bird used to be considered by the holy man to be a queen.'
   b. CiRiyaa-**ko**/Ø Anjum-dwaaraa jaa-ne di-yaa   ga-yaa.
      bird-KO   Anjum-by   go-INF give-PERF go-PERF
      'The/A bird was let go by Anjum.'
      (Rajesh Bhatt, personal communication; Veneeta Dayal, personal communication)

Mohanan's test suggests, then, that the argument of a small clause or a permissive predicate in an active sentence may be represented in the mental grammar of Hindi speakers as dative or accusative.

Next, let us turn to causatives. In Hindi, the causative morpheme is an incorporating suffix. This grammatical difference between Hindi on the one hand and Persian and Spanish on the other yields empirical consequences. I start with an example in which the causative morpheme selects for an unaccusative verb. When the complement of a causative is unaccusative, *-ko* is optional on the causee. When *-ko* is not present, the resulting reading recalls incorporation (Veneeta Dayal, personal communication).

(57) Mãĩ-ne ciRiyaa-**ko**/Ø cal-a-yaa.
    I-ERG   bird-KO   walk-CAUS-PERF
    'I made the bird walk.'

This phenomenon is different from what we found in Spanish, where a causee needs to be a marked accusative. However, this difference between Spanish and Hindi is fully expected within my assumptions. In Spanish, the causative verb is not an incorporating verb, but the Hindi causative is incorporating. Thus, the derivation depicted in (58) is available. The nominal *ciRiyaa* 'bird' is merged as a complement of the verbal root *cal* 'walk' and therefore can incorporate into it. The second step of the derivation in (58) consists of the incorporation of the complex head [*ciRiyaa* + *cal*-] into the causative affix *-a-*. This incorporation of the subordinate verb into the causative predicate is the step crucially absent in Spanish. Eventually, the causative affix incorporates into V and the latter incorporates into v, giving rise to a configuration in which the Case requirement of *ciRiyaa* is satisfied.

(58)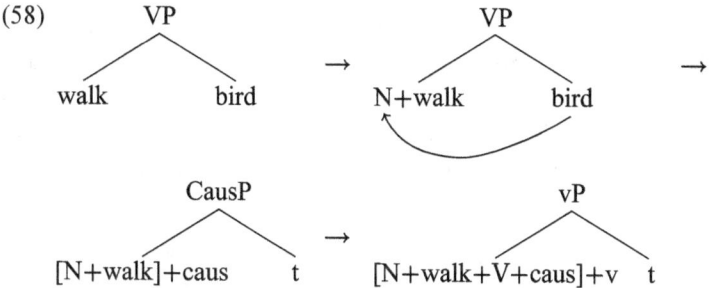

If the subordinate verb is transitive, the causee cannot be a bare noun.

(59) Atif-ne kutte-se/*Ø ciRiyaa pakaR-vaa-yii.
     Atif-ERG dog.INST   bird   catch.CAUS.PERF
     'Atif made the dog catch a bird.'
     (Rajesh Bhatt, personal communication)

Again, this follows from my framework. The causee of a transitive predicate is initially merged as the EA of the predicate (see chapter 2 and López 2001). Therefore, it can't incorporate and it can't be a bare noun. In this example, the causee appears with the oblique case marker -*se*.[5]

With unergatives, the judgments get a little murkier. A bare noun as a causee is not entirely rejected.

(60) Atif-ne kutte-**ko/?Ø** dauR-vaa-yaa.
    Atif-ERG dog-KO run-CAUS-PERF
    'Atif made the dog run.'
    (Rajesh Bhatt, personal communication)

This is only mildly surprising, since the distinction between unergative and unaccusative is somewhat fluid. As is well-known (Hoekstra and Mulder 1990) in Dutch it is possible for a verb like *springen* 'jump' to take a 'have' or a 'be' auxiliary depending on the situation being described—in essence, it is possible for an unergative verb to take on unaccusative syntax.

Thus, causatives in Hindi contrast with causatives in Spanish in a manner that my assumptions fully predict. In Spanish, the subordinate predicate does not incorporate into the causative predicate. In such a configuration, incorporation of the DP into the predicate would never give rise to a Case-satisfying configuration. In this language, the causee must always raise for Case reasons and therefore it will end up exhibiting a mark. In Hindi, the subordinate predicate incorporates into the causative suffix. Therefore, a causee that is initially merged as an internal argument can be unmarked because it can satisfy its Case requirement by incorporation. On the other hand, if the causee is an EA, it must satisfy its Case requirement by raising and it will have to show up as -*ko* (or oblique).

Now let us turn to object control. A controlled infinitive in Hindi can be bare, can be suffixed with -*ko*, or can be introduced by a postposition. In any case, the presence of -*ko* on the controller is obligatory. For instance, the verb *kah*- 'tell' takes an infinitive that can bear the -*ko* suffix. However, the controller should probably be considered dative, since the accusative case is taken by the infinitive.

(61) Anjum-ne ciRiyaa-**ko/*Ø** haar banaa-ne-ko kah-aa.
    Anjum.ERG bird-KO necklace make-INF-KO say-PERF
    'Anjum told the bird to make a necklace.'
    (based on an example in Butt 1995, 58)

More revealing is the verb *majbuur ki*- 'force', which takes an infinitive that bears the postposition *par*, a locative postposition. Since the controlled clause is headed by a P, the possibility arises that the controller bears an accusative *-ko*. I predict that, given that controlling objects are merged in a specifier position, the controller must bear *-ko*. This prediction is fulfilled.

(62) Radhaa-ne *ciRiyaa*-**ko**/*Ø kitaab parh-ne-par majbuur ki-yaa.
     Radhaa-ERG bird-KO   book   read-INF-LOC force   do-PERF
     'Radhaa forced a bird to read a book.'

Is this *-ko* accusative or dative? My consultants agree that the passive of (62) allows *-ko* to be retained, which means that *ciRiyaa-ko* may be dative or accusative.

4.3.4 Existential and Possessive

Next, let us take up prediction (iii): existentials and possessives. Since *-ko* can only be interpreted as specific/definite, it is not surprising to find that the pivot of an existential construction or the possessee cannot be marked. Again, it is worth showing that this is the case before moving on.

Example (63) shows that the pivot of an existential cannot be suffixed by *-ko*.

(63) Jangal meN sher hE. / *Jangal meN sher-**ko** hE.
     jungle in   lion is
     'There is a lion in the jungle.'
     (Sinha and Thakur 2005, 250)

Interestingly, *sher* 'lion' can scramble. The outcome of this scrambling is that *sher* ends up being interpreted as a definite nominal (as is generally the case with scrambled bare nominal phrases).

(64) Sher jangal meN hE.
     lion jungle in   is
     'The lion is in the jungle.'
     (Sinha and Thakur 2005, 250)

Possessive constructions are very similar to existentials in Hindi. The pivot of the possessor cannot bear the *-ko* suffix. Instead, the possessor can bear *-ko* or a postpositional locative like *-ke*.

(65) Ram-ke ek beti   hE. / *Ram-ke ek beti-ko hE.
     Ram-LOC a daughter is
     'Ram has a daughter.'
     (Kachru 1970, 37)

(66) Bacce-ko buxar hE.   /   *Bacce-ko buxar-**ko** hE.
child-KO fever is
'The child has a fever.'
(Kachru 1970, 38)

These data are consistent with my analyses in chapter 3. The existential construction depends on incorporation of the pivot into $BE_{(p,c)}$; therefore, -*ko* is not permitted. Scrambling of the pivot prevents incorporation and BE_{loc} appears without incorporation—in other words, the result is a regular locative sentence (it is worth remarking that -*ko* is also ungrammatical in (64), for reasons that I do not know). The possessor is $BE_{(p,c)}$ with an affected argument.

4.3.5 Scope

Finally, let us consider point (iv): scope. My analyses predict that a marked object in Hindi can take scope over other sentential operators even outside an island, whereas an unmarked object cannot do so. Fortunately, Hindi is a scope-rigid language (Kidwai 2000, 7), which facilitates our work in the manner explained in chapters 1 and 3: if an indefinite takes wide scope, we know it must do so because of the effect of a choice function.

Dayal (2011) discusses some examples that clearly contrast a -*ko* object and a bare object, showing that the -*ko* object can (marginally) take wide scope with respect to negation and (more easily) over a subject quantifier. A bare animate object can only take narrow scope. Although the following examples all feature a singular bare noun, plural bare nouns behave the same way (Dayal 2011, 128):

(67) a. Anu bacca nahii sambhaalegii.
Anu child not will.look.after
'Anu will not look after children.'
$\neg > \exists$
$*\exists > \neg$

b. Anu ek bacce-**ko** / bacce-**ko** nahii sambhaalegii.
Anu one child-KO / child-KO not will.look.after
'Anu will not look after a particular child / the child.'
$\neg > \exists$
$??\exists > \neg$

(68) a. Har aurat bacca sambhaal rahii thii.
every woman child is.looking.after
'Every woman is looking after a child / children.'
$\forall > \exists$
$*\exists > \forall$

b. Har aurat ek bacce-**ko** / bacce-**ko** sambhaal rahii thii.
every woman one child-KO / child-KO is.looking.after
'Every woman is looking after a particular child / the child.'
$\forall > \exists$
$\exists > \forall$

Again, these scope facts have a direct account within my framework. The -*ko* arguments scramble and include a choice function variable. The (indefinite) bare arguments stay in situ and incorporate (or pseudo-incorporate; Dayal 1999, 2011) and they are interpreted by means of Restrict.

To conclude my discussion of -*ko*: the data available to me at this point show that the properties of marked and unmarked objects in Hindi fall together with those of Persian and Spanish, while providing new corroborating data.

At this point, it becomes necessary to approach the two issues that I brushed aside earlier: the structure of DP, and the nature of object agreement in Hindi and whether it correlates with specificity.

4.3.6 Nominal Structure

Let me summarize the facts about Hindi nominal phrase structure as I understand them. I take as a starting point the assumption that nominal phrases in Hindi can project a bare noun, a #P, a DP, or a KP. This is different from Spanish, where at least a #P needs to be projected and bare count nouns are (mostly) prohibited (see the appendix to chapter 2). The possibility of bare nouns in Hindi adds substantial complexity to the phenomena surrounding nominal structure. In the following paragraphs, I discuss, in turn, nominals that surface as bare nouns, nominals that bear a plural affix, nominals that have an overt indefinite determiner, and -*ko* nominals.

Dayal (1999, 2011) argues that bare nouns in object position are pseudo-incorporated into V. This sort of bare noun is number neutral, as shown in (69). I take this number neutrality to be evidence that the nominal phrase involves no #P.

(69) Anu botal ikaTThaa kartii hai.
Anu bottle collects
'Anu collects bottles.'
(Dayal 2011, 141; see also chapter 2 above)

Dayal shows that the number neutrality of bare nouns depends on Aspect. That is, an example like (69) is grammatical because the habitual or iterative interpretation of imperfective aspect allows us to see the noun *botal* as referring to more than one. In Spanish, on the other hand, although the imperfect/perfect dichotomy is rich in grammatical consequences, an example equivalent to (69) is ungrammatical even in the imperfect. So, there is something about the structure of the Hindi nominal phrases that differs from the structure of their counterparts in Spanish. I claim that in Spanish, the functional category Number is obligatory in a nominal phrase; in Hindi, it is not.[6]

Pseudo-incorporated bare nouns agree in gender with the T-V complex. This coheres with the assumption that Hindi bare nouns may not project any functional categories if we take gender to be an inherent feature of nouns (as in Carstens 2000) and not a functional category.

Bare animate nouns in singular or plural form can be interpreted as kind NPs or as definite NPs. However, as argued by Dayal (2011), bare nouns cannot be interpreted as specific indefinites. Consider example (70). The first instance of *bacce* is a nonspecific indefinite. It cannot mean something like 'some of the children'. The second instance of *bacce* refers back to the aforementioned group of children in its totality, not to a subset of them; it is definite, not specific indefinite.

(70) Kuch bacce   andar aaye. Bacce   bahut khush the.
     some children inside came children very happy were
     'Some children came in. The children were very happy.'
     (Dayal 2011, 129)

I take it that bare nouns in Hindi that are not pseudo-incorporated include a #P and are headed by a silent $D_{[definite]}$ or $D_{[generic]}$ head. In object position, a bare noun can be definite only if inanimate.

A nominal phrase can also include the indefinite determiner *ek*. Since it precedes the nominal phrase, *ek* should probably be regarded as an instance of Spec,D. Quantifiers such as *har* 'every' also precede the nominal phrase and therefore can also be regarded as instances of Spec,D.

Objects in Hindi can appear with the suffix *-ko*. If *-ko* affixes to a bare noun, the resulting KP is interpreted as definite. If *-ko* attaches to a DP with *ek* in its specifier, the resulting KP is interpreted as a specific indefinite (see also the discussion of Persian in the previous section). The suffix *-ko* also attaches obligatorily (modulo animacy) to strong quantifiers, proper names, and definite pronouns.

With this information, we can already fill in some more details about the structure of nominal phrases in Hindi. The tree in (71) collapses several choices available in the grammar of Hindi: a KP in Hindi can consist of (i) a quantifier and the *-ko* suffix, (ii) plural morphology and the *-ko* suffix, or (iii) the indefinite D *ek* and the *-ko* suffix; or (iv) *-ko* can attach to a silent definite D. Since inanimate bare nouns in object position can be definite/specific, I assume that K can also be silent if the noun is inanimate.

(71)
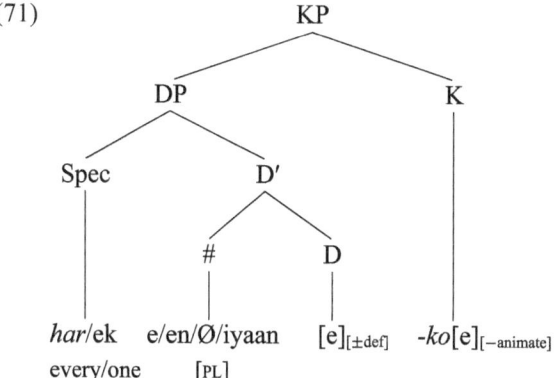

4.3.7 Object Agreement

Let us now turn to object agreement. Recall that Mahajan (1989, 1990, 1992) claims that object agreement in Hindi is related to specificity. This makes it necessary to say a few words about object agreement.

Object agreement is exemplified in (72).

(72) Ram-ne   roTii   khaa-yii.
Ram(M)-ERG bread(F) eat-PERF.F.SG
'Ram ate bread.'
(Mahajan 1990, 189)

Object agreement is only possible if the EA bears overt case morphology. This overt case morphology acts as a barrier for any external probe. Similar phenomena are found in Icelandic, Spanish, and many other languages, including Indo-Aryan languages other than Hindi. EAs in this language bear overt case morphology in perfect clauses, like the one in (72). An experiencer EA of a psych verb also bears overt case morphology (-*ko*). Finally, goal EAs also bear -*ko*. Let me articulate these facts in more detail.

In imperfect clauses, the subject appears without overt case morphology and T agrees with it. The direct object can also appear without case morphology, as in (73), or it can appear with -*ko*, as in (74).

(73) Ram   roTii   khaataa   thaa.
Ram(M) bread(F) eat.IMP.M.SG be.PERF.M.SG
'Ram eats bread.'
(Mahajan 1990, 189)

(74) Ram   rote-**ko**   khaataa   thaa.
     Ram(M) bread(F).KO eat.IMP.M.SG be.PERF.M.SG
     'Ram eats bread.'
     (Mahajan 1990, 189)

In perfect clauses, the EA bears an overt piece of case morphology, *-ne*. Overt case morphology prevents agreement in Hindi, with the result that the finite T may end up agreeing with the object, as in (75), or surfacing in a default masculine singular form.

(75) Ram-ne   roTii   khaa-yii.
     Ram(M)-ERG bread(F) eat-PERF.F.SG
     'Ram ate bread.'
     (Mahajan 1990, 189)

The following example involves a goal EA. The goal EA appears with *-ko*, and agreement again takes place with the object.

(76) Tusaar-ko kitaab   mil-ii.
     Tushar-KO book(F) receive-PERF.F.SG
     'Tushar received a book.'
     (Mohanan 1994, 141)

Mahajan (1989, 1990, 1992) claims that agreeing objects raise to a Spec,Agr position located outside the VP. As noted earlier, he further claims that object agreement correlates with specificity. To support his claim that agreeing objects move, Mahajan (1990) provides data concerning the interpretation of adverbs. However, he does not present an argument that agreeing objects are specific; that is, he does not present any minimal pairs of agreeing/nonagreeing objects, place them in a context, and solicit native speaker judgments.

Butt (1993) argues that the specific reading of agreeing objects is possible but not necessary and claims that specificity should be separated from agreement. Up to this point, I could assume that object agreement in Hindi is similar in some important respects to Spanish accusative A. Both are optionally specific and both, apparently, scramble. However, Mohanan (1994) presents clear evidence that agreeing objects in Hindi can incorporate, since they have the compound interpretation of incorporated objects.

(77) Anil-ne   kitaabẽ   bec-ĩĩ.
     Anil-ERG book.F.PL sell-PERF.F.PL
     'Anil sold books.' or 'Anil did book-selling.'
     (Mohanan 1994, 106)

Crosslinguistic Predictions

As I argued in chapter 2, accusative A in Spanish always scrambles, even if minimally. But the Hindi agreeing object does not have to scramble. Thus, there is a substantial difference between Hindi object agreement and Spanish accusative A. In particular, I am convinced by Mohanan's (1994) evidence that object agreement does not implicate specificity.

4.3.8 Conclusions

I have suggested that Hindi nominal phrases can be merged as NPs, #Ps, DPs, and KPs. Both N and # incorporate; D possibly does so, too. As I outlined it in chapter 2, I take incorporation to consist of copying the highest nominal head of the phrase. Assume that a bare noun is merged in Compl,V. This bare noun must incorporate (or pseudo-incorporate). The incorporated noun ends up included as a part of v or T (as we saw in chapter 2). This inclusion satisfies its Case requirement and allows for gender agreement. Gender agreement between the object and T arises if the EA bears overt case morphology, turning it opaque to probes. Since there is no Number head, the noun is neutral with respect to number.

Assume that a #P is merged in Compl,V. This can also incorporate, and the resulting nominal phrase appears in plural form.

Finally, assume that a KP is merged in Compl,V. Like KPs in Spanish and Persian, it scrambles to Spec,α. K selects for a DP whose head, if definite, is phonetically null. K spells out as -*ko* under the animacy conditions specified above. -*ko* prevents agreement.

Once the complex phenomena of Hindi nominal phrases are teased apart, the following conclusions can be drawn. Hindi shows evidence that marked objects scramble and that scrambled objects can take wide scope. Scrambled objects take the suffix -*ko*, with the usual caveat that the appropriate environmental conditions must hold. Unmarked objects incorporate and can only take narrow scope. The properties of Hindi marked objects match those of marked objects in Spanish and Persian.

4.4 Head-Marked DOM: Kiswahili

In Kiswahili, DOM appears as agreement morphology on the verb. In the following examples, object agreement is boldfaced and glossed as *OA*. Subject agreement is glossed as *SA*. Notice that the Kiswahili DP lacks an overt D head (Carstens 1991). (Regarding the sources of examples in this section, see note 7.)

(78) a. Juma a-li-**mw**-ona   mtu.
     Juma 3SA-PAST-3OA-see person
     'Juma saw the/a person.'
  b. Juma a-li-ona   mtu.
     Juma 3SA-PAST-see person
     'Juma saw a person.'
  c. Juma a-li-**mw**/*Ø-ona kila mtu.
     Juma 3SA-PAST-3OA-see every person
     'Juma saw every person.'
  d. Juma a-li-**mw**/*Ø-ona Fatuma.
     Juma 3SA-PAST-3OA-see Fatuma
     'Juma saw Fatuma.'
  e. Juma a-li-**mw**/*Ø-ona yeye.
     Juma 3SA-PAST-3OA-see her/him
     'Juma saw her/him.'

Consider (78a,b). The difference between using and not using agreement with a bare noun is expressed in the translations. Agreement favors a specific/definite reading on the object, without making it obligatory. At least, that is the case when the object is animate. When the object is inanimate, agreement is also possible, although the conditions for OA with inanimates are somewhat elusive to me. As is my by-now-routine strategy, I stick to examples with animate objects.[7] When the object is a strong quantifier, animate and definite, or a pronoun, as in (78c,d,e), the agreement marker is obligatory.

As with Spanish, Persian, and Hindi DOM, I take it that Kiswahili DOM reflects a local relationship between v and the DO. In this case, this local relationship results in overt agreement rather than the spell-out of K.

(79) [EA v$_{[u\varphi]}$ [DO$_{[\varphi]}$ . . .]]

Kiswahili provides additional evidence for some of the claims developed in chapters 2 and 3. Let us start with scope. The DOM object can take scope over a subject, over negation, and outside of a conditional. The object without OA can only take narrow scope. This is shown in the following examples. (80) and (81) are identical, except that the latter bears OA. The difference in scope is as indicated: only if there is OA can the DO take scope over the subject.

(80) Kila mwanamume a-na-penda   mwanamke.
     every man   3SA-PRES-love woman
     'Every man loves a woman.'
         $\forall > \exists$
         *$\exists > \forall$

(81) Kila mwanamume a-na-**m**-penda mwanamke.
every man 3SA-PRES-3OA-love woman
'Every man loves a woman.'
$\forall > \exists$
$\exists > \forall$

The following examples involve the relative scope of negation and the indefinite object. Only if there is OA can the DO take scope over negation.

(82) Juma ha-**wa**-pend-i watoto.
Juma NEG.3SA-3PL.OA-love-NEG children
'Juma doesn't like the/some children.'

(83) Juma ha-pend-i watoto.
Juma NEG.3SA-love-NEG children
'Juma doesn't like children.'

Finally, we have our "philosopher" examples once again. And once again, scope over the conditional is dependent on OA.

(84) Ikiwa Bert a-ta-**mw**-alika mwanafalsafa, Lud a-ta-kasirika.
if Bert 3SA-FUT-3OA-invite philosopher Lud 3SA-FUT-be.upset
'If Bert invites a philosopher, Lud will be upset.'

(85) Ikiwa Bert a-ta-alika mwanafalsafa, Lud a-ta-kasirika.
if Bert 3SA-FUT-invite philosopher Lud 3SA-FUT-be.upset

Kiswahili requires DOM with (animate) *wh*-questions, just like Spanish and as expected under my approach. Unlike Spanish, Kiswahili is a *wh*-in-situ language.

(86) Juma a-na-**m**-penda nani?
Juma 3SA-PRES-3OA-love who
'Who does Juma love?'

(87) *Juma anapenda nani?
Juma loves who

In object control contexts, OA is also obligatory.

(88) Ni-li-**wa**-shawishi watoto kubusu mama zao.
1SA-PAST-3PL.OA-persuade children kiss.INF mom their
'I persuaded the/some children to kiss their mom.'

On the other hand, other predictions of the theory cannot be tested with Kiswahili because of its own grammatical properties. For instance, there is nothing like small clauses in Kiswahili: their equivalents involve subordination of a finite clause.

Additionally, it is not possible to test whether the DO with OA scrambles over the IO. As Kiswahili ditransitives are a matter of some interest, I discuss them here in detail. There are two frames for Kiswahili ditransitives: one in which the IO is introduced by the preposition *kwa*, exemplified in (89a); and the applicative frame, in which the IO triggers OA, exemplified in (89b). In (89b), the OA marker agrees with *Fatuma* and not with *chakula* 'food'. This is apparent because of the Bantu class system. *Fatuma* is a member of class 1 and *chakula* is a member of class 7. The OA marker *-m-* is a marker for class 1 nominals.

(89) a. Juma a-li-pika   chakula cha asubuhi kwa Fatuma.
         Juma 1SA-PAST-cook food   of   morning for   Fatuma
         'Juma cooked breakfast for Fatuma.'
    b. Juma a-li-**m**-pik-ia   Fatuma chakula cha asubuhi.
         Juma 1SA-PAST-3OA-cook-APPL Fatuma food   of   morning
         'Juma cooked breakfast for Fatuma.'

In the applicative frame, the IO c-commands the DO, as shown by Marantz (1993). In (90), the quantifier *kila* 'every' binds the variable *chake* 'his'.

(90) Ni-li-**m**-som-e-a   kila   mwandishi kitabu chake.
      1SA-PAST-3OA-read-APPL-FV every writer   book   his
      'I read for each author his book.'
      (Marantz 1993, 117)

In the languages we have explored so far, it was possible to look at an example with an applicative or applicative-like ditransitive and a marked object and check their c-command relations (the marked object always c-commands the IO). In Kiswahili, the applicative frame only allows for the IO to c-command the DO.

I would like to speculate that this difference between Kiswahili and the other languages lies in the structure of the predicate phrase. In the languages that we have looked at so far, the head α bundles the applicative and the inner aspect features. Following Marantz (1993) and many others, I have taken the IO to be merged in Spec,α and the DO in Compl,V. The marked DO scrambles to a higher Spec,α in Spanish, Persian, and Hindi.

Crosslinguistic Predictions

(91) 1. [$_{vP}$ EA v [$_{αP}$ IO α [$_{VP}$ V DO]]] →
    2. [$_{vP}$ EA v [$_{αP}$ DO [IO α [$_{VP}$ V t(DO)]]]]

I propose that in Kiswahili, the Applicative head is an independent verbal head. Applicative is selected by v and itself selects inner aspect. Applicative introduces the IO and assigns Case to the DO. Under the assumption that Case assignment is local (see chapter 2), the DO scrambles to Spec,Asp. The Kiswahili applicative structure is exemplified in (92).

(92) 1. [$_{vP}$ EA v [$_{ApplP}$ IO Appl [$_{AspP}$ Asp [$_{VP}$ V DO]]]] →
    2. [$_{vP}$ EA v [$_{ApplP}$ IO Appl [$_{AspP}$ DO Asp [$_{VP}$ V t(DO)]]]]

The structure in (92) accounts for the two properties of Kiswahili double object constructions that distinguish Kiswahili from the other DOM languages we have discussed: The IO triggers OA because the IO is the argument that stands closest to v. The IO c-commands the DO because the latter scrambles only to the lower Spec,Asp.

One might wonder why a freestanding Applicative head can assign Case while α, which includes [applicative] among its features, cannot do so. I surmise that Applicative is embedded within the structure of α, leaving its Case feature inaccessible. In other words, the syncretic head α is headed by Aspect and Applicative is embedded within it.

(93)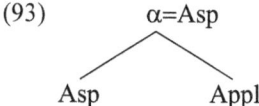

The separation of α into two heads, resulting in a freestanding Applicative head with a Case feature, also sheds light on another empirical challenge. Kiswahili has a morphological causative (*-sha*). The incorporating nature of this causative morpheme would lead one to expect the causee to behave in a manner similar to its counterpart in Hindi: DOM on the causee should be optional in unaccusatives, where the nominal can incorporate into the subordinate verb, and obligatory in transitive and unergative predicates. However, my consultant finds OA optional in every case.

Why does the causee not trigger OA obligatorily? If the causative morpheme is a form of applicative (Marantz 1993) and can assign Case, then we would have two alternative structures for Kiswahili causatives. In (94a), the causative morpheme does not have a Case feature to assign. Consequently, the causee raises to Spec,Cause, where it is probed by v and OA is triggered. In (94b), *-sha* comes fully equipped with a Case-assigning feature. In this instance, the causee does not raise to Spec,Cause and does not trigger OA.

(94) a. [vP EA v [CausP causee -*sha* [vP t(causee) v [vP V]]]]
    b. [vP EA v [CausP -*sha* [vP causee v [vP V]]]]

Now, let us consider existentials and possessives. Existentials in Kiswahili are constructed with a locative prefix and the morpheme *na*, which can be translated as 'have', 'with', or 'and', depending on the environment. An example is given in (95).

(95) Ku-na   watu   hapa.
    LOC-HAVE people here
    'There are people here.'

There is no agreement of any kind between the predicate *kuna* and the pivot *watu*. Possessives are constructed with *na*. There is SA but they reject OA.

(96) a. Juma a-na   watoto.
        Juma 3SGSA.PRES-HAVE children
        'Juma has children.'
    b. *Juma a-**wa**-na   watoto.
        Juma 3SGSA-3PLOA-PRES-HAVE children

To conclude: Kiswahili does not provide evidence for scrambling. However, it has provided more data that allow us to connect DOM with choice functions and unmarked objects with Restrict.

4.5 Dependent- and Head-Marked DOM: Romanian

4.5.1 DOM in Romanian

In the canonical examples, Romanian is morphologically the most complex DOM language discussed here, since it combines a clitic of pronominal origin and a preposition or case marker on the object. DOM in Romanian is sensitive to "humanness" and is generally ungrammatical with animals or inanimate objects. Thus, in this section I once again control for this factor and present only examples with human objects. In (98), the clitic and the DOM morpheme are boldfaced.

(97) Caut   un student.
    seek(1) a student
    'I'm looking for a student.'
    (Mardale 2004, 64)

(98) Il   caut   pe un student.
    CL.ACC seek(1) PE a student
    'I'm looking for a student.'
    (Mardale 2004, 64)

The literature provides examples suggesting that the requirement that the clitic and *pe* go together can be mitigated. Sometimes *pe* is possible without the clitic, and there are even examples in which *pe* is obligatory while the clitic is forbidden. The latter involve the nominal phrases equivalent to the English indefinite quantifiers *someone* and *no one*.

(99) **Pe/*Ø** nimeni n-am   supărat.
    PE   no.one NEG-AUX.1SG annoyed
    'I have annoyed no one.'
    (Dobrovie-Sorin 1984, 220)

(100) **Pe/*Ø** cineva   trebuie   să   superi tu în fiecare zi.
     PE   somebody must.2SG SUBJ upset you in every   day
     'You must upset somebody every day.'
     (Dobrovie-Sorin 1984, 220)

These two examples lead to the issue of the interpretive import of *pe*. Regarding canonical examples like (98), Romanian speakers agree that the DO must be specific. However, examples (99) and (100) show that the requirement is not categorical, at least when the clitic is not present. In light of these examples, I conclude that the association of *pe* with specificity is a strong preference rather than a grammatical requirement.

This leads to another prediction. In languages where DOM does not require obligatory specificity (Spanish, Kiswahili), we expect to find DOM on *wh*-phrases because the Vocabulary insertion rule that inserts DOM into the K slot can proceed unimpeded (while in languages where DOM is categorically linked to specificity, non-D-linked *wh*-phrases cannot be marked). I predict that Romanian DO *wh*-phrases bear *pe*. This is in fact the case.

(101) **Pe/*Ø** cine ai   văzut?
     PE   who AUX.2SG seen
     'Who have you seen?'
     (Dobrovie-Sorin 1984, 198)

Dobrovie-Sorin (1984) argues that D-linked *wh*-phrases require clitic doubling while non-D-linked *wh*-phrases forbid it, as in example (101). Interestingly, *all* object *wh*-phrases must have *pe* (modulo "humanness," of course). Thus, we have already confirmed one of the predictions made in section 4.1.

DOM in Romanian is also obligatory with personal pronouns and names as well as strong quantifiers, along familiar lines (although my language consultants find this requirement to be less strict with some strong quantifiers such as *aproapi toti* 'most').[8]

(102) Televiziunea m-a ales **pe/*Ø** mine.
television CL.1SG-AUX.3SG chosen PE me
'Television has chosen me.'
(Klein 2007, 1)

(103) **L**-am lovit **pe/*Ø** Mihai.
CL.ACC.3SG-AUX.1 hit PE Mihai
'I/We have hit Mihai.'
(Klein 2007, 1)

(104) Isus iubeşte **pe/*Ø** fiecare.
Isus loves PE every
'Isus loves everyone.'

DOM is optional with definite and indefinite DPs.[9]

(105) **L**-am lovit **pe/Ø** copil-ul vecin-ul-ui.
CL.ACC.3SG-AUX.1 hit PE child-DEF neighbor-DEF-GEN
'I/We have hit the neighbor's child.'

(106) a. **L**-am lovit **pe** un copil.
CL.ACC.3SG-AUX.1 hit PE a child
'I have hit a child.'
(Klein 2007, 1)
b. Am lovit un copil.
'I have hit a child.'
(Klein 2007, 2)

In existential sentences, the pivot is not introduced by *pe*—unsurprisingly, since the pivot acts as a morphosyntactic subject. With respect to possessives, Romanian works like Spanish, at least partially. Recall that in Spanish, possessive individual-level structures do not allow DOM, while possessive stage-level ones do. In Romanian, *pe* is prohibited in an individual-level possessive structure, and possible in a stage-level possessive structure—just as my analyses predict.

Crosslinguistic Predictions

(107) Maria are *pe/Ø o fică.
      Maria has PE   a daughter

(108) A   avut-o   pe cealaltă.
      has had-CL.ACC.3SG PE other
      'She/He had the other one.'

On the other hand, the possessive followed by a secondary predicate does not allow *pe* (as we saw in chapters 1 and 3, Spanish allows accusative A in this context).

(109) Maria are *pe/Ø unul dintre copii   în armată.
      Maria has PE   one among children in army
      'Maria has one of her children in the army.'

This datum is consistent with my assumptions, since nothing in my framework prevents unmarked objects with a possessor and a secondary predicate. However, I do not know the reason for this prohibition against *pe*. For detailed discussions of the distribution of DOM in Romanian, see Mardale 2004 and references therein.

I take as my starting point that *pe* is a spell-out of K, as shown in (110). The clitic is part of the verbal morphology (although sometimes attached to negation).

(110)

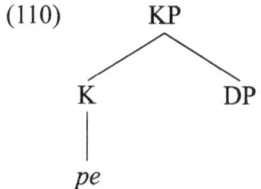

In the next two sections, I test the predictions of my analyses on the Romanian data. In section 4.5.2, I argue that *pe*-marked objects in Romanian are scrambled to a position where they c-command an IO. In section 4.5.3, I show evidence that marked objects take scope outside islands. A new datum is that QR can apply to unmarked indefinite objects in Romanian.

4.5.2 Scrambling

Both word order and the standard quantifier-variable tests provide evidence that the DOM object c-commands the IO in Romanian. Example (111) has the reading in which there is a distribution of prisoners and sons.

(111) Duşmanii   nu   l-au   cedat   pe nici un prizonier fiului
      enemies.DEF NEG CL.ACC.3SG-AUX yielded PE NEG a   prisoner son.3.DAT
      lui.
      his
      'The enemies yielded no prisoner to his son.'

The order DO-IO is quasi obligatory. The order IO-DO is awkward.

(112) ?Duşmanii   nu   l-au   cedat   fiului   lui pe nici un
      enemies.DEF NEG CL.ACC.3SG-AUX yielded son.3.DAT his PE NEG a
      prizonier.
      prisoner

If the DO does not bear *pe*, the natural order is IO-DO. The bound variable reading for *lui* is not possible.

(113) Duşmanii   nu   i-au   cedat   fiului   lui un prizonier.
      enemies.DEF NEG CL.DAT.3SG-AUX yielded son.DAT his a prisoner
      'The enemies yielded no prisoner to his son.'

4.5.3 Scope

The scope data in Romanian confirm the analyses I have proposed in previous sections, while adding a new twist. In fact, the data suggest that in Romanian marked indefinite objects are interpreted by means of choice functions and unmarked indefinites can be subject to QR.

I begin with conditional clauses. An indefinite introduced by *pe* can take scope outside a conditional clause, while an indefinite not introduced by *pe* cannot.

(114) Dacă Bert invită pe un filozof,   Lud se va   supără.
      if   Bert invites PE a philosopher Lud CL AUX.FUT annoy
      'If Bert invites a philosopher, Lud will be annoyed.'
         → > ∃
         ∃ > →

(115) Dacă Bert invită un filozof,   Lud se va   supără.
      if   Bert invites a philosopher Lud CL AUX.FUT annoy
      'If Bert invites a philosopher, Lud will be annoyed.'
         → > ∃
         *∃ > →

According to the analyses presented so far, this indicates that only *pe* nominal phrases include a choice function variable.

This difference between marked and unmarked indefinites is not obvious if we look only at simple sentences. As has been noted before (Dobrovie-Sorin 1994; Geist and Onea 2007), Romanian is not a scope-rigid language. The following sentences are all ambiguous, including (118), without *pe*:[10]

(116) O femeie iubeşte **pe** fiecare barbat.
   a woman loves PE every man
   'A woman loves every man.'
   $\forall > \exists$
   $\exists > \forall$

(117) Fiecare barbat iubeşte **pe** o femeie.
   every man loves PE a woman
   'Every man loves a woman.'
   $\forall > \exists$
   $\exists > \forall$

(118) Fiecare barbat iubeşte o femeie.
   every man loves a woman
   'Every man loves a woman.'
   $\forall > \exists$
   $\exists > \forall$

These sentences show that QR is alive and well in Romanian, and able to apply to indefinite DPs. I surmise that the latter can be shifted to the type $\langle\langle e,t\rangle,t\rangle$ and moved by QR to Spec,T. The scopal ambiguity of these sentences adds a new factor to the analyses—a factor absent from (e.g.) Spanish, a language that lacks QR. Both *pe* indefinite objects and unmarked indefinite objects can take wide scope within a clause. This wide scope could be accounted for by application of QR or choice functions. However, only *pe* indefinites can take scope outside the conditional island, as shown in (114). This means that only *pe* indefinites—those indefinites that scramble—include a choice function variable. Exploring the implications of these data for semantic theory is a matter I will have to leave for future research.

4.5.4 Small Clauses, Clause Union, and Object Control

Small clauses in Romanian follow the patterns found in the previously discussed languages. The morpheme *pe* is obligatory, with or without clitic doubling.

(119) a. Ion (îl)   consideră **pe**/*Ø student tîmpit.
      Ion CL.ACC.3SG considers PE   student stupid
      'Ion considers a/the student stupid.'

b. Obama (l)-a numit **pe/*Ø** senator ministr-ul
   Obama CL.ACC.3SG-AUX named PE senator secretary-DEF
   sănătăţi-i.
   health-GEN
   'Obama designated a senator health secretary.'

With clause union and object control clauses, both the object clitic and *pe* are required by my consultants (absence of a clitic gives rise to mild ungrammaticality). In (120), I use a permissive clause as a representative of clause union.

(120) Ion l-a lăsat **pe/*Ø** un copil să joace Nintendo.
      Ion CL.ACC.3SG-AUX let PE a child C play Nintendo
      'Ion let a/the child play Nintendo.'

(121) exemplifies object control.

(121) Ion l-a fortat **pe/*Ø** un baiat să-i faca
      Ion CL.ACC.3SG-AUX forced PE a boy C-CL.ACC.3PL do
      temele.
      homework.DEF
      'Ion has forced a boy to do his homework.'

To summarize this section: We have seen that Romanian *pe* marks a class of indefinite objects that scramble and take wide scope over islands. Additionally, *pe* marks all *wh*-phrases, and it marks the arguments of small clauses, clause union, and controlling objects. Thus, Romanian adds more empirical evidence for a framework that connects scope outside islands, scrambling, and DOM.

4.6 No (Apparent) Marking: German

German is a language without overt DOM. However, it has scrambling and specificity effects derived from scrambling, so it does look like a good language to round out my overview of crosslinguistic phenomena. Moreover, German formed the main empirical basis for Diesing's (1992) Mapping Hypothesis, so any analysis of scrambling and interpretation would be incomplete without considering German.

Let us start by going back to the tree in (1). This tree makes the claim that there are three possible positions for indefinite nominals: P1, P2, and P3, the first two being crucial for my proposals. In this chapter, I am trying to find evidence for scrambling of indefinite objects into P2. If such scrambling exists, my approach makes clear predictions: the scrambled object can take wide scope, be specific, and so on, while the unscrambled object cannot.

Recall Diesing's (1992) Mapping Hypothesis:

(122) a. Material from VP is mapped into the nuclear scope.
b. Material from IP is mapped into a restrictive clause.
(Diesing 1992, 10)

Recall that in Diesing's framework, the VP is where all the arguments of the verb are merged. The predicate phrase does not split into vP and VP, and there are no functional categories in between. Thus, the target of scrambling is always the IP area.

A substantial subset of Diesing's empirical data for the Mapping Hypothesis comes from her analysis of German scrambling. As we have seen, Diesing claims that scrambled DPs are located outside the VP, thus triggering a partition of the clause into the three-part structure proposed by Heim (1982): Quantifier [Restrictive clause] Nuclear Scope. Material outside VP—that is, the scrambled object—ends up in the restrictive clause.

(123) [$_{IP}$ ... Obj [$_{VP}$ ... t(Obj)]]
　　　└─────┘ └─────┘
　　　Restr. cl.　Nuc. scope

In terms of the assumptions made here, Diesing argues that objects scramble to P3.

A scrambled indefinite object is taken to be a strong quantifier. Quantifier strength leads to specific or generic interpretations.

The landmarks that Diesing uses as VP boundaries in her German data are adjuncts such as *immer* 'always', *gestern* 'yesterday', and *ja doch* 'indeed'. She assumes they stand at the left border of the VP.

(124) [$_{IP}$ ... [$_{VP}$ immer / gestern / ja doch [$_{VP}$ ...]]]

Granting this assumption, it is clear that any object to the left of these adjuncts must have scrambled. Further, Diesing argues that such an object must have a strong reading. Consider the following examples:[11]

(125) a. ... daß Otto immer Bücher über Wombats liest.
　　　　　　that Otto always books　over wombats reads
　　　　'... that Otto always reads books about wombats.'
　　　　(Diesing 1992, 107)
b. ... daß Otto Bücher über Wombats immer liest.
　　(Diesing 1992, 108)

In (125a), the object is to the right of the adverb *immer* 'always'. According to Diesing, the only possible reading for the object is the existential one, represented in (126a) (using English lexical items for convenience). According to this reading, the adverb *always* binds a variable for times, with the result that Otto spends most of his time reading books about wombats. In (125b), the object is to the left of the adjunct. In this position, the only natural reading for the indefinite is a strong one, bound by the adverb. In this reading, it is generally the case that if Otto finds a book about wombats, he will read it.

(126) a. Always(t) [t a time] ∃(x) x a book ∧ Otto reads x at t
= Otto spends most of his time reading books about wombats
b. Always(x) [x a book] Otto reads x
= Otto reads most of the books about wombats that he can find

Diesing's data have been criticized by de Hoop (1996) and Frey (2001), both of whom argue that an indefinite to the right of *immer* or similar adverbs like *ja doch* can have a strong reading. The following sentence exemplifies this:

(127) ... weil   Otto ja   doch Fußballübertragungen anschaut.
         because Otto PRT PRT soccer.broadcasts   watches
Possible LF: GEN(x) [x a soccer game] Otto watches x
Reading for this LF: Generally speaking, if there is a soccer game on TV, Otto watches it.
(Frey 2001, 138)

Frey argues that it is possible to have a generic reading for the object in (127), as shown in the very free translation that I provide.

The Spanish DOM data discussed in this monograph do not fit Diesing's model either. Spanish seems to fail in the other direction, since the scrambled object does not need to have a strong reading—scrambling simply opens up this possibility. However, we have also seen that the scrambling discussed in this monograph is different from the type that Diesing studied: the Spanish DOM object moves to P2, a position lower than the initial Merge position of the EA. When we reconsider the German data in light of the structural assumptions presented in (1), a question arises. The ambiguity reported in (127) for the indefinite object may in fact be the by-product of a structural ambiguity: *Fußballübertragungen* 'soccer broadcasts' could be in P2 or P3. This is in essence Frey's (2001) point. To put it in the terms of my theory:

(128) a. [$_{VP}$ ja doch [$_{αP}$ Fußballübertragungen α [$_{VP}$ t(DO) anschaut]]]
             indeed   soccer.broadcasts   watches
         → Generic reading

b. [$_{vP}$ ja doch [$_{αP}$ α [$_{VP}$ Fußballübertragungen anschaut]]]
   → Existential reading

In order to pinpoint the actual position of the DO, Frey undertakes a fine-grained analysis of object positions in German using a broader range of adverbs than Diesing considered. He identifies a class of adverbs—manner, instrumental, and locative—that are merged in a position lower than *immer, ja doch*, or *gerade*. Let's take it that the latter adverbs are vP (or higher) adjuncts while the former, lower ones are VP adjuncts.

Frey shows that a lower adverb can help us inspect the readings of indefinites in more detail. An indefinite that has been scrambled to the left of a low adverb can have a weak (existential) or a strong (generic) reading. But if the object stays to the right of the low adverb, only the existential reading is possible.

(129) a. Heute hat Otto Kolleginnen zärtlich umarmt.
today has Otto colleagues tenderly embraced
= GEN(x) [x a colleague] Otto has embraced x
= ∃(x) x is a colleague ∧ Otto has embraced x
b. Heute hat Otto zärtlich Kolleginnen umarmt.
today has Otto tenderly colleagues embraced
≠ GEN(x) [x a colleague] Otto has embraced x
= ∃(x) x is a colleague ∧ Otto has embraced x
(Frey 2001, 141)

The same possibility regarding strong and weak readings obtains if the DO is scrambled over the IO. Again, if the DO is not scrambled over the IO, it can only have the existential reading.

(130) a. ... weil   ein Kollege   Pressemitteilungen   einer Kollegin   t
because a   colleague.M   press.statements.ACC   a.DAT colleague.F
vorliest.
reads
'... because a male colleague reads press statements to a female colleague.'
b. ... weil   ein Kollege   einer Kollegin   Pressemitteilungen
because a   colleague.M   a.DAT colleague.F   press.statements.ACC
vorliest.
reads
'... because a male colleague reads press statements to a female colleague.'
(Frey 2001, 142)

Next, consider (131a,b). These examples contain two adverbs. By assumption, *gründlich* 'thoroughly' is attached to VP while *neulich* 'recently' is attached to vP. In (131b), a generic reading for *Akten* 'documents' is possible, together with the existential reading. In (131a), only the existential reading is possible. This example pinpoints the ambiguous position as being the one between the two adverbs: to the left of *neulich*, only strong readings are possible; to the right of *gründlich*, only weak readings are possible. In my framework, this position must be Spec,α.

(131) a. Der Kanzler   hat neulich gründlich Akten   studiert.
        the chancellor has recently thoroughly documents studied
        'The chancellor has recently studied documents thoroughly.'
    b. Der Kanzler   hat neulich Akten   gründlich studiert.
        the chancellor has recently documents thoroughly studied
        (Frey 2001, 146)

Let us explore further the position adjacent to the lexical verb. Let's take it to be P1, Compl,V. In section 3.3.5 I claimed, following Carlson (2003), that only constituents of type ⟨e,t⟩ occur in this position. This hypothesis entails that strong quantifiers cannot be found in Compl,V. Consequently, we should not find strong quantifiers to the right of low adjuncts. Frey argues that this is in fact the case.

(132) a. ??Der Kanzler   hat heute gründlich   diese Akten   studiert.
        the chancellor has today thoroughly these documents studied
    b. *Der Kanzler   hat heute gründlich   jede Akte   studiert.
        the chancellor has today thoroughly every document studied
        (Frey 2001, 146)

Thus, with the help of Frey's work, we can begin to glimpse the correspondences between the German and Spanish data. The set of German object DPs that cannot be found in a position adjacent to the verb is exactly the set of Spanish objects that need accusative A. When an indefinite DP, in German or Spanish, undergoes short scrambling to P2, the possibility of strong readings opens up.

Frey's discussion can be summarized with the help of the following diagram (where > signifies the left-to-right order and, by assumption, the c-command hierarchy):

(133)   DO³ > *immer/gestern* > DO² > manner/instr adj > IO > DO¹ > V
            ↑   ↑   ↑
         √strong   √strong   √weak
         *weak   √weak   *strong

This diagram corresponds point by point to my own theory, as presented in the previous sections. DO^2 is in position P2, and DO^1 is in position P1. DO^3 could be in position P3 (i.e., Spec,v), since it seems to have an information structure "topic" component (see section 2.2).

(134) [$_{vP}$ DO^3 [$_{v'}$ Adv v [$_{\alpha P}$ DO^2 (IO) α [$_{VP}$ Adv [$_{v'}$ (IO) DO^1 V]]]]]

Finally, let us consider scope. My theory predicts that only the scrambled object can take scope outside an island. A "philosopher" example confirms this.

(135) Wenn Bert höflich einen Philosophen einlädt, ärgert sich Lud.
     if   Bert politely a   philosopher invites angers REFL Lud
    'If Bert politely invites a philosopher, Lud will be annoyed.'
    $\forall > \exists$
    *$\exists > \forall$

(136) Wenn Bert einen Philosophen höflich einlädt, ärgert sich Lud.
     if   Bert a   philosopher politely invites angers REFL Lud
    $\forall > \exists$
    $\exists > \forall$

My consultants report that the scrambled DP *einen Philosophen* can take wide scope over the conditional in (136), while the unscrambled object in (135) cannot (with one exception, a speaker who found no wide scope for either example).[12]

4.7 Conclusions

Table 4.1 summarizes the findings in this chapter. The following paragraphs describe the column headings in the table:

Table 4.1
Crosslinguistic properties of marked objects

	Specificity	Scope	Scrambling	Affectee	*Wh*-phrase
Spanish	√	√	√	√	√
Persian	√	√	√	√	?
Hindi	√	√	√	√	?
Kiswahili	√	√	?	?	√
Romanian	√	√	√	√	√
German	√	√	√	N/A	N/A

1. Specificity: Marked objects are/can be specific. This is not surprising, of course, since a language must have this property to be included in the list.

However, it is worthy of note that in *none* of these languages can unmarked objects be specific (modulo "animacy," as usual). The check mark in the cell for German means that we can identify two distinct positions (even if there is no morphological correlate), one that allows for strong indefinites and one reserved for weak indefinites.

2. Scope: Marked objects can take scope over islands. Unmarked objects cannot. In Romanian, unmarked objects—as well as strong quantifiers in object position—can take wide scope within their clause, suggesting that QR is operative in this language and freely able to affect indefinite nominal phrases. Again, the check mark in the cell for German refers to a scrambled position.

3. Scrambling: Marked objects undergo very short scrambling while unmarked objects stay in situ. The question mark in the cell for Kiswahili indicates that scrambling of marked objects in this language is not apparent, which I attributed to the split of α into two different heads in this language.

4. Affectee: The affectee of a clause union (without predicate incorporation), the object controller, and the argument of a small clause must be marked in Spanish, Persian, Romanian, and, at least in the case of object control, Kiswahili. In Hindi, the head of the clause union is incorporated, in which case the unaccusative argument can only be optionally marked. In Kiswahili, there is predicate incorporation in causatives, but DOM, unexpectedly, is optional for all types of arguments; an account of this apparent counterexample has been sketched, based again on the properties of the functional categories involved.

5. *Wh*-phrase: DO *wh*-phrases must be marked. The stars in the cells for Persian and Hindi indicate that this generalization does not hold in these languages. The reason is, I suggest, that in these two languages the connection between specificity and DOM is categorical rather than optional. If the connection between specificity and DOM is categorical, non-D-linked *wh*-phrases will not be able to exhibit DOM.

It is surprising to find this convergence of properties among genetically unrelated DOM phenomena. Without the theory presented in earlier chapters, these coincidences would be mysterious: why should the properties of morphological marking, scrambling, and wide scope come together? One could imagine a language that has some other combination of properties. To gauge the novelty of the results obtained here, consider Lasnik and Saito 1992. In this work, the authors show that Ā-movement freezes operators in place. So, if an operator Ā-moves to an intermediate position, it cannot take scope higher up; but if an operator surfaces in situ, it can take wide scope (which Lasnik and Saito take to entail covert movement). In this light, it would surely be surprising to find that scrambling of indefinites allows for wide scope while in-situ indefinites can only take narrow scope. But in the light of my proposals in chapters 2 and 3, this constellation of features—the constellation exhibited by the languages described here—is exactly what we would expect. I submit that what I have described in these pages is a feature of the language faculty.

This is the hypothesis I have tried to argue for throughout this monograph: The narrow faculty of language incorporates a mechanism of short scrambling that opens up the possibility that indefinite objects can be composed by Function Application (via type-shifting). Without scrambling, indefinite objects in situ must be composed by a different mode of semantic composition, which Chung and Ladusaw (2004) call Restrict. Whether an indefinite object is composed by means of Function Application or by means of Restrict has consequences for its final interpretation. Since DOs can appear in two different configurations, the possibility of developing rules of Vocabulary insertion that affect DOs in one configuration and not the other also emerges—and thus, DOM.

Appendix: Inuit

Prompted by an anonymous reviewer, I end this chapter with a discussion of Inuit. The anonymous reviewer presents the following objection: in Inuit languages, an unmarked object (bearing absolutive or nominative morphology, expressed overtly only in the plural form) is the one that takes wide scope, while a marked object (bearing the *-mik* suffix, sometimes glossed as comitative or instrumental) takes obligatory narrow scope. On the face of it, this datum makes Inuit look very different from the other languages studied in this monograph and warrants investigation. My discussion of Inuit is brief, focused on the canonical cases; and I do not try to make a contribution to the already voluminous literature on the language. My goal instead is the very limited one of showing that the difference between Inuit and the other languages discussed in this monograph is superficial, a direct consequence of ergativity and the presence of the antipassive morpheme. I do so by building especially on the work of Bittner (1994), Bok-Bennema (1991), Van Geenhoven (1998), and Wharram (2003).

In Inuit, predicates that are conceptually transitive appear in three different syntactic frames, which I refer to as Type 1, Type 2, and Type 3 (see table 4.2 for a summary). In Type 1, the EA is in absolutive (ABS) case, the IA (internal argument) is incorporated, and the verb exhibits absolutive agreement morphology. The absolutive argument, in this and all the other frames, takes obligatory wide scope. The incorporated IA takes narrow scope (Van Geenhoven 1998).

Table 4.2
Case, agreement, and scope in Inuit

	Case	Agreement	Scope of indefinites
Type 1	EA: ABS	ABS	EA: wide
	IA: incorporated		IA: narrow
Type 2	EA: ERG	ERG/ABS	EA: wide/narrow
	IA: ABS		IA: wide
Type 3	EA: ABS	ABS	EA: wide
	IA: ADP		IA: narrow

In the Type 2 frame, the EA appears in ergative (ERG) case and the IA appears in absolutive case. The absolutive argument again takes wide scope. The ergative argument takes wide scope obligatorily in Inuktitut and optionally in Kalaallisut (West Greenlandic) (Wharram 2003, 43). The verb agrees with both arguments.

Finally, in the Type 3 frame, the one with which we are concerned, the EA is in absolutive case while the IA exhibits the *-mik* suffix, which I choose to gloss as ADP (adposition) (at the risk of somewhat prejudging the matter). In Type 3, the verb usually bears a suffix called the *antipassive* (AP). Even when no AP is overt, the specialists normally assume a covert version. There are several types of AP morphemes, each with its own shade of meaning (Bittner 1987).

The following sentences exemplify these patterns. (138) is a Kalaallisut example; the other two are Inuktitut.

(137) *Type 1*
    Tuttu-p-puq.
    caribou-catch-3SG.ABS
    'He caught a caribou.'
    (Bok-Bennema 1991, 162)

(138) *Type 2*
    Anguti-up nutaraq takuv-aa.
    man-ERG child.ABS see-3SG.ERG.3SG.ABS
    'The man sees the child.'
    (Wharram 2003, 24)

(139) *Type 3*
    Arnaq pisir-mik imngiq-tuq.
    woman.ABS song-ADP sing-3SG.ABS
    'The woman sings a song.'
    (Bok-Bennema 1991, 247)

We need to establish the hierarchical relations among the arguments. The binding properties in Inuit are complex, but it seems clear that the ergative argument c-commands the absolutive argument. For instance, as Bobaljik (1993) argues, a reflexive possessive in the absolutive argument can be bound by the ergative argument but the reverse is ungrammatical.

(140) Piita-up anaana-ni nagligi-jaNa.
Piita-ERG mother-POSS.ABS love-3SG.ERG.3SG.ABS
'Pita loves his mother.'
(Bobaljik 1993, 12)

(141) *Anaana-mi Piita nagligi-jaNa.
mother-POSS.ERG Piita.ABS love-3SG.ERG.3SG.ABS
(Bobaljik 1993, 12)

I take ergative and absolutive to be structural cases assigned by structural case assigners (T or C for ergative and v for absolutive).[13] I take the -*mik* morpheme to be an adposition. In my discussion, I ignore dative case (as well as other morphological cases), under the assumption that it does not affect my conclusions.

Let us now look at the configurations of the three types of sentences described above. Type 1 is the classic case of incorporation, most productively studied by Van Geenhoven (1998). The IA incorporates into the lexical verb, it is composed by Restrict or Van Geenhoven's Semantic Incorporation, and it is immediately closed by an existential operator. Additionally, I take it that absolutive case on the EA is assigned by v. Within the framework developed in chapter 1, nothing prevents the valuation of an unvalued Case feature of the EA argument by v because they are in a local relationship, as described in section 2.2.1.

Following Wharram (2003), I take it that absolutive indefinites include a choice function variable that gives rise to the possibility of wide scope. I am not aware of any account that explains why the wide scope of absolutive arguments is categorical rather than optional.

Next, consider Type 2. In this type, the object raises to a position where it can receive absolutive case: Spec,α, I would suggest. In this position, the DO can be probed by v. The EA receives ergative case from T or C. Ergative case arguments also take wide scope, narrow scope being available in Kalaallisut but not in Inuktitut (Wharram 2003).

Finally, consider Type 3, the antipassive frame. I take it that the structure of a VP with an AP morpheme is as shown in (142) (see, e.g., Bok-Bennema 1991; Wharram 2003).

(142)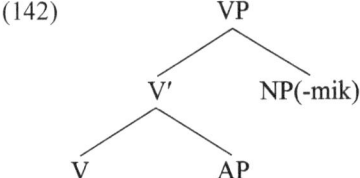

The oblique argument obligatorily takes narrow scope, although it shows no sign of being incorporated. The absolutive argument takes wide scope as usual.

As for the semantics of the construction, I take inspiration from Wharram 2003. I take it that the AP morpheme is a predicate variable. Additionally, I assume that Restrict can conjoin a lexical verb ($\lambda x\, \lambda e\, [\text{Verb}(x)(e)]$) with a predicate variable ($\lambda P\, \lambda x\, [P(x)]$). The *-mik* argument is of type $\langle e,t \rangle$. It is merged as a second object and composed by means of Function Application. Existential closure then applies, yielding narrow scope for the *-mik* argument.

(143) Merge ($\lambda x\, \lambda e\, [\text{Verb}(x)(e)]$, AP: $\lambda P\, \lambda x\, [P(x)]$)
  → $\lambda P\, \lambda x\, \lambda e\, [\text{Verb}(x)(e) \land P(x)]$
  Merge ($\lambda P\, \lambda x\, \lambda e\, [\text{Verb}(x)(e) \land P(x)]$, NP-mik)
  → $\lambda x\, \lambda e\, [\text{Verb}(x)(e) \land \text{NP-mik}(x)]$
  $\exists x\, \lambda e\, [\text{Verb}(x)(e) \land \text{NP-mik}(x)]$

Now we can address the anonymous reviewer's concerns. The *-mik* argument is marked because it is not merged in Compl,V and subsequently incorporated—the Compl,V position being taken by the AP morpheme. However, if we assume that the *-mik* argument is an indefinite nominal phrase and therefore of type $\langle e,t \rangle$, it follows that it is merged within the VP (see my discussion of Carlson 2003 in chapter 3). The narrow scope of *-mik* follows from the mechanics of Function Application and existential closure detailed above.

The absolutive argument is in an intermediate position and takes wide scope. Unlike in the other languages surveyed in this monograph, the DO that scrambles is unmarked relative to the DO that stays in the VP, the *-mik* DO. However, absolutive case morphology is not entirely unmarked: in fact, plural absolutive case is spelled out as *-t* . Indeed, one could argue that the absolutive DO is marked relative to the incorporated DO. One consequence of my perspective on DOM is that markedness is a relatively superficial property, consequence of applying a particular Vocabulary insertion rule to a DO in a particular position.

All the features of the analysis presented in this appendix are sketchy; turning them into a theory would require serious argumentation. However, I think they are plausible and coherent with the analyses of the other languages discussed here; thus, I believe they fulfill my modest goal of showing that my approach is not incompatible with what is known about the Inuit languages.

Notes

Chapter 1

1. There are, of course, other traditions in the treatment of indefinites; and even within the approaches I discuss, there are works I will not have space to mention. The literature on indefinite nominal phrases has grown exponentially in recent years, forcing scholars to make drastic choices about what can be included in a monograph on the topic.

2. One could still wonder if it would be possible to apply QR to a scrambled object. However, Lasnik and Saito (1992) show that covert movement cannot follow overt movement.

3. I have not tried to carry out a thorough investigation of accusative A in other dialects. Anecdotal evidence suggests that its usage has expanded in at least some varieties of Latin American Spanish. On the other hand, Montrul (2004) shows that varieties in contact with English do not use accusative A in contexts where other speakers find it obligatory.

4. Definite nonreferential DPs, of the type Quine (1960) studied, do not need accusative A.

(i) Juan busca la mujer perfecta.
    Juan seeks the woman perfect
    'Juan is looking for the perfect woman.'

I will not discuss this sort of example in depth in this monograph; but see note 12.

5. A note is in order concerning quantifiers in Spanish. There are two determiners that could translate the logical existential quantifier: *un-* and *algun-*. Both *un-* and *algun-* inflect for gender and number. For an analysis, see Martí 2008 and references therein. As for the universal quantifier, Spanish has three candidates:

(i) a. *cada*   Cada hombre tiene un burro.
    b. *tod-*   Todo hombre tiene un burro.
    c. *tod-*+art Todos los hombres tienen un burro.
       'Every man has a donkey.'

Cada is the most straightforward one; it is a distributive quantifier equivalent to *each*. *Tod-* resembles *every*, but its range cannot easily be contextually restricted. Thus, (ii) sounds infelicitous.

(ii) #Todo hombre en esta habitación tiene un burro.
  'Every man in this room has a donkey.'

A variant *of tod-* is *todo el mundo* (literally, 'all the world'; idiomatically, 'everyone'). *Tod-* inflects for gender (*todo(m)*, *toda(f)*). *Tod-*+art is the one closest to English *every*. It inflects for gender and number. Although it formally looks like 'all the', it can bind a variable just as 'every' does.

(iii) Todos los cerdos tienen   su   Sanmartín.
  all   the pigs   have.3PL POSS.3SG Saint Martin's
  'Every pig has its "St. Martin's Day,"' (cf. *All the pigs have its St. Martin's Day.)

In this monograph, I use *tod-* and *tod-*+art more or less interchangeably, since their differing properties do not affect my conclusions.

6. Focus on the determiner/numeral and on the noun alters this picture somewhat, but detailed discussion would take us too far afield.

7. *Cualquiera*, which is postnominal and invariable, should not be confused with the prenominal modifier *cualquier-*. *Cualquier-* agrees in gender and number with the noun and seems to be equivalent to free-choice *any*.

8. We can take the complement of *haber* to be an object rather than a subject because (i) it can be replaced by an accusative clitic and (ii) there is no agreement—at least in the dialect described in this monograph. There are some dialects in which agreement is possible in some tenses. See López 2010 and Rodríguez-Mondoñedo 2007 for analyses and references.

9. Spanish bare plurals have a restricted syntactic distribution and have only an existential reading. English bare plural generics are usually translated with a "definite" plural determiner. In Spanish, accusative A is obligatory.

(i) a. *Juan odia abogados.
     Juan hates lawyers
  b. Juan odia **a los** abogados.
     Juan hates the lawyers
     'Juan hates lawyers.'

Plurals without a determiner can be modified or can be subject to contrastive focus. In these cases, accusative A is possible.

(ii) Yo contrato solo **a/Ø** traductores cualificados.
   I   hire   only   translators qualified
   'I only hire qualified translators.'

(iii) Yo contrato **a/Ø** TRADUCTORES, no **a/Ø** REDACTORES.
   'I hire translators, not editors.'

These data will be discussed in section 3.3.2.

10. I say "almost" because the Maori *tētahi* determiners can be external arguments and complements of prepositions, while in Spanish only direct objects are marked.

11. Accusative A and dative *a* can be teased apart because (i) the morphology of the pronominal clitics that replace or double them is distinct (*le* for dative, *lo/la* for mascu-

line accusative and feminine accusative, respectively), and (ii) accusative A has an animacy requirement that a dative argument does not have.

12. There is another problem with the definiteness scale that I do not discuss in this monograph (but for detailed discussion, see von Heusinger 2002 and Rodríguez-Mondoñedo 2007). The problem is that definite DPs can be specific or nonspecific, just like indefinite DPs (see also note 4), and this affects accusative A. So, instead of a scale (Definiteness > Specificity > Nonspecificity), we have binary features ([±definite], [±specific]), which can combine in any possible way. The following example includes a nonspecific definite DP in object position. The use of the subjunctive in the relative clause ensures that there is no doubt that the object is nonspecific. Accusative A is optional.

(i) Juan busca **a/Ø** la mujer perfecta que le prepare el desayuno por
 Juan seeks the woman perfect who CL.DAT prepares.SUBJ the breakfast for
 las mañanas.
 the mornings
 'Juan is looking for the perfect woman who prepares his breakfast in the morning.'

As an anonymous reviewer points out, Carlson and Sussman (2005) discuss what they call "weak definites": DPs that are formally definite but are interpreted as indefinite.

(ii) He went to the hospital (cf. He went to the building); Scarface is in the pen (cf. Scarface is in the cage).

Although related, this is a different phenomenon. As Carlson and Sussman show, the requirement of a definite determiner in (ii) is a property of the noun itself (compare *He went to the hospital* with *He went to school*), and it disappears when the noun is modified (*He went to the Children's Hospital*). The nonspecific definite in (i) is not a property of the noun (the sentence could have any noun instead of *mujer*), and the nonspecific interpretation does not disappear when the noun is modified, as (i) itself shows.

Chapter 2

1. Neither Torrego (1998) nor Rodríguez-Mondoñedo (2007) presents empirical arguments for (21). Torrego (1998, 46) writes, "The empirical evidence for which specifier of v is filled by object raising in Spanish (such as word order matters) is extremely elusive. In fact, I rely solely on theory-internal arguments to postulate overt object raising for Spanish marked accusatives."

2. In chapter 4, I argue that unmarked nominals in Spanish are DPs or #Ps, while in other languages they can be just NPs.

3. Baker (2009) argues that at least some forms of head movement take place in the syntax. If so, it follows that at least some items in List 1 will come into the derivation specified as affixes.

4. Some examples with unergative bare plurals are grammatical. However, to my ear, they only sound felicitous under contrastive focus.

(i) En este parque juegan niños.
   in this park play boys
   Felicitous context: . . . *no niñas.* 'not girls'
   Infelicitous context: *This neighborhood is very pleasant. For instance . . .*

When a contrastive focus context is harder to devise, bare plural subjects of unergatives sound ungrammatical.

(ii) *Estornudan perros.
    sneeze dogs

Transitive bare plural subjects are uniformly ungrammatical (see Suñer 1982, 212).

The very similar distribution of bare plurals in Italian leads Longobardi (1994) to propose that there is indeed a phonetically null D in the structure that requires licensing by means of some form of lexical government, a condition that would be fulfilled in Compl,V but not in a specifier position. However, the arguments presented by Martí (2008) and others that bare plurals are small nominal phrases are, in my view, convincing. Chierchia (1998, 355–356) argues that a null D is necessary in bare plurals in Spanish because a bare noun is of type $\langle e,t \rangle$ in this language and therefore cannot compose with the verb. In chapter 3, I will investigate an alternative mode of semantic composition that makes Chierchia's conclusion unnecessary.

5. We can tell that the causee is dative with transitive predicates because (i) the case marker *a* is obligatory even if the causee is inanimate and (ii) it is doubled by a dative clitic.

6. With one apparent exception: Johns (2009) shows some examples of incorporated proper names in an Inuit dialect. Mohawk, particularly as described by Baker (1996), also does not fit in.

Chapter 3

1. Since Legate 2003, it has commonly been assumed that unaccusatives and passives include a version of v that does not introduce an EA. It is not clear to me what semantics this version of v should have. Fortunately, this is an issue that does not need to be resolved here.

2. I realize that by adopting this assumption, I gloss over a lively debate on the status of DPs, NumPs, and NPs; the role of D; the structure of bare nouns; and so on. See Alexiadou, Haegeman, and Stavrou 2007 for a detailed discussion of the issues.

3. I abstract away from the internal syntax of nominal phrases. So *a man* is written simply as *man*.

4. If K selects for a DP of type $\langle e \rangle$ or $\langle \langle e,t \rangle, t \rangle$, K cannot be associated with **f**. In that configuration, K does not trigger any type-shifting. K is never irrelevant for semantics, though, since it forces scrambling, which is crucial for nominal phrases to find a denotation.

Reinhart (1997) has D itself carry out the type-shifting. However, everything we have seen in this monograph clearly indicates that K is the functional head that carries out this job.

5. It is unusual to have a DP of type $\langle e,t \rangle$. However, consideration of examples such as *John is looking for the perfect woman* leads me to think that at least some DPs are properties (see Zimmermann 1993; von Heusinger 2002).

6. If α introduces an argument (as in example (2) of chapter 2), α can be taken to be composed by Event Identification (Pylkkänen 2008). Otherwise, its semantic contribution is limited to inner aspect.

7. As far as I can tell, there is nothing wrong formally with an operation defined as follows, with the lower VP unsaturated:

(i)   **f**   **g**   →   **h**
$\langle e,\langle s,t \rangle \rangle$ $\langle e,\langle s,t \rangle \rangle$ $\langle e,\langle e,\langle s,t \rangle \rangle \rangle$
λxλe Init(x)(e)   λyλe V'(x)(e)   λxλyλe [Init(x)(e) ∧ V'(y)(e)]

I am working on the assumption that Event Identification applies exactly in the environment proposed by Kratzer (1996) and that v therefore cannot compose as in (i).

8. A language in which K does not necessarily trigger (13) and therefore KP can be interpreted by Restrict is conceivable. That would not be a DOM language, though. Rather, it would be a language in which objects always receive the same case morphology.

9. Traces are generally assumed to be of type $\langle e \rangle$ (Heim and Kratzer 1998) (but see Sauerland 2004 for arguments that they can also be of type $\langle e,t \rangle$). In my analyses, scrambling is a movement rule that takes a nominal phrase in Compl,V and moves it to Spec,α, leaving a trace behind. There are at least two possible approaches to this problem. The simplest one is to claim that the output of applying Function Application to a trace and a lexical verb remains an eventuality with a denotation in **E**. Alternatively, anything but weak indefinites could be externally merged in Spec,α.

10. As an anonymous reviewer points out, a note is in order concerning intensional verbs. If intensional verbs are interpreted in their initial Merge position, my analysis predicts that marked objects will always take scope over scopal material introduced by the verb. In fact, marked objects in Spanish can be interpreted within the scope of intensional verbs, as shown in chapter 1. One possible approach is to assume that lexical verbs do not necessarily take scope in their initial Merge position; rather, they take scope higher in their extended projection (maybe at the head of the v phase). Alternatively, one could adopt a type-shifting analysis of intensional verbs like Zimmermann's (1993). In this context, it is worth remarking on Deal's (2010) analysis of DOM in Nez Perce. In this language, marked objects must occur outside the scope of intensional verbs, although in other respects the DOM phenomenon seems similar to that of Spanish.

11. See Milsark 1974 for an analysis of English *there is* in terms of existential quantification. See McNally 2011 for a survey of semantic theories of existentials. My proposal for *haber* is not meant to make a claim for a universal theory of existentials, which is beyond my purview. Moreover, as McNally suggests, existentials may have different semantic properties in different languages.

12. As Gutiérrez-Rexach (2003, 208) argues, *haber* expresses existence restricted to a space-time parameter. Díaz (2004) presents supporting evidence, while Rodríguez-Mondoñedo (2005) expresses a dissenting view.

13. The uses of *estar* are broader than I present here, since it can also work as a copula for stage-level predicate adjectives and as a selector for the progressive participle. For present purposes, we can ignore these uses here.

14. Much interesting work has been done on thematic hierarchies, the field being divided between those who argue for absolute hierarchies and those who argue for relative ones. Baker (1997) presents an excellent overview of the issues from his point of view as a proponent of an absolute hierarchy (his Uniformity of Theta Assignment Hypothesis).

Chapter 4

1. I gloss the examples in this chapter as in the original sources. Since I use different sources, what appears to be the same word in two different examples may end up spelled somewhat differently.

2. -EZ is short for a morpheme referred to in the Persian grammatical tradition as *ezafe*. Simplifying somewhat, it is a relator. See Ghomeshi 1997 for detailed discussion.

3. Contemporary Persian has no clause union. In Persian, the sort of predicate that yields typical clause union sentences in other languages ('make', 'let', etc.) yields complex clauses with the complement in the subjunctive and no affectee in the matrix clause. There was a morphological causative in Classical Persian, but apparently it is no longer productive (Lotfi 2008). Object control clauses are also subjunctive, but since the controller is in the main clause, they still allow us to check predictions.

4. Karimi (2003) argues that the marked object cannot take scope over the subject unless the marked object scrambles overtly over the subject. Thus, she claims that in the following example, *ye she'r-ro* can only take narrow scope:

(i) Har dâneshju-i ye she'r-ro bâyad be-xun-e.
    every student-INDEF one poem-RÂ must SUBJ-read-3SG
    'Every student must read a poem.'
    (Karimi 2003, 109)

However, my consultants provided examples with *hame* 'every' such as (30) in the text that did allow scope ambiguity. I am not sure why *har* and *hame* differ in this way. I venture that *har* might have a distributive meaning (apparent in the expression *har dū* 'both of you'). Distributive quantifiers tend very strongly to take wider scope than any other quantifier in the clause.

5. Saksena (1982) argues that the choice of *-se* or *-ko* on the causee depends on the feature [affected]; when the causee is affected, *-ko* is used.

6. Dayal (2011) argues that the effect of plurality is brought about by a pluractional operator that selects the verb.

7. My characterization of Kiswahili is based on the judgments of Zeyana Hamid, a native of Zanzibar, obtained with the help of Vicki Carstens, and on additional examples by Jonathan Choti.

In standard or literary Kiswahili, object agreement with animates is supposed to be obligatory (see Morimoto 2002). However, this characterization does not seem to describe spoken Kiswahili; it certainly does not agree with my consultants' intuitions, and a Google search yields numerous examples of indefinite object animates that do not agree. This does not mean that *all* Kiswahili speakers will agree that OA indicates specificity; I am in no position to make any claims about the Kiswahili speech community as a whole. Additionally, most Kiswahili speakers either are simultaneous bilinguals or speak Kiswahili as a second language. The contact situation adds confounding variables, since the properties of OA vary among the Bantu languages (see Marten and Kula 2011 for an overview of object agreement in Bantu).

8. Unattributed examples in this section have been supplied by Ioana Chitoran, Remus Gergel, and Edward Göbbel.

9. However, *pe* is prohibited with bare definite nouns (Chiriacescu 2009). This is part of a more general requirement, since this restriction affects all prepositions as well. *Pe* cannot be regarded as a preposition in contemporary Romanian, as the binding facts that I show in section 4.5.2 make clear, but it was historically a preposition (von Heusinger and Onea 2008; Stark 2011). Additionally, notice the difference between Spanish and Romanian with regard to definite DPs: optionality of DOM in Spanish is more limited than in Romanian. For a comparative study of Spanish and Romanian DOM, see Stark 2011.

10. However, QR does not make the bound variable reading possible in (113), a matter I will have to postpone for future research.

11. The Germanic literature on strong/weak readings discusses specific/nonspecific contrasts for singular indefinites and generic/existential contrasts for bare plurals, as in the German examples in the text. In Spanish, bare plurals are always existential (see section 1.2.4) and generic plurals are introduced by the so-called definite determiner. Thus, discussion of strong readings in Spanish must be limited to the specific/nonspecific contrast. However, the discussion of German in the text uses bare plurals, to stay close to Frey's (2001) argumentation, which is the backbone of this section.

12. On the other hand, scope judgments involving quantifiers in the same clause resulted in a variety of readings from which I could gather no firm conclusions.

13. This assumption roughly follows Bobaljik 1995. Woolford (2006), among others, argues instead that ergative case is an inherent case assigned by little v.

References

Abusch, Dorit. 1994. The scope of indefinites. *Natural Language Semantics* 2, 83–135.

Aissen, Judith. 2003. Differential object marking: Iconicity vs. economy. *Natural Language and Linguistic Theory* 21, 435–483.

Alexiadou, Artemis, Liliane Haegeman, and Melita Stavrou. 2007. *Noun phrase in the generative perspective*. Berlin: Mouton de Gruyter.

Anagnostopoulou, Elena. 2003. *The syntax of ditransitives: Evidence from clitics*. Berlin: Mouton de Gruyter.

Bach, Emmon. 1986. The algebra of events. *Linguistics and Philosophy* 9, 5–16.

Baker, C. L. 1970. Notes on the description of English questions: The role of the abstract question morpheme. *Foundations of Language* 6, 197–219.

Baker, Mark. 1988. *Incorporation*. Chicago: University of Chicago Press.

Baker, Mark. 1996. *The polysynthesis parameter*. Oxford: Oxford University Press.

Baker, Mark. 1997. Thematic roles and syntactic structure. In *Elements of grammar*, ed. by Liliane Haegeman 73–137. Dordrecht: Kluwer.

Baker, Mark. 2009. Is head movement still needed for noun incorporation? The case of Mapudungun. *Lingua* 119, 148–165.

Baker, Mark, Roberto Aranovich, and Lucía Golluscio. 2005. Two types of noun incorporation: Noun incorporation in Mapudungun and its typological implications. *Language* 81, 138–177.

Baker, Mark, and Chris Collins. 2006. Linkers and the internal structure of vP. *Natural Language and Linguistic Theory* 24, 307–354.

Basilico, David. 1998. Object position and predication forms. *Natural Language and Linguistic Theory* 16, 541–595.

Belletti, Adriana. 1988. The case of unaccusatives. *Linguistic Inquiry* 19, 1–34.

Bhatia, Archna. 2006. Testing Cinque's hierarchy: Adverb placement in Hindi. In *LSO working papers in linguistics*. Vol. 6, *Proceedings of WIGL 2006*, ed. by Blake Rodgers, 10–25. Madison: University of Wisconsin, Linguistics Student Organization.

Bhatt, Rajesh. 2005. Long distance agreement in Hindi-Urdu. *Natural Language and Linguistic Theory* 23, 757–807.

Bhatt, Rajesh. 2007. Unaccusativity and case licensing. Handout of talk delivered at McGill University, May 7.

Bhatt, Rajesh, and Elena Anagnostopoulou. 1996. Object shift and specificity. In *CLS 32*, ed. by Lise M. Dobrin, Kora Singer, and Lisa McNair, 11–22. Chicago: University of Chicago, Chicago Linguistic Society.

Bittner, Maria. 1987. On the semantics of the Greenlandic antipassive and related constructions. *International Journal of American Linguistics* 53, 194–231.

Bittner, Maria. 1994. *Case, scope and licensing.* Dordrecht: Kluwer.

Bleam, Tonia. 2003. Properties of the double object construction in Spanish. In *A Romance perspective on language knowledge and use*, ed. by Rafael Núñez-Cedeño, Luis López, and Richard Cameron, 233–252. Amsterdam: John Benjamins.

Bleam, Tonia. 2005. The role of semantic type on differential object marking. *Belgian Journal of Linguistics* 19, 3–27.

Bobaljik, Jonathan David. 1993. Ergativity and ergative unergatives. In *Papers on case and agreement II*, ed. by Colin Phillips, 45–88. MIT Working Papers in Linguistics 19. Cambridge, MA: MIT, MIT Working Papers in Linguistics.

Bobaljik, Jonathan David. 1995. Morphosyntax: The syntax of verbal inflection. Doctoral dissertation, MIT.

Bobaljik, Jonathan David, and Dianne Jonas. 1996. Subject positions and the roles of TP. *Linguistic Inquiry* 27, 195–236.

Boeckx, Cedric, and Kleanthes Grohmann. 2007. Putting phases in perspective. *Syntax* 10, 204–222.

Bok-Bennema, Reineke. 1991. *Case and agreement in Inuit.* Dordrecht: Foris.

Bossong, Georg. 1985. *Empirische Universalienforschung: Differentielle Objektmarkierung in den neuiranischen Sprachen.* Tübingen: Narr.

Bruening, Benjamin. 2010. Ditransitive asymmetries and a theory of idiom formation. *Linguistic Inquiry* 41, 519–562.

Brugè, Laura. 2000. *Categorie funzionale del nome nelle lingue romanze.* Milan: Cisalpino.

Brugè, Laura, and Gerhard Brugger. 1996. On the accusative *a* in Spanish. *Probus* 8, 1–51.

Butt, Miriam. 1993. Object specificity and agreement in Hindi/Urdu. In *CLS 29*, ed. by Katharine Beals, Gina Cooke, David Kathman, Sotaro Kita, Karl-Erik McCullough, and David Testen, 1:89–103. Chicago: University of Chicago, Chicago Linguistic Society.

Butt, Miriam. 1995. *The structure of complex predicates in Urdu.* Stanford, CA: CSLI Publications.

Cardinaletti, Anna, and Michal Starke. 1999. The typology of structural deficiency: A case study of the three classes of pronouns. In *Clitics in the languages of Europe*, ed. by Henk van Riemsdijk, 145–235. Berlin: Mouton de Gruyter.

Carlson, Greg. 2003. Weak indefinites. In *From NP to DP*. Vol. 1, *The syntax and semantics of noun phrases*, ed. by Martine Coene and Yves D'hulst, 195–210. Amsterdam: John Benjamins.

Carlson, Greg. 2006. The meaningful bounds of incorporation. In *Non-definiteness and plurality*, ed. by Svetlana Vogeleer and Liliane Tasmowski, 35–50. Amsterdam: John Benjamins.

Carlson, Greg, and Rachel S. Sussman. 2005. Seemingly indefinite definites. In *Linguistic evidence: Empirical, theoretical, and computational perspectives*, ed. by Stephan Kepser and Marga Reis, 71–86. Berlin: Mouton de Gruyter.

Carstens, Vicki. 1991. The structure of DP in Kiswahili. Doctoral dissertation, UCLA.

Chierchia, Gennaro. 1998. Reference to kinds across languages. *Natural Language Semantics* 6, 339–405.

Chierchia, Gennaro. 2001. A puzzle about indefinites. In *Semantic interfaces*, ed. by Carlo Cecchetto, Gennaro Chierchia, and Maria Teresa Guasti, 51–89. Stanford, CA: CSLI Publications.

Chiriacescu, Sofiana. 2009. Indefinite NPs and *PE*-marking in Romanian. Ms., University of Stuttgart.

Chomsky, Noam. 1981. *Lectures on government and binding.* Dordrecht: Foris.

Chomsky, Noam. 1995. Categories and transformations. In *The Minimalist Program*, 219–394. Cambridge, MA: MIT Press.

Chomsky, Noam. 2000. Minimalist inquiries: The framework. In *Step by step: Essays on minimalist syntax in honor of Howard Lasnik*, ed. by Roger Martin, David Michaels, and Juan Uriagereka, 89–156. Cambridge, MA: MIT Press.

References

Chomsky, Noam. 2001. Derivation by phase. In *Ken Hale: A life in language*, ed. by Michael Kenstowicz, 1–52. Cambridge, MA: MIT Press.

Chomsky, Noam. 2008. On phases. In *Foundational issues in linguistic theory*, ed. by Robert Freidin, Carlos Otero, and Maria Luisa Zubizarreta, 133–166. Cambridge, MA: MIT Press.

Chung, Sandra, and William Ladusaw. 2004. *Restriction and saturation*. Cambridge, MA: MIT Press.

Chung, Sandra, and William Ladusaw. 2006. Chamorro evidence for compositional asymmetry. *Natural Language Semantics* 14, 325–357.

Contreras, Heles. 1976. *A theory of word order with special reference to Spanish*. Leiden: Elsevier.

Cuervo, Cristina. 2003. Datives at large. Doctoral dissertation, MIT.

Davison, Alice. 2004. Structural case, lexical case and the verbal projection. In *Clause structure in South Asian languages*, ed. by Veneeta Dayal and Anoop Mahajan, 199–225. Dordrecht: Kluwer.

Dayal, Veneeta. 1999. Bare NP's, reference to kinds, and incorporation. In *Proceedings of SALT 9*, ed. by Tanya Matthews and Devon Strolovich, 34–51. Available at http://elanguage.net/journals/index.php/salt/issue/view/292.

Dayal, Veneeta. 2011. Hindi pseudo incorporation. *Natural Language and Linguistic Theory* 29, 123–167.

Deal, Amy. 2010. Topics in the Nez Perce verb. Doctoral dissertation, University of Massachusetts, Amherst.

Déchaine, Rose-Marie. 1994. Ellipsis and the position of subjects. In *NELS 34*, ed. by Mercè Gonzàlez, 47–63. Amherst: University of Massachusetts, Graduate Linguistic Student Association.

Déchaine, Rose-Marie, and Martina Wiltschko. 2002. Decomposing pronouns. *Linguistic Inquiry* 33, 409–442.

de Hoop, Helen. 1996. *Case configuration and noun phrase interpretation*. New York: Garland.

Demonte, Violeta. 1995. Dative alternation in Spanish. *Probus* 7, 5–30.

Depraetere, Ilse. 1995. On the necessity of distinguishing between (un)boundedness and (a)telicity. *Linguistics and Philosophy* 18, 1–19.

de Swart, Peter. 2007. *Cross-linguistic variation in object marking*. Utrecht: LOT.

Díaz, Miriam. 2004. Las oraciones existenciales en español en el marco minimista. MA thesis, University of Arizona.

Diesing, Molly. 1992. *Indefinites*. Cambridge, MA: MIT Press.

Diesing, Molly. 1996. Semantic variables and object shift. In *Studies in comparative Germanic syntax, vol. II*, ed. by Samuel David Epstein and Höskuldur Thráinsson, 66–84. Dordrecht: Kluwer.

Diesing, Molly, and Eloise Jelinek. 1995. Distributing arguments. *Natural Language Semantics* 3, 123–176.

Dikken, Marcel den. 2006. *Relators and linkers*. Cambridge, MA: MIT Press.

Dixon, R. M. W. 1992. *Ergativity*. Cambridge: Cambridge University Press.

Dobrovie-Sorin, Carmen. 1994. *The syntax of Romanian*. Berlin: Mouton de Gruyter.

Enç, Mürvet. 1991. The semantics of specificity. *Linguistic Inquiry* 22, 1–25.

Farkas, Donka. 1994. Specificity and scope. In *Langues et grammaires 1*, ed. by Léa Nash and George Tsoulas, 119–137.

Farkas, Donka. 1997. Dependent indefinites. In *Empirical issues in formal syntax and semantics*, ed. by Francis Corblin, Danièle Godard, and Jean-Marie Marandin, 243–267. Frankfurt: Peter Lang.

Farkas, Donka, and Henriëtte de Swart. 2003. *The semantics of incorporation*. Stanford, CA: CSLI Publications.

von Fintel, Kai, and Lisa Matthewson. 2008. Universals in semantics. *The Linguistic Review* 25, 139–201.

Frampton, John, and Sam Gutmann. 2002. Crash-proof syntax. In *Derivation and explanation in the Minimalist Program*, ed. by Samuel David Epstein and T. Daniel Seely, 90–105. Oxford: Blackwell.

Freeze, Ray. 1992. Existentials and other locatives. *Language* 68, 553–595.

Frey, Werner. 2001. About the whereabouts of indefinites. *Theoretical Linguistics* 27, 137–161.

Gair, James, and Kashi Wali. 1989. Hindi agreement as anaphor. *Linguistics* 27, 45–70.

García, Marco. 2007. Differential object marking with inanimate objects. In *Proceedings of the Workshop "Definiteness, Specificity and Animacy in Ibero-Romance Languages,"* ed. by Georg Kaiser and Manuel Leonetti, 63–84. Arbeitspapier 122. Konstanz: Universität Konstanz, Fachbereich Sprachwissenschaft.

Geist, Ljudmila, and Edgar Onea. 2007. Specificity and implicatures. In *Proceedings of the Sixteenth Amsterdam Colloquium*, ed. by Maria Aloni, Paul Dekker, and Floris Roelofsen, 109–114. Amsterdam: University of Amsterdam, Institute for Language, Logic and Computation.

Ghomeshi, Jila. 1997. Topics in Persian VPs. *Lingua* 102, 133–167.

Ghomeshi, Jila. 2008. Markedness and bare nouns in Persian. In *Aspects of Iranian linguistics*, ed. by Simin Karimi, Vida Samiian, and Donald Stilo, 85–111. Newcastle upon Tyne, UK: Cambridge Scholars Press.

Grimshaw, Jane. 1991. Extended projection. Ms., Brandeis University.

Guasti, Maria Teresa. 1992. *Causative constructions in Romance.* Turin: Rosenberg and Sellier.

Gutiérrez-Rexach, Javier. 2003. *La semántica de los indefinidos.* Madrid: Visor.

Halle, Morris, and Alec Marantz. 1993. Distributed Morphology and the pieces of inflection. In *The view from Building 20: Essays in linguistics in honor of Sylvain Bromberger*, ed. by Kenneth Hale and Samuel Jay Keyser, 111–176. Cambridge, MA: MIT Press.

Heim, Irene. 1982. The semantics of definite and indefinite noun phrases. Doctoral dissertation, University of Massachusetts, Amherst.

Heim, Irene, and Angelika Kratzer. 1998. *Semantics in generative grammar.* Oxford: Blackwell.

von Heusinger, Klaus. 2002. Specificity and definiteness in sentence and discourse structure. *Journal of Semantics* 19, 245–274.

von Heusinger, Klaus. 2011. Specificity. In *Semantics: An international handbook of natural language meaning, vol. 2*, ed. by Klaus von Heusinger, Claudia Maienborn, and Paul Portner, 1025–1058. Berlin: Mouton de Gruyter.

von Heusinger, Klaus, and Georg Kaiser. 2005. The evolution of differentiated object marking in Spanish. In *Specificity and the evolution/emergence of nominal determination systems in Romance*, ed. by Elisabeth Stark, Klaus von Heusinger, and Georg Kaiser, 33–69. Arbeitspapier 119. Konstanz: Universität Konstanz, Fachbereich Sprachwissenschaft.

von Heusinger, Klaus, and Edgar Onea. 2008. Triggering and blocking effects in the diachronic development of DOM in Romanian. *Probus* 20, 71–116.

Hintikka, Jaakko. 1986. The semantics of 'a certain'. *Linguistic Inquiry* 17, 331–336.

Hoekstra, Teun, and René Mulder. 1990. Unergatives as copular verbs: Locational and existential predication. *The Linguistic Review* 7, 1–79.

Johns, Alana. 2009. Additional facts about noun incorporation in Inuktitut. *Lingua* 119, 185–198.

Johnson, Kyle. 1991. Object positions. *Natural Language and Linguistic Theory* 9, 577–637.

Kachru, Yamuna. 1970. A note on possessive constructions in Hindi-Urdu. *Journal of Linguistics* 6, 37–45.

Karimi, Simin. 1990. Obliqueness, specificity and discourse functions. *Linguistic Analysis* 20, 139–191.

Karimi, Simin. 2003. Object positions, specificity and scrambling. In *Word order and scrambling*, ed. by Simin Karimi, 91–125. Oxford: Blackwell.

Karimi, Simin. 2005. *A minimalist approach to scrambling.* Berlin: Mouton de Gruyter.

References

Kayne, Richard. 1994. *The antisymmetry of syntax*. Cambridge, MA: MIT Press.

Keenan, Edward. 1987. On the definition of 'indefinite NP'. In *The representation of (in)definiteness*, ed. by Eric Reuland and Alice ter Meulen, 286–317. Cambridge, MA: MIT Press.

Kidwai, Ayesha. 2000. *XP-adjunction in Universal Grammar*. Oxford: Oxford University Press.

Kiparsky, Paul. 1998. Partitive case and aspect. In *The projection of arguments: Lexical and syntactic constraints*, ed. by Wilhelm Geuder and Miriam Butt, 265–308. Stanford, CA: CSLI Publications.

Klein, Udo. 2007. Clitic doubling and differential object marking in Romanian. Handout, University of Stuttgart.

Koizumi, Masatoshi. 1995. Phrase structure in the Minimalist Program. Doctoral dissertation, MIT.

Koopman, Hilda, and Dominique Sportiche. 1982. Variables and the Bijection Principle. *The Linguistic Review* 2, 139–160.

Kornfilt, Jacqueline. 2003. Scrambling, subscrambling and case in Turkish. In *Word order and scrambling*, ed. by Simin Karimi, 127–155. Oxford: Blackwell.

Koul, Omkar. 2008. *Modern Hindi grammar*. Springfield, VA: Dunwoody Press.

Kratzer, Angelika. 1988. Stage-level and individual-level predicates. In *Genericity in natural language*, ed. by Manfred Krifka, 247–284. SNS-Bericht 88-42. Tübingen: University of Tübingen, Department of Linguistics.

Kratzer, Angelika. 1996. Severing the external argument from its verb. In *Phrase structure and the lexicon*, ed. by Johan Rooryck and Laurie Zaring, 109–137. Dordrecht: Kluwer.

Kratzer, Angelika. 1998. Scope or pseudoscope? Are there wide-scope indefinites? In *Events and grammar*, ed. by Susan Rothstein, 163–196. Dordrecht: Kluwer.

Lasnik, Howard, and Mamoru Saito. 1992. *Move α*. Cambridge, MA: MIT Press.

Lenerz, Jürgen. 1977. *Zur Abfolge nominaler Satzglieder im Deutschen*. Tübingen: Narr.

Leonetti, Manuel. 2004. Specificity and differential object marking in Spanish. *Catalan Journal of Linguistics* 3, 75–114.

Lewis, David. 1975. Adverbs of quantification. In *Formal semantics of natural language*, ed. by Edward L. Keenan, 3–15. Cambridge: Cambridge University Press.

Li, Yafei. 1990. X^0-movement. Doctoral dissertation, MIT.

Lidz, Jeffrey. 2006. The grammar of accusative case in Kannada. *Language* 82, 1–23.

Longobardi, Giuseppe. 1994. Reference and proper names: A theory of N-movement in syntax and Logical Form. *Linguistic Inquiry* 25, 609–665.

López, Luis. 2001. On the (non)complementarity of θ-theory and checking theory. *Linguistic Inquiry* 32, 694–716.

López, Luis. 2002. On agreement: Locality and feature valuation. In *Theoretical approaches to universals*, ed. by Artemis Alexiadou, 165–209. Amsterdam: John Benjamins.

López, Luis. 2007. *Locality and the architecture of syntactic dependencies*. London: Palgrave Macmillan.

López, Luis. 2009a. *A derivational syntax for information structure*. Oxford: Oxford University Press.

López, Luis. 2009b. Ranking the Linear Correspondence Axiom. *Linguistic Inquiry* 40, 239–278.

López, Luis. 2010. Había(n). In *Cuestiones gramaticales del español, últimos avances*, ed. by Marta Luján and Mirta Groppi. *Cuadernos de la ALFAL*, Nueva Serie 1:132–140.

López, Luis. 2011. When the external argument is a THEME. Ms., University of Illinois, Chicago.

Lotfi, Ahmad. 2008. Causative constructions in Modern Persian. *California Linguistic Notes* 33.2. Available at http://hss.fullerton.edu/linguistics/cln/Spring-08.htm.

Mahajan, Anoop. 1989. Agreement and Agreement Phrases. In *Functional heads and clause structure*, ed. by Itziar Laka and Anoop Mahajan, 217–252. MIT Working Papers in Linguistics 10. Cambridge, MA: MIT, MIT Working Papers in Linguistics.

Mahajan, Anoop. 1990. The A/A' distinction and movement theory. Doctoral dissertation, MIT.

Mahajan, Anoop. 1992. The Specificity Condition and the CED. *Linguistic Inquiry* 23, 510–516.

Marantz, Alec. 1984. *On the nature of grammatical relations*. Cambridge, MA: MIT Press.

Marantz, Alec. 1991. Case and licensing. In *Proceedings of the Eighth Eastern States Conference on Linguistics*, ed. by German Westphal, Benjamin Ao, and Hee-Rahk Chae, 234–253. Columbus: Ohio State University, Department of Linguistics.

Marantz, Alec. 1993. Implications of asymmetries in double object constructions. In *Theoretical aspects of Bantu grammar*, ed. by Sam A. Mchombo, 113–151. Stanford, CA: CSLI Publications.

Mardale, Alexandru. 2004. Sur l'object direct prépositionnel en roumain. In *Actes des VIIèmes Rencontre des Jeunes Chercheurs. ED 268 langage et langues*, 62–68. Paris: Université Paris 3—Sorbonne Nouvelle.

Marten, Lutz, and Nancy C. Kula. 2011. Object marking and morphosyntactic variation in Bantu. Ms., University College London and University of Essex.

Martí, Luisa. 2008. The semantics of plural indefinite noun phrases in Spanish and Portuguese. *Natural Language Semantics* 16, 1–37.

Massam, Diane. 2001. Pseudo noun incorporation in Niuean. *Natural Language and Linguistic Theory* 19, 153–197.

Matthewson, Lisa. 1999. On the interpretation of wide scope indefinites. *Natural Language Semantics* 7, 79–134.

May, Robert. 1985. *Logical Form*. Cambridge, MA: MIT Press.

McGinnis, Martha. 1998. Locality of A-movement. Doctoral dissertation, MIT.

McNally, Louise. 1997. *An interpretation for the English existential construction*. New York: Garland.

McNally, Louise. 2004. Bare plurals in Spanish are interpreted as properties. *Catalan Journal of Linguistics* 3, 115–133.

McNally, Louise. 2011. Existential sentences. In *Semantics: An international handbook of natural language meaning, vol. 2*, ed. by Klaus von Heusinger, Claudia Maienborn, and Paul Portner, 1829–1874. Berlin: Mouton de Gruyter.

Milsark, Gary. 1974. Existential sentences in English. Doctoral dissertation, MIT.

Mithun, Marianne. 1984. The evolution of noun incorporation. *Language* 62, 32–38.

Mohanan, Tara. 1994. *Argument structure in Hindi*. Stanford, CA: CSLI Publications.

Montrul, Silvina. 2004. Subject and object expression in Spanish heritage speakers: A case of morpho-syntactic convergence. *Bilingualism: Language and Cognition* 7, 125–142.

Morimoto, Yukiko. 2002. Prominence mismatches and differential object marking in Bantu. In *Proceedings of the LFG02 Conference*, ed. by Miriam Butt and Tracy H. King, 292–314. Stanford, CA: CSLI Publications.

Orbell, Margaret, transl. 1992. *Traditional Maori stories*. Auckland: Reed.

Ordóñez, Francisco. 1998. Post-verbal asymmetries in Spanish. *Natural Language and Linguistic Theory* 16, 313–346.

Pensado, Carmen. 1995. El complemento directo preposicional: Estado de la cuestión y bibliografía comentada. In *El complemento directo preposicional*, ed. by Carmen Pensado, 11–59. Madrid: Visor.

Pesetsky, David, and Esther Torrego. 2001. T-to-C movement: Causes and consequences. In *Ken Hale: A life in language*, ed. by Michael Kenstowicz, 355–426. Cambridge, MA: MIT Press.

Pylkkänen, Liina. 2008. *Introducing arguments*. Cambridge, MA: MIT Press.

Quine, Willard Van Orman. 1960. *Word and object*. New York: Wiley.

References

Ramchand, Gillian. 1997. *Aspect and predication.* Oxford: Clarendon Press.

Ramchand, Gillian. 2008. *Verb meaning and the lexicon.* Cambridge: Cambridge University Press.

Reinhart, Tanya. 1997. Quantifier scope: How labor is divided between QR and choice functions. *Linguistics and Philosophy* 20, 335–397.

Reinhart, Tanya. 2006. *Interface strategies.* Cambridge, MA: MIT Press.

Ritter, Elizabeth, and Sarah T. Rosen. 2001. The interpretive value of object splits. *Language Sciences* 23, 425–451.

Rivero, María Luisa. 1979. Referencia y especificidad. In *Estudios de gramática generativa del Español*, 123–161. Madrid: Cátedra.

Rodríguez-Mondoñedo, Miguel. 2005. Case and agreement in Spanish existential constructions and beyond. Ms., University of Connecticut, Storrs. Available at http://ling.auf.net/lingBuzz/000164.

Rodríguez-Mondoñedo, Miguel. 2007. The syntax of objects: Agree and differential object marking. Doctoral dissertation, University of Connecticut, Storrs.

Saksena, Anuradha. 1982. *Topics in the analysis of causatives with an account of Hindi paradigms.* Berkeley and Los Angeles: University of California Press.

Sauerland, Uli. 2004. The interpretation of traces. *Natural Language Semantics* 12, 63–127.

Sapir, Edward. 1911. The problem of noun incorporation in American languages. *American Anthropologist* 13, 250–282.

Sigurðsson, Halldór Ármann. 1991. Icelandic case-marked pro and the licensing of lexical arguments. *Natural Language and Linguistic Theory* 9, 327–363.

Silverstein, Michael. 1976. Hierarchy of features and ergativity. In *Grammatical categories in Australian languages*, ed. by R. M. W. Dixon, 112–171. Atlantic Highlands: Humanities Press.

Sinha, R. Mahesh K., and Anil Thakur. 2005. Translation divergence in English-Hindi MT. In *EAMT 2005 conference proceedings*, 245–254. Available at http://www.mt-archive.info/EAMT-2005-TOC.htm.

Solà, Jaume. 1992. Agreement and subjects. Doctoral dissertation, Universitat Autònoma de Barcelona.

Stark, Elisabeth. 2011. Fonction et développement du marquage différentiel de l'objet direct (MDO) en roumain, en comparaison avec l'espagnol péninsulaire. In *Mémoires de la Société de Linguistique de Paris 19: L'évolution grammaticale à travers les langues romanes*, ed. by Société de Linguistique de Paris, 35–61. Leuven: Peeters.

Suñer, Margarita. 1982. *The syntax and semantics of Spanish presentational sentence types.* Washington, DC: Georgetown University Press.

Svenonius, Peter. 2004. On the edge. In *Peripheries: Syntactic edges and Their effects* ed. by David Adger, Cécile De Cat, and George Tsoulas, 261–287. Dordrecht: Kluwer.

Torrego, Esther. 1998. *The dependencies of objects.* Cambridge, MA: MIT Press.

Torrego, Esther. 1999. El complemento directo preposicional. In *Gramática descriptiva de la lengua española, vol. 2*, ed. by Ignacio Bosque and Violeta Demonte, 1779–1806. Madrid: Espasa Calpe/Real Academia Española de la Lengua.

Travis, Lisa. 1984. Parameters and effects of word order variation. Doctoral dissertation, MIT.

Travis, Lisa. 1992. Inner aspect and the structure of VP. *Cahiers de Linguistique de l'UQAM* 1, 130–146.

Travis, Lisa. 2010. *Inner aspect.* Dordrecht: Springer Verlag.

Uriagereka, Juan. 1995. Clitic placement in Western Romance. *Linguistic Inquiry* 26, 79–123.

Vainikka, Anne. 1989. Deriving syntactic representations in Finnish. Doctoral dissertation, University of Massachusetts, Amherst.

Van Geenhoven, Veerle. 1998. *Semantic incorporation and indefinite descriptions.* Stanford, CA: CSLI Publications.

Villalba, Xavier. 2000. The syntax of sentence periphery. Doctoral dissertation, Universitat Autònoma de Barcelona.

Wharram, Douglas. 2003. On the interpretation of (un)certain indefinites in Inuktitut and related languages. Doctoral dissertation, University of Connecticut, Storrs.

Winter, Yoad. 1997. Choice functions and the scopal semantics of indefinites. *Linguistics and Philosophy* 20, 399–467.

Woolford, Ellen. 2006. Lexical Case, inherent Case, and argument structure. *Linguistic Inquiry* 37, 111–130.

Yatsushiro, Kazuko. 1999. Case licensing and VP structure. Doctoral dissertation, University of Connecticut, Storrs.

Zimmermann, Thomas. 1993. On the proper treatment of opacity in certain verbs. *Natural Language Semantics* 1, 149–179.

Zubizarreta, Maria Luisa. 1998. *Prosody, focus, and word order*. Cambridge, MA: MIT Press.

Index

Accusative A. *See* Differential Object Marking
Agree, 34–36
Aissen, Judith, 10, 26–29

Baker, Mark, 33, 47, 50, 96, 103
Bare plural, 20–21, 23, 52–53, 54–55, 93–94
Bare singular, 67, 128–131
Belletti, Adriana, 23, 51, 55
Bleam, Tonia, 21, 33, 34, 47, 71

Carlson, Greg, 67, 68, 80–82, 116, 148, 154
Choice function, 7, 9, 11, 16, 22–23, 29, 69, 77, 97–98, 101, 115–117, 138, 142
Chung and Ladusaw, 8, 21–23, 50, 69–79, 82, 98
Clitic-right-dislocation, 43–44

Dayal, Veneeta, 47, 67–68, 118, 128–131
De Hoop, 4, 23, 51, 55, 71, 95
Definiteness scale. *See* Differential object marking
Diesing, Molly, 3, 4, 5, 11, 42, 69–70, 80, 97, 145–146
Differential object marking (DOM), 1, 9–12, 26–29
  accusative A, 1, 2, 12–29, chapter 2, chapter 3, 106
  and clause union, 10, 23–26, 53, 56–58, 102–105, 123–126, 137–138, 143–144, 149–150
  context of, 59–64
  and definiteness scales, 10, 26–29, 60–61
  and Distributed Morphology, 38–39, 59–64
  and object control, 10, 23–26, 53, 58, 102–105, 111–113, 126–127, 135, 143–144, 149–150
  and scope 13–16, 101, 115–117, 128–129, 134–135, 142–143, 149–150
  and specificity 16–20, 101, 109–110, 149–150
Distributed Morphology 37–38, 59–60, 86, 93, 110. *See also* Differential object marking

Ditransitives, 32, 33–34, 36–37, 39–42, 136–137
Dutch, 3, 4

English, 8, 42
Event Identification, 72–73, 79
Existentials, 20–21, 84–89, 114–115, 127, 138, 140–141

Finnish, 61–62
Frey, Werner, 6, 146–149
Function Application, 7, 8, 75, 82, 88, 97–98

German, 3, 4, 6, 8, 101, 103, 105, 108, 144–150
Ghomeshi, Jila, 106–108

Hindi-Urdu, 59, 60, 67, 101, 103, 104, 105, 118–133, 149–150
Hungarian, 67

Incorporation, 47–48, 52, 56–58, 64–65, 65–68, 86, 89, 91, 92, 103–105, 116–117
  Causative, in Hindi-Urdu, 104, 125–126
  Semantic, 82
Inuit, 8, 151–154

Japanese, 87–88

K and KP (Kase Phrase), 46, 48–51, 52, 54, 57, 58–65, 77–78, 80–81, 83, 94, 95, 99, 106–108, 119, 130, 131, 133, 141
Karimi, Simi, 106–117
Kiswahili, 32, 59, 60, 101, 103, 104, 105, 133–138, 149–150
Kratzer, Angelika, 71, 72–73, 75

Leonetti, Manuel, 40–41
LF-Lowering, 5–6, 42

Maori, 21–23, 29, 50, 69, 74
Mapping Hypothesis, 4, 5, 6, 70, 97, 145

Massam, Diane, 47, 65–66
Move, 35

Niuean, 65–66

P-movement, 43, 44
Persian, 59, 101, 103, 105, 106–117, 149–150
Possessors, 20–21, 89–93, 127–128, 138, 140–141

Quantifier Raising (QR), 1, 39, 70, 71, 115, 142–143, 150

Reinhart, Tanya, 1, 7, 11, 69, 70, 75, 95, 101
Restrict, 8, 11, 22–23, 67, 69, 72, 73–80, 82, 86–87, 89, 93–94, 96–98, 99, 101, 117, 129, 138, 153
Rodríguez-Mondoñedo, Miguel, 42–43
Romanian, 59, 60, 101, 103, 105, 138–144, 149–150

Satisfy, 73–77
Scope, 2, 76. *See also* Accusative A; Differential Object Marking; Scrambling
  narrow scope indefinites, 8, 14–15, 21–23
  wide scope indefinites, 1, 6, 11, 13–16, 21–23
Scrambling, 3, 4, 10, 11, 29, 31–64, 69–84, 105, 120–123, 133, 144–145
Scrambling and differential object marking 39–48, 64–65, 110–114, 134–135, 141–142, 149–150
Scrambling and scope, 70, 133
Specificity, 2, 11, 16–20, 83–84. *See also* Accusative A; Differential object marking
  epistemic, 17–18
  and mood in the relative clause, 2, 18, 19
  and object agreement in Hindi–Urdu, 131–133, 134
  partitive, 18
  and scope 19–20
  and syntactic configuration, 4–6
Strong indefinites, 4, 70, 81

Torrego, Ester, 12, 42–43, 45–46, 83, 108
Turkish, 71

Unmarked objects 45–48, 69, 105, 116. *See also* Incorporation

Van Geenhoven, Veerle, 7, 8, 47, 67, 71, 82–83, 116, 151, 153
Von Heusinger, Klaus, 17, 19, 28, 72, 83–84, 102

Weak indefinites, 3, 70
Wh-phrases, 26, 94–95, 103, 105, 110, 135, 139, 149–150

Linguistic Inquiry Monographs
Samuel Jay Keyser, general editor

1. *Word Formation in Generative Grammar*, Mark Aronoff
2. *X Syntax: A Study of Phrase Structure*, Ray Jackendoff
3. *Recent Transformational Studies in European Languages*, S. Jay Keyser, editor
4. *Studies in Abstract Phonology*, Edmund Gussmann
5. *An Encyclopedia of AUX: A Study of Cross-Linguistic Equivalence*, Susan Steele
6. *Some Concepts and Consequences of the Theory of Government and Binding*, Noam Chomsky
7. *The Syntax of Words*, Elisabeth O. Selkirk
8. *Syllable Structure and Stress in Spanish: A Nonlinear Analysis*, James W. Harris
9. *CV Phonology: A Generative Theory of the Syllable*, George N. Clements and Samuel Jay Keyser
10. *On the Nature of Grammatical Relations*, Alec P. Marantz
11. *A Grammar of Anaphora*, Joseph Aoun
12. *Logical Form: Its Structure and Derivation*, Robert May
13. *Barriers*, Noam Chomsky
14. *On the Definition of Word*, Anna-Maria Di Sciullo and Edwin Williams
15. *Japanese Tone Structure*, Janet Pierrehumbert and Mary E. Beckman
16. *Relativized Minimality*, Luigi Rizzi
17. *Types of Ā-Dependencies*, Guglielmo Cinque
18. *Argument Structure*, Jane Grimshaw
19. *Locality: A Theory and Some of Its Empirical Consequences*, Maria Rita Manzini
20. *Indefinites*, Molly Diesing
21. *Syntax of Scope*, Joseph Aoun and Yen-hui Audrey Li
22. *Morphology by Itself: Stems and Inflectional Classes*, Mark Aronoff
23. *Thematic Structure in Syntax*, Edwin Williams
24. *Indices and Identity*, Robert Fiengo and Robert May
25. *The Antisymmetry of Syntax*, Richard S. Kayne
26. *Unaccusativity: At the Syntax–Lexical Semantics Interface*, Beth Levin and Malka Rappaport Hovav
27. *Lexico-Logical Form: A Radically Minimalist Theory*, Michael Brody
28. *The Architecture of the Language Faculty*, Ray Jackendoff
29. *Local Economy*, Chris Collins
30. *Surface Structure and Interpretation*, Mark Steedman
31. *Elementary Operations and Optimal Derivations*, Hisatsugu Kitahara
32. *The Syntax of Nonfinite Complementation: An Economy Approach*, Željko Bošković

33. *Prosody, Focus, and Word Order*, Maria Luisa Zubizarreta

34. *The Dependencies of Objects*, Esther Torrego

35. *Economy and Semantic Interpretation*, Danny Fox

36. *What Counts: Focus and Quantification*, Elena Herburger

37. *Phrasal Movement and Its Kin*, David Pesetsky

38. *Dynamic Antisymmetry*, Andrea Moro

39. *Prolegomenon to a Theory of Argument Structure*, Ken Hale and Samuel Jay Keyser

40. *Essays on the Representational and Derivational Nature of Grammar: The Diversity of* Wh-*Constructions*, Joseph Aoun and Yen-hui Audrey Li

41. *Japanese Morphophonemics: Markedness and Word Structure*, Junko Ito and Armin Mester

42. *Restriction and Saturation*, Sandra Chung and William A. Ladusaw

43. *Linearization of Chains and Sideward Movement*, Jairo Nunes

44. *The Syntax of (In)dependence*, Ken Safir

45. *Interface Strategies: Optimal and Costly Computations*, Tanya Reinhart

46. *Asymmetry in Morphology*, Anna Maria Di Sciullo

47. *Relators and Linkers: The Syntax of Predication, Predicate Inversion, and Copulas*, Marcel den Dikken

48. *On the Syntactic Composition of Manner and Motion*, Maria Luisa Zubizarreta and Eunjeong Oh

49. *Introducing Arguments*, Liina Pylkkänen

50. *Where Does Binding Theory Apply?*, David Lebeaux

51. *Locality in Minimalist Syntax*, Thomas S. Stroik

52. *Distributed Reduplication*, John Frampton

53. *The Locative Syntax of Experiencers*, Idan Landau

54. *Why Agree? Why Move?: Unifying Agreement-Based and Discourse-Configurational Languages*, Shigeru Miyagawa

55. *Locality in Vowel Harmony*, Andrew Nevins

56. *Uttering Trees*, Norvin Richards

57. *The Syntax of Adjectives*, Guglielmo Cinque

58. *Arguments as Relations*, John Bowers

59. *Agreement and Head Movement*, Ian Roberts

60. *Localism versus Globalism in Morphology and Phonology*, David Embick

61. *Provocative Syntax*, Phil Branigan

62. *Anaphora and Language Design*, Eric J. Reuland

63. *Indefinite Objects: Scrambling, Choice Functions, and Differential Marking*, Luis López

www.ingramcontent.com/pod-product-compliance
Lightning Source LLC
Chambersburg PA
CBHW061448300426
44114CB00014B/1887